Piet Schreuders

The Book of Paperbacks
A Visual History of the Paperback

Translated from the Dutch by Josh Pachter

Virgin

Virgin Books · London

First published in Great Britain in 1981 by Virgin Books Ltd., 61-63 Portobello
Road, London WII 3DD.

Copyright © Piet Schreuders, 1981

ISBN 0 907080 18 9

Originally published as *Paperbacks U.S.A.* by Loeb Publishers, Amsterdam in
January 1981

PRINTED
IN
HOLLAND

by C. Haasbeek B.V., Alphen a/d Rijn

The author and publisher are indebted to the following publishers for permission
to include copyright material in this book. Every effort has been made to trace the
copyright holders of the book covers. In the event of any accidental infringement
of copyright, the author and publisher offer their apologies and undertake to make
the necessary corrections in future editions.
Ace Books, New York; Avon Books, New York; Ballantine Books, New York;
Bantam Books, New York; Dell Publishing, New York; New American Library,
New York; Pocket Books, New York; Popular Library, New York.

Book Design: Piet Schreuders
Cover Design: Peter Saville
Cover photo: Trevor Key
Reproductions: Loe van Nimwegen and Jan Noot

Virgin Books are distributed by Hamlyn Paperbacks, Banda House, Cambridge
Grove, Hammersmith, London, W6 OLE.

For Robert and Lisl

CONTENTS

PART TWO

Paperback Covers

PART THREE

Appendices

Preface

This book has had a complicated history. I first came up with the idea of doing something with my then very modest collection of paperbacks in 1976; I was thinking along the lines of an exhibition. Two other collectors, Bert Haagsman and Ed Schilders, had similar ideas, and we decided to work together. A few years later I began collecting in earnest, and I went from Holland to the United States to do some necessary research.

The results? An exhibition after all, in the Gemeentemuseum in The Hague, and this book. Neither would have been possible without Schilders and Haagsman and their ceaseless interest and assistance. They have written articles, interviewed artists, carried on correspondence, made lists and shared their bountiful enthusiasm with me.

During my visits to America I have always been able to count on the hospitality of Thomas L. Bonn and his family. Even though Bonn has spent 10 years preparing his own book on this subject, he has not let that stop him from encouraging me and helping me gather material along the way; in late 1979, for example, we wrote to about 50 cover artists together. Our mutual interest has become the basis for a valuable friendship. That same comment applies to Françoise Berserik, who concerns herself more with British paperbacks than with those from America, but who read through large sections of my manuscript and made valuable suggestions all the same. Bert Haagsman has also made many corrections; his feeling for language and his knowledge of the subject have enabled me to correct most of my mistakes in time. The job of editing the Dutch text could not have been trusted to a better person than Bert.

My grateful thanks to Robert Jonas for his friendship and trust; to George Hornby for his unique knowledge of the world of American publishing, which he kindly shared with me; to Paul Shaw for his information about George Salter; to Paul F. Payne for his information about Bantam of Los Angeles; and to William H. Lyles, the Dell historian, for many facts and much news.

Stanley Meltzoff, who you will be reading about shortly, has reacted enthusiastically towards this project from its inception. He has an excellent memory and a wealth of outspoken opinions about the paperback era, qualities which, to the compiler of a book like this one, are priceless. Other artists who have responded extensively to my questions are James Avati, Charles Andres, George T. Erickson, Louis Glanzman, Gerald Gregg, Mitchell Hooks, Casey Jones, Paul Kresse, Leo Manso, Rafael Palacios, Verne Tossey and Stanley Zuckerberg. Also, art directors Al Allard, Walter Brooks, Bill Gregory, Sol Immerman, Roy Lagrone, John Legakes, Leonard Leone, Ed Rofheart and Gobin Stair have patiently answered all my questions and filled in many gaps in my knowledge.

When Ed Schilders and I approached the Gemeentemuseum in The Hague, our idea of an exhibition was immediately taken seriously. A date was set, so I had a real deadline for the completion of this book; if Theo van Velzen, Flip Bool, Kees Broos and Donald Janssen had not been interested, it might have taken me five more years to finish it, and for that I say to them as well: thanks!

The dirty old books which started this whole thing off can still be picked up at rummage sales and in secondhand bookstores. I actually ought to thank such sources for selling me many valuable volumes at very low prices, but maybe I'd better just let sleeping dogs lie. I *will* thank Tony Scheeuwe, Françoise Berserik, Melville C. Hill, Thomas L. Bonn, Atse van der Hoek and the Escher family for lending me, selling me and giving me important additions to my collection. The transformation of often cracked, curled and partially-powdered book covers into beautiful illustrations was in the hands of photographers Loe van Nimwegen and Jan Noot.

I want to put a stop to this list of thank-you's before I start sounding like a sentimental grandfather, but I simply can't, at least not without mentioning a host of people who gave advice, wrote letters, showed interest, or supported me through difficult moments: Bert Bakker, Louis Black, Ron Boonstra, Jill Bossert, Glenn Bray, Eiko Bron, Terry Brown, Jared Carter, Lance Casebeer, Joseph J. Cronin, Evelyn Deitchman, Har van Fulpen, Evert Geradts, Bert Jan Hardenbol, A.J. Heerma van Voss, Anton Hermus, Klaas Hoek, Harry Hoogstraten, Dola de Jong-van Leer, Jan de Jong, Halbo C. Kool, Jan Kuijzer, Billy C. Lee, Peter Loeb, David Madden, Tonie van Marle, Emily McWhinney, Terese Nehrbauer, Geoffrey O'Brien, Huib Opstal, Tobias Oudejans, W.H. van Proosdij, Peter Schaap, Mark Schaffer, Peter Schröder, Roger E. Stoddard, Edu van Wermeskerken and a woman who is, unfortunately, always placed last in lists of this sort: Lena Zwalve.

P.S.

Amsterdam, May-October, 1980

Preface to the English Edition

Many people provided valuable assistance during the preparation of this revised and updated edition, and I would like to take this opportunity to offer them my heartfelt thanks for their contributions.

William and Patricia Lyles read through the entire English manuscript and suggested numerous corrections and additions for the chapter on Dell and the *First Hundred* appendix; Bert Haagsman gave me much new information for *From Avati to Zuckerberg*; Kurt Enoch read the *European Prelude* and rewrote large sections of it. Of special help were Agnes Salter, Kenneth Cirlin and Philip Grushkin (who supplied information about and pictures of George Salter, Edgard Cirlin and H.L. Hoffman), as well as Sol and Rosalynd Immerman, Phillip Album and Paul Payne. Artists Hermanus Berserik and Stanley Meltzoff made some corrections in the section on types of paint; Arthur Getz, Gerald Gregg, John Groth, Robert Jonas, Victor Kalin, Frank J. Lieberman and Isador N. Steinberg have provided new information about themselves. I would also like to thank Michael S. Barson, Thomas L. Bonn, Rinus Ferdinandusse, Mark Haworth-Booth, Anton Hermus, Lotte Jacobi, Sidney B. Kramer, Leonard Leone, Thomas Lesser, Riki Levinson, Maury Nemoy, Walt Reed, Mark Schaffer, J.J. Strating and Ava Morgan Weiss for their hints, advice and help. And, finally, I am deeply indebted to James Avati, who flew from America to Holland to attend the opening of the "Paperbacks, U.S.A." exhibition in The Hague.

Working with Josh Pachter, who translated and edited the text, has been a treat. He suggested many additions, deletions and changes, brought inconsistencies to my attention, and cheerfully allowed me to complicate his work with my own frequent alterations. He did a fine job, and our collaboration has been a wonderful experience for me.

P.S.

Amsterdam, April, 1981

Why is it more interesting to spend an evening with this book than with a beautiful woman?

A DELL BOOK

A COMPARISON TEST CHART

| BOOK ⬇ | WOMAN ⬇ |

49%	☜	TEXTURE	☞	100%
100%	☜	AVAILABILITY	☞	2-100% (depending on competition)
60,000	☜	NUMBER OF WORDS	☞	11
97%	☜	LAUGHTER PRODUCTION	☞	3% average
0	☜	MISERABILITY (capacity to make you feel terrible)	☞	73%
80%	☜	INSOMNIABILITY (ability to keep you up all night, one way or another)	☞	79%
100%	☜	OVERCOATABILITY (ease of placing in overcoat pocket)	☞	11%
25¢	☜	COST	☞	$45 for dinner (wine and cabs not included)

From *What A Body!*, Dell 483 (1951)

"*Let's not fool ourselves, look at the trend!*"

From *Doubleday Book News* (July, 1946)

Introduction

T HIS BOOK IS NOT INTENDED as a history of American publishing. It is a sketch of the *graphic* development of American paperbacks through the years. It may seem to you as though you're on the wrong side of Alice's looking-glass, but in this volume the designers and artists of book *covers* will receive more attention than will authors, editors, printers, binders, distributors and salesmen. Some insight into the history of the major paperback publishers will be necessary, however, to get the picture of this graphic development, and I hope to give the reader that insight in Part One.

Pocket Books was the first American paperback publisher founded for that purpose and for that purpose only; Penguin Books, Bantam Books and Ballantine Books, which followed, could also make the claim: "Paperbacks are our business—our *only* business." Other firms (Avon, Dell, Popular Library, Graphic, Checkerbooks, Pyramid, Lion, Fawcett, Ace, Berkley) were originally magazine or pulp publishers which, when the time seemed ripe, began issuing paperbacks as well.

All of these companies are or were producers of *mass-market* paperbacks, which today have an average impression of 200,000 copies and are distributed to bookstores, newsstands, supermarkets and train-station, bus-station and airport kiosks. There are also *trade* paperbacks, published by firms which cropped up in the 1950s as affiliates of hardback publishers; trade paperbacks are larger than mass-market paperbacks, and are sold mainly by the major bookshops. And then there are paperback textbooks, paperback releases from university presses, religious paperbacks and other types of softcovered books. But we'll be dealing here only with the most important of the mass-market publishers.

The chapters are in chronological order according to the year in which each company began publication. Penguin Books and Signet Books, which are really two different names for the same firm, are dealt with in separate chapters; it might help to consider Penguin a pre-World War II publisher and Signet a post-World War II publisher.

The period we're interested in runs from 1939 to 1959. Why those particular years? On the one hand, there *were* no really important American paperback series before Pocket Books was established in 1939; on the other hand, however, there have indeed been important paperback publishers active *since* 1959. I've chosen '59 as a cut-off point only because it ended the 20-year period in which the most interesting softcovered books appeared. Most collectors agree that 1959 is a good place to stop, not because "I'm only interested in the first 20 years" sounds particularly impressive, but because that unique element which makes the older paperbacks attractive to collect seemed to disappear at the beginning of the 1960s: the charming, naive, artistic, daring covers, covers used as testing grounds for new graphic forms, covers whose designs were not 100% dictated by sales departments, covers executed by H. Lawrence Hoffman, Rudolph Belarski, Robert Jonas, Leo Manso, James Avati and a slew of their colleagues. In comparison with today's product, the paperbacks of the 1940s and '50s have so much personality that you are often strongly aware of their having been created by human beings, rather than by some sterile marketing policy.

By the way, I'm not claiming that no good work has been done since 1959—I find some covers from the 1960s highly inspiring. But when I see that I have collected around 2,000 paperbacks from before 1959 and only 200 from later years, that indicates (to *me*, anyway) a definite difference in quality. Maybe the fact that Avon Books was bought out by Hearst in 1958—and that, later, Signet was bought by MCA, Dell by Doubleday, Popular Library by CBS, Bantam by Bertelsmann Verlag and Pocket Books by Gulf & Western—has had some influence on this decline in quality, but that remains to be proven. In any case, if someone out there disagrees with me and thinks that "every day in every way, paperback covers are getting better and better," I welcome him to write his own book about the years 1960 to 1980. I'll be sure to buy a copy.

Since an objective study, dealing more in facts than in opinions and interpretations, is of the most value to the art historian, the collector and the interested reader, I've tried to limit myself to, as Joe Friday would have put it, "just the fac's." I have to admit, though, that I haven't completely succeeded. I have personal preferences for certain paperback series and for certain cover artists, and those preferences are noticeable throughout this book.

The amount of information presented varies from chapter to chapter, as historical data on paperback publishers are always hard to come by and often nonexistant. It might be possible to write an exhaustive study of all American paperback publishers in the '40s and '50s anyway, but that's probably more a project for a research team at some American university than for one collector working on his own in Europe.

To date, there have been practically no publications *about* paperbacks. The books and articles which do exist pay shamefully little attention to cover paintings and graphic form, although according to George Delacorte, the founder of Dell Books, covers are of great importance to a publisher: "If you've got a lousy book that you're stuck with, you hire your best artist to put the finest cover on it, have your best blurb writer give it the greatest blurb, and you won't lose *too* much money." That may be just a bit exaggerated, but it gives a good idea of the standard American approach: a cover is good if it looks like some other good cover, and the lousiest books wind up with the best cover illustrations.

Whatever criteria you may use, when you're talking about paperback covers you're not exactly talking about Art. Americans do use the term "cover art," but you'll notice they spell it with a small "a." Anyway, whether paperback covers are "Art" or merely "art," they often radiate a wonderful charm, even though they are frequently the product of clichéd thinking. It seems that, at least in the '40s and '50s, an appeal to mass taste did not necessarily exclude the possibility of daring, eccentricity, sensitivity and, yes, even creativity.

The heroes and, at the same time, the victims of the paperback era were the artists. Most of them were forced to specialize in some particular genre: Frank McCarthy and A. Leslie Ross did many Westerns, Avati did exclusively novels and Jonas primarily nonfiction, while Stanley Meltzoff, Richard Powers and Earle Bergey were science fiction men. Because of the restrictions, the deadlines, the lack of artistic recognition and the unimpressive fees, a good artist made sure that his "apprenticeship" in paperback cover art was as short as possible; a bad artist also disappeared quickly from the field, although for other reasons.

If you're hoping to learn everything there is to know about the work of Stanley Borack or Verne Tossey from this volume, you will find my Who's Who of artists, *From Avati to Zuckerberg*, disappointingly superficial. Such giants as Hoffman, Jonas and Avati naturally get more space than lesser-knowns like Nappi and Bacon. There were many artists about whom I would gladly have included more information if I could only have uncovered more, but such information is often difficult or impossible to obtain. And then there are the extreme cases, the artists whose work was done anonymously and whose identities remain a mystery to us today.

The identification of cover artists is, unfortunately, a difficult task. Usually, cover illustrations were not signed and the artists were not credited anywhere in the book. Sometimes artists were mentioned on an inside page or a back cover, but these credits were not always accurate: it often happened that a new cover by a different artist was substituted for the credited cover at the last minute, or that new covers were glued onto old books before sending them out for a second chance on the stands, or, simply, that mistakes were made. If you can find his name signed clearly at the bottom of the cover itself, only then can you be fairly certain that you are indeed dealing with the work of a given artist.

Avati, the master of emotional realism, is the only one of them who was there at the beginning, who dug a niche for himself and who stayed at it his whole life; he was not only successful, he was *good*. Of the non-realists, Jonas was indisputably the best. It wouldn't surprise me if, 25 years from now, the names Erskine Caldwell and James T. Farrell are forgotten, while those of Jonas and Avati, who created covers for their books, are still remembered.

This year, the Gemeentemuseum in The Hague featured a large exhibition of paperback covers. Perhaps that exhibition will turn out to have been the beginning of a period of recognition for a group of skilled popular artists who, until recently, have sadly often found it embarrassing to admit what they do for a living.

I hope so.

The gaps and missing information in some parts of this book will make it obvious that my research has not been complete. I've been fooling myself for some time that I'd eventually really finish, that I'd bring together in one publication *all* existing information on American paperbacks. I've used that ambitious line as a pretext for holding back the release of this book for the last few years, but that's all over now. The book is out, and if its shortcomings inspire others to study paperbacks, maybe even to send in additions and corrections for future editions, I'll be satisfied.

Send all correspondence to:
Piet Schreuders
Postbus 70053
1007 KB Amsterdam
The Netherlands

The History of the Paperback

European Prelude

T HE "PAPERBACK" is not just a book which, for one of many possible reasons, has been published in a soft cover instead of a hard one. It is rather a type of book which, for the purpose of creating a mass audience for books, has been designed for the cheapest possible production and in a format most handy for mass display and reading comfort.

In this modern sense of the term, the paperback book made its first appearance in Europe, early in the 19th century.

Beginning in 1809, printer-publisher Karl Christoph Traugott Tauchnitz made a name for himself by issuing an inexpensive series of Greek and Roman classics, bound in paper covers. In 1837, in Leipzig, Christian Bernhard (later Baron) Tauchnitz, Karl Christoph's nephew, began to release his own series of paper-bound books: the TAUCHNITZ EDITIONS. Edward Bulwer, Lord Lytton, was the first author published in a Tauchnitz Edition; the second was Charles Dickens.

The series, consisting mainly of reprints of English and, later, American works, soon became popular in Europe. They were bought by Frenchmen and Germans who wanted to learn English, and especially by British travelers stocking up on reading material in Paris before boarding the Orient Express, preparing themselves for 48 hours in a cramped sleeping car on their way to Eastern Europe. They even found a market in South America and the Middle East.

Officially, Tauchnitz Editions were not distributed in English-speaking countries. The agreement not to sell them in Britain was, in fact, a gentleman's agreement with no legal standing, as the current international copyright conventions did not yet exist.

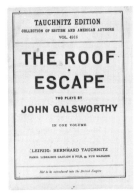
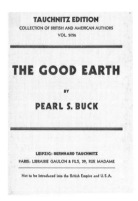
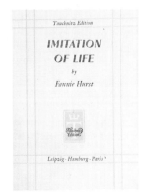

Tauchnitz Editions from 1930, 1932, 1935, 1938, 1942 and 1948

Baron Tauchnitz wanted his relationships with authors to be mutually beneficial: he paid them royalties although he was not legally obliged to do so and, at the end of the century, his son, Christian Karl Bernhard, was making regular visits to England to maintain contact with such authors as Dickens, Disraeli and Thackeray.

The "look" of these earliest of early paperbacks was not very impressive. Like French books, the pages were uncut, so that anyone who actually wanted to *read* a Tauchnitz Edition had to do the cutting himself, winding up with a volume of ragged-edged pages in his hands. The pages themselves were too wide, the type was too small, the lines of print were too long to be comfortably readable. Still, the books were successful: by the 1930s there were some 5,000 titles in the series, an average of about one new title a week for almost a century!

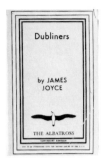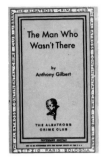

The Albatross Modern Continental Library

Except for minor adjustments of the cover typography, there were no signs of a move to adapt to changing tastes in book design and editorial interest until the 1930s, which made the company vulnerable to an attack on the quasi-monopoly which it had enjoyed for about a century. Then, in 1932, a new competitor appeared on the scene with a new paperback series of British and American reprints, based on the same system of uniform format and price, regular monthly releases and market restrictions, but with a number of changes which made their product more attractive to readers and booksellers alike.

That competitor, THE ALBATROSS MODERN CONTINENTAL LIBRARY, was organized and managed by British publisher John Holroyd-Reece and German publisher Kurt Enoch. Its editor was Max Christian Wegner, a former Tauchnitz executive. Financially backed principally by Sir Edmond Davis (with Kurt Enoch as minority partner), the main office was in Hamburg at Schauenburgerstrasse 14, the editorial office was in Paris at 37 Rue Boulard, and there was a temporary production office in the Via Milasso in Bologna. Like the Tauchnitz Editions, the Albatross books were officially only to be distributed on the European Continent; in each volume were printed the words, "Not to be introduced into the British Empire or the U.S.A." An average volume cost 1.80 German Reichsmarks, or 12 French francs, or 9 Italian lira. Four new titles were published each month; early authors included James Joyce (his *Dubliners* was the very first Albatross), Aldous Huxley, Sinclair Lewis, Hugh Walpole, Virginia Woolf, A. A. Milne and Edgar Wallace.

Special new features of the Albatross series included, in the first place, a completely new overall book design by Giovanni Mardersteig, at that time art director of Mondadori printers. He created a new format of 11.1 × 18 cm ($4\frac{1}{3}'' \times 7''$), which permitted a longer type page and established a width which easily fit into a coat pocket. He used economical and readable type faces, designed an attractive standard cover pattern and a stylized picture of an albatross as a colophon, and also used better paper.

Another important feature was Albatross' system of color coding of the covers (red, blue, yellow, green, orange, silver and gray) to indicate the genre of each volume (literary novels, mysteries, romance, etc.); also, a short blurb about the author and the contents of the book in English, French and German inside the cover made it easier for the customer to choose and the seller to sell, especially if either of them did not speak English.

In addition to these new features, the close British connections, the location of the editorial office in Paris instead of Leipzig and generally a better adaptation to the new literary trends developing outside the more and more politically isolated Germany resulted in editorial offerings more appealing to the market than had been available from Tauchnitz.

Consequently, with rapidly increasing Albatross sales and popularity, Tauchnitz's weakening position led to discussions of a merger of the two companies. Objections by the Nazi regime to a takeover of the old German firm by British interests were resolved by an arrangement according to which the printer of Tauchnitz, Oscar Brandstetter in Leipzig, purchased the Tauchnitz Company but turned over all editorial, design and marketing activities to Albatross. For all practical purposes, this meant a merging of Tauchnitz into Albatross except for the printing.

As a result, all new features used in the production of Albatross books were gradually also applied to Tauchnitz. The size of the Tauchnitz books became identical with those of Albatross, and a modern, standardized cover design and a new, eye-catching Tauchnitz colophon made Tauchnitz books equally appealing. Editorially, an attempt was made to give the Tauchnitz Editions a more conservative traditional tone in contrast to Albatross' more modern or experimental coloration.

This arrangement was well on its way to success when, in July of 1935, PENGUIN BOOKS, a new British paperback reprint series, appeared on the market. In its technical aspects it began as a somewhat cheaper version of Albatross. All books were of a standard size (the same as that designed by Mardersteig!), they were released periodically in groups, there was a standard design for all covers (including a bird colophon), and a color code for the covers was used for genre identification. The typography and paper, however, were inferior, and there were two other important differences. The reprint licenses for Penguin Books included the British Empire and home markets, which permitted substantially larger print runs and, consequently, substantially lower sales prices: a Penguin Book cost only sixpence.

The guiding force behind Penguin was Allen Lane, who worked for The Bodley Head, a hardcover publisher. At first, The Bodley Head was not enthusiastic about Lane's suggestion of an English-language paperback series; such series had appeared on a small scale in England in the early years of the 20th century and even during the 19th century, specializing in cheap reprints and mainly available at W. H. Smith kiosks. Most of these publishing ventures were short-lived, and the books themselves were of generally poor quality.

Allen Lane persevered, though, and eventually succeeded in establishing Penguin Books, Ltd. His biggest early triumph was a thousand-book order placed by the Woolworth's chain, which at that time sold only articles priced at sixpence. There is a story that, just as he was about to be sent away from Woolworth's without an order, the director's wife happened into the office where Lane and her husband were meeting. Her husband asked her, as a typical British consumer, if *she* would buy Pen-

Seven Penguins and a Pelican (released 1935-1938, except for *Hiroshima*, which appeared in 1946)

guins at Woolworth's. She looked over Lane's samples, said yes, and the rest is history.

Twenty Penguin titles were published during the company's first year, 50 the second year. Fifty new titles a year became Penguin's average, even through most of World War II (although only 33 appeared in 1941 and 37 in 1942); furthermore, Penguin Books, Ltd. started several additional lines. The first of these, PELICAN, was a series of educational books covering scientific subjects; the first Pelican, published in the spring of 1937, was George Bernard Shaw's *The Intelligent Woman's Guide to Socialism and Fascism*. Shaw wrote two new chapters especially for the Pelican edition, and this was the first time that Penguin published *original* work, as opposed to strictly reprints. It was not to be the last.

In the autumn of 1937, as the threat of a second European war became grimmer and grimmer, Penguin introduced a series of books dealing with the current world situation. These volumes, mostly originals, were called PENGUIN SPECIALS. The first title, *Germany Puts the Clock Back*, came out in November, 1937; 18 Specials were published in 1938 and 30 in 1939. They sold so well that, when paper rationing began, Penguin was able to claim and receive a large share of England's available stocks.

Several other new series appeared during the war years, such as KING PENGUINS (deluxe editions with colored illustrations and hard covers, selling for a shilling), PENGUIN HANSARDS (dealing with specialized, war-related subjects), PUFFIN PICTURE BOOKS and PUFFIN STORY BOOKS for children, and PENGUIN HANDBOOKS.

The characteristic style of the Penguin covers—horizontal colored bands at top and bottom (such as, for example, orange for works of fiction) with the words "Penguin Books" in the top band and a drawing of a penguin in the bottom band—was developed by Edward Young, a 21-year-old employee of The Bodley Head who "dabbled" in sketching. He drew the original Penguin penguin himself, after a special study trip to the London Zoo.

It may be interesting to stop for a moment to study this worthy bird in his various Penguin manifestations. Young's 1935 penguin stares off to the reader's left, a rather dumb-looking beast. He was, however, clever enough to survive for three years, until Penguin decided that he was not quite the ideal mascot for a modern publisher. In 1938, a period of animal experimentation began. The 1938 Penguin Specials auditioned a penguin walking towards the right, a penguin with a wrinkled tummy *dancing* towards the right, and a bolder, more self-assured version of the original penguin-staring-off-left, all drawn by Edward Young, who was head of production until 1939. In that year, the third of the 1938 ingenues (who most resembles the bird currently in use), began to appear both outside and inside the regular Penguin series in addition to the Specials. He received more and more competition from a flock of rightwards-dancing cousins, though, who occasionally seemed to be suffering from severe stomach cramp. The battle for dominance was still raging fiercely in 1942, but by 1946-48 the dancing (or hopping) bird clearly had the upper hand (or foot). Variations on both themes cropped up on certain special volumes, such as *Penguin New Writing* (1946), *New Biology* (1947), *Penguin Music Magazine* and *Penguin Parade* (1948). In the autumn of 1949, typographer Jan Tschichold, who had spent several years with Penguin, put, once and for all, an end to the muddle by taking the 1938 towards-the-upper-left-gazing veteran, cleaning him up a bit and exalting him to the position of Only True Penguin. (What happened to the American bird, by the way, is another story.)

From the beginning. the orange Penguins were fiction, the green were thrillers, the blue travel and adventure stories, the cherry-red biographies and the yellow miscellaneous. Later, a light-blue cover was introduced for Pelicans, along with grey for books on world affairs, red for plays and purple for collections of essays.

Tauchnitz began to lose business when Albatross entered the market-place, and Penguin and Pelican took sales away from both of them. That was the situation when deteriorating political conditions in Germany

| 1935 | 1938 | 1942 (U.S.) | 1946 | 1946 | 1947 |

| 1938 | 1938 | 1944 | 1948 | 1948 | 1949 |

necessitated further reorganization of the Tauchnitz-Albatross concern. In 1936 Kurt Enoch left Germany and moved to Paris. There and in London he organized two new companies (the Continenta SRL in Paris and the Imperia Book Co., Ltd. in London) as bases for new publishing and distributing activities abroad. At the same time, Max Christian Wegner resigned his position and moved back to Germany, where he acquired all of Enoch's German publishing and distributing businesses. The editiorial activites of the Albatross concern were taken over by the office of Holroyd-Reece in Paris. After a short interval, during which Enoch continued sales of Albatross and Tauchnitz to markets outside Germany, that function too was turned over to the Paris office.

When the war broke out Enoch left for London, where he sold French books for a time. Meanwhile, in Leipzig, the Tauchnitz-Albatross concern came under new management, which made sure that a series of German-language Tauchnitz books was published during the war years: the DEUTSCHE TAUCHNITZ-REIHE. Where the English Tauchnitz Editions could not be sold in Britain or America, each volume of this wartime German series carried the legend: "Nur zum Verkauf ausserhalb Grossdeutschlands" ("Only for sale outside Greater Germany").

After the war, Wegner made several attempts to revive Albatross and Tauchnitz. New offices were opened in Paris and London and, just as in 1932, Albatross books were again printed by Mondadori in Verona; they were also printed in Leyden (The Netherlands), in Paris and in Scotland. The Tauchnitz NEW SERIES began in 1947, published in Hamburg and printed in Heide in Holst (both in West Germany); at the beginning of the '50s, Bernhard Tauchnitz Verlag moved to Stuttgart (still in West Germany) and had a firm in Verona handle all printing. But international copyright conventions and legal problems plagued both Tauchnitz and Albatross, and neither survived.

Tauchnitz and Albatross were not only important publishers in their own right. In addition, they served as the forerunners for what later became known as the "paperback revolution," the worldwide production and distribution of inexpensive mass-marketed books, universally and widely available at prices most people could afford.

American Prelude

The earliest American paperbound books had little in common with paperbacks as we know them today.

The Boston Society for the Diffusion of Knowledge began printing inexpensive books, bound in paper, in 1829, and started their AMERICAN LIBRARY OF USEFUL KNOWLEDGE in 1831. In 1839, New York journalists Park Benjamin and Rufus Griswold started a weekly magazine, *Brother Jonathan*; each issue included, in paperback form, a complete British novel. A year later, *New World*, another new magazine, adopted the same gimmick; their first paperback supplement was Charles Lever's *Charles O'Malley*. Immediately, *Brother Jonathan* used the same novel as *its* book-of-the-week—and at a lower price.

By the time the first Tauchnitz Editions appeared in Europe, a war was being fought by American publishers, a war in which the weapons were dirt-cheap paperbacks, mainly editions of British novels. Every publisher wanted to dominate this new market, and the result was incredible competition and prices as low as $12\frac{1}{2}$ cents for a normal-format paperback and $6\frac{1}{4}$ cents for books printed in a smaller format. Even serious firms like Harpers joined the fray and began releasing paperbacks. By 1845 the market was flooded, and new postal regulations made the mailing of softcovered books less attractive.

In the 1860s, the Civil War years, the first dime novels appeared—on battlefields, in hospitals, in military barracks and private homes. They were published by Erastus F. Beadle, whose *Dime Song Books* had made him rich, Beadle's brother Irwin, and Robert Adams. Similar series, also offering complete novels for 10 cents, were begun by Robert M. DeWitt & Company in New York (DEWITT'S TEN-CENT ROMANCES) and by Elliot, Thomas & Talbot in Boston (TEN-CENT NOVELETTES).

Ten years later, the introduction of the rotary press made it possible to produce paperbacks at an even lower cost. The *New York Tribune* used its own presses to print the TRIBUNE NOVELS; the LAKESIDE LIBRARY in Chicago began issuing a new title every 14 days in 1875, later upping production to a new book a week; the FIRESIDE LIBRARY (from Beadle & Adams), the PEOPLE'S LIBRARY and the HOME LIBRARY quickly appeared to keep their Lakeside colleagues company; and the SEASIDE LIBRARY was the busiest of them all, with a new novel added to their list every day! In 1877 there were 14 of these paperback series, by 1887 there were 20. Again the market flooded and, when an international copyright law took effect in 1891, it delivered a death blow to most of the smaller firms.

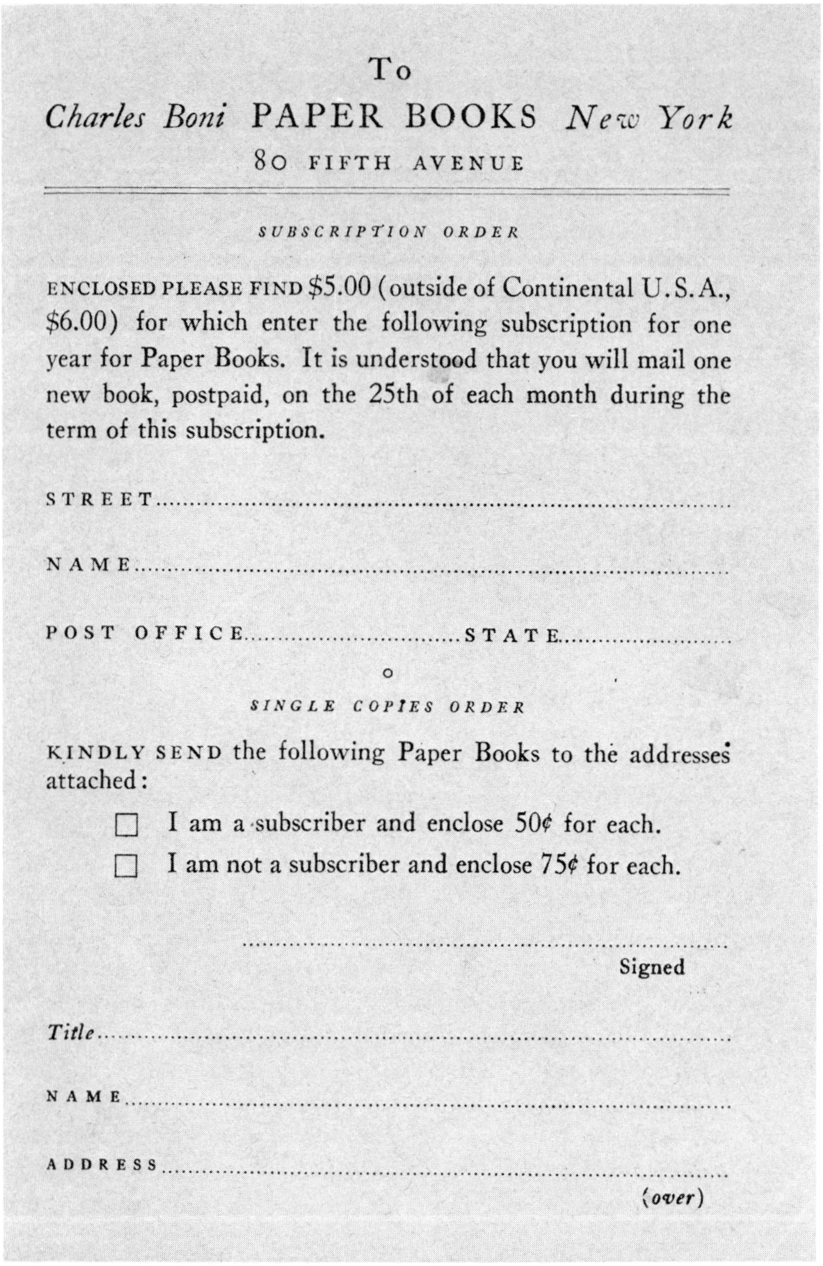

To

Charles Boni PAPER BOOKS New York

80 FIFTH AVENUE

ENCLOSED PLEASE FIND $5.00 (outside of Continental U.S.A., $6.00) for which enter the following subscription for one year for Paper Books. It is understood that you will mail one new book, postpaid, on the 25th of each month during the term of this subscription.

STREET..

NAME..

POST OFFICE......................STATE........................

o

SINGLE COPIES ORDER

KINDLY SEND the following Paper Books to the addresses attached:

- ☐ I am a subscriber and enclose 50¢ for each.
- ☐ I am not a subscriber and enclose 75¢ for each.

....

Signed

Title..

NAME..

ADDRESS...

(over)

Subscription form for Boni Paper Books (1929)

The first 10 years of the 20th century saw the birth of the pulp novel; the midwives were publishers like Street & Smith and A.L. Burt. Street & Smith were already known for their dime novels featuring Buffalo Bill (beginning in 1869), Nick Carter (1886) and Frank Merriwell, the All-American Boy (1896). Their first pulp was *Popular Magazine* (1903), followed by *Detective Story*, *Western Story*, *Love Story*, *Sea Story* and *Sport Story*.

In 1922, capitalizing on a demand for *war* stories, George T. Delacorte founded the Dell Publishing Company and began releasing pulps titled *Navy Stories* and, naturally, *War Stories*. To keep costs down, the first issues were completely filled with reprints of books Delacorte had purchased for next to nothing at a flea market in London. Dell was the first pulp publisher to put a number on the cover of each pulp publication instead of a date, so that unsold copies could be shipped to Canada and the West Coast for sale as new issues.

Amazing Stories, *Weird Tales*, *Western Round-Up*, *Western Tales*, *Western Story Magazine*, *Black Mask*, *Doc Savage*, *Nick Carter*, *Secret Agent "X,"* *The Shadow*, *Thrilling Adventures*, *Blue Book*, *Crime Busters*, *The Avenger*, *The Phantom Detective*, *Doctor Death*... these pulps are of course interesting as the stages on which Max Brand, Dashiell Hammett, Ray Bradbury, Tennessee Williams, Raymond Chandler and many others debuted as writers, and because some of their publishers (Dell, Fawcett, Popular Library, Ace) would later turn from pulps to paperbacks, but their covers are also worthy of our attention. Especially in the 1920s and '30s, a huge number of pulp novels was being published, and there was a school of artists who, while earning a living drawing pulp covers, were also learning a trade. A number of pulp artists were later to become paperback artists, including Frank Tinsley (whose pulp work was largely done for aviation stories and mysteries), Rudolph Belarski (also aviation and mysteries), H.W. Scott (mysteries and Westerns), George Rozen *(The Shadow)*, Earle Bergey (romance and science fiction), Norman Saunders (Westerns and mysteries) and A. Leslie Ross (Westerns).

As the pulps were developing, several publishers experimented with the idea of selling mail-order paperbacks: in 1920, Emanuel Haldeman-Julius started sending his series of LITTLE BLUE BOOKS (mostly dealing with philosophical and psychological problems) out of Girard, Kansas; almost a decade later, Charles Boni launched the BONI PAPER BOOKS.

Charles and Albert Boni were partners in the publishing firm Boni and Liveright. They lost all of their shares in the company to Liveright in 1928, on a bet. Looking for something to do, Charles came up with the idea of a club, whose members would receive inexpensive, attractive books by mail. He had Rockwell Kent design a cover and endpapers and, in May of 1929, he published a trial volume, Thornton Wilder's *The Bridge of San Luis Rey*. That sample generated enough interest to justify the establishment of the club.

One became a member by sending five dollars to Charles Boni Paper Books, 80 Fifth Avenue, New York. Beginning in September, a new selection would be available on the 25th of every month; members would pay 50 cents per volume while the cost to non-members would be 75 cents.

It's not clear exactly why, but after the appearance of the 16th Paper Book (including *The Bridge of San Luis Rey*), Charles Boni closed down his mail-order business and began to put out BONIBOOKS instead. The 16 Paper Books were all rereleased as Bonibooks, and at least 27 other titles were added; they were sold in bookstores at 50 cents a copy. Rockwell Kent's covers and endpapers were beautiful; except for *Wandering Women* (September, 1930), with its cover by John Barbour, Kent provided covers for the whole series. The paper and the typography were of a quality which was, and still is, rare for paperbacks. Unfortunately, the series died in 1932, a victim of the Depression and the collapse of Charles Boni's distribution network.

In 1932-33, the National Home Library Foundation in Washington, D.C. issued a series of paperbacks using the same format as Albatross and the later Penguins: the JACKET LIBRARY. There were 15 titles in all, mostly classics and light classics from around the world. Number 13 was *Cyrano de Bergerac*, by Edmond Rostand; it was later rereleased, unnumbered, still as a part of the Jacket Library but retitled *The Art of Love: A Parisian Casanova*. This was the only Jacket book with an illustrated cover; the other covers were solid brown with black type.

The Postman Always Rings Twice, James M. Cain's first and finest novel, was published in hardcover in 1934. It was reprinted in 1937 as the first of the AMERICAN MERCURY BOOKS, one of Lawrence E. Spivak's Mercury Publications. At first American Mercury introduced one new title every other month; after 1938 production doubled to one a month and in March, 1940, the series split into MERCURY MYSTERIES and BESTSELLER MYSTERIES. The books were handsomely designed: the covers, the typography, even the logos were all the work of George Salter, a German calligrapher who had been designing book covers for various American publishers since emigrating to the United States in 1934. At Mercury Publications, Salter was the art director: the combination of a pulp-like

George Salter teaching at the Cooper Union for Advancement of Science and Art

design, a low price and Salter's refined typography made the Mercury Mysteries, Bestseller Mysteries and JONATHAN PRESS MYSTERIES (which first appeared in 1942) an unusual cross between the hardcovers and the pulps. All these books used the so-called "digest" format, which, like the *Reader's Digest*, is generally wider than standard paperbacks, with the text usually printed in double columns.

At the end of the 1930s, the New York publisher Modern Age Books (founded in 1937 by Richard S. Childs) produced the last of the "prehistoric" paperback series, at first subdivided into BLUE SEAL BOOKS (which cost 25 cents), GOLD SEAL BOOKS (which were more expensive) and RED SEAL BOOKS (which were reprints of well-known titles), but as of 1938 all called, simply, SEAL BOOKS. They were printed on the *Reader's Digest*'s rotary presses and used the digest format. In December of 1939, as the first Pocket Books appeared in New York, Modern Age left the paperback field and began publishing hardcovered books.

Pocket Books, 1939-1959

POCKET BOOKS was not only America's first major paperback house—it has also been the most many-sided. Gertrude the Kangaroo's company has had, from the very beginning, something different about it, even back when there was no competition to compare it with. That "something different" has often been changed and adapted, not for any want of a coherent style (as was the case with Avon Books), but simply out of a desire to keep getting newer and better. Pocket Books are characterized more by a general impression of care and inventive design than by specific features, although the specific features are there as well: the dark-red endpapers, for example, which date back to the early years, the Gertrude endpapers from the end of the '40s, the silver spines from the '50s. Most of these physical characteristics were the work of Sol Immerman, who became the house's art director shortly after World War II and held that position until the 1970s. Sol Immerman truly *created* the Pocket Book "look."

There were various distinct periods in the graphic development of Pocket Books, and each period has its fans. The most attractive books were probably those where the cover illustrations appeared within a rectangle with rounded-off corners, a style which was introduced in the autumn of 1942 and which lasted for three years; this was also the period when H. L. Hoffman and Leo Manso were active cover artists. There are, however, also those who prefer the exuberant and colorful covers of the late '40s or the books of the silver-spine era. Individual Pocket Books may sometimes be less interesting than individual volumes from other publishers, but, on the whole, as a series, Pocket Books has always been far ahead of the rest of the field.

Dr. Benjamin Spock's *Pocket Book of Baby and Child Care* is the all-time bestselling paperback. Other successful Pocket Book titles have been *How to Win Friends and Influence People* by Dale Carnegie, *See Here, Private Hargrove* by Marion Hargrove and *The Pocket Book of Erskine Caldwell Stories*. And then there are the books by Thorne Smith and William P. McGivern and, of course, Erle Stanley Gardner's Perry Mason series.

Robert Fair DeGraff, who worked for Country Life Press (a subsidiary of Doubleday), started Pocket Books. At the time, DeGraff answered the question "Why should Pocket Books become a success?" with another question: "What possible reason could the public have for *not* wanting to buy paperbacks?"

"It had almost become an axiom in publishing that they wouldn't,"

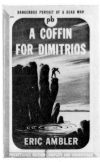

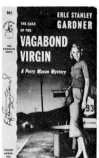

Pocket Books with covers by, among others, Sol Immerman, H. L. Hoffman, E. McKnight Kauffer and Leo Manso

DeGraff has said, "because there had been so many failures in the last 30 or 40 years. Possibly it was my persistent nature that urged me to prove once and for all that it really *wouldn't* work that tempted me to try it.... I felt that if a first-class book, editorially and physically, could be made, the turnover would be sufficiently rapid that the wholesaler and retailer would not require the usual large margin."

The normal discount to bookstores at that time was 30-35%; DeGraff offered 20%. Distributors usually received 46% of a book's cover price; they only got 36% from Pocket Books. Author's royalties, customarily 10% of the retail price, were dropped to 4%, which the author had to share with the publisher of the original hardcover edition. All this allowed Pocket Books to hit the stands priced at 25 cents, making them, as advertised, "the best books for the largest number of people at the lowest possible prices."

The original idea was to call the series 20th Century Books and to sell them for 20 cents, but DeGraff finally decided on the higher price and the name Pocket Books: "I picked this name because I felt it should be made clear that this was a book that could be carried in the pocket and, at the start, we did a good deal of promotion on selling the public on the convenience of a book that could be carried in a man's pocket or a lady's purse."

Like Charles Boni had done nine years earlier, DeGraff first tested the market with a sample book. In September, 1938, he printed 2,000 copies of *The Good Earth*, for which Pearl S. Buck was to receive that year's Nobel Prize for Literature. The book was distributed in New York City only: the first day, a small cigar store near the Pocket Books offices sold 110 copies and Macy's department store sold 695. Subsequent sales figures were equally encouraging, and the first 10 "official" titles soon followed.

Pocket Books was a collaborative enterprise between Robert DeGraff and three directors from the hardcover publisher Simon and Schuster: Richard L. Simon, M. Lincoln Schuster and Leon Shimkin. The corporate structure underwent some changes over the years: in 1944, Pocket Books was sold to Marshall Field's Field Enterprises, Inc.; DeGraff stayed on as president, Shimkin became treasurer and Simon and Schuster were placed on the Board of Directors. Freeman "Doc" Lewis became an executive vice-president a year later and, in 1954, he replaced DeGraff as president. After Marshall Field's death in 1956, Pocket Books was sold to Publishing Enterprises and managed by Leon Shimkin and James M. Jacobson.

Robert F. DeGraff holding a poster simultaneously advertising Pocket Books and U.S. Defense Bonds (Photo courtesy of Thomas L. Bonn; originally published in *Cue* magazine, October 25, 1941)

Let us go back now to 1939 and the earliest Pocket Books, which appeared in June of that year. The first 10 titles (including James Hilton's *Lost Horizon*, Agatha Christie's *The Murder of Roger Ackroyd* and Thornton Wilder's *The Bridge of San Luis Rey*) were distributed in New York in editions of 10,000 copies each (except for number 6, Dorothy Parker's *Enough Rope*, of which 7,600 copies were printed). These books, like *The Good Earth*, had dark-red endpapers, with the added attraction of a drawing of a kangaroo. That marsupial, designed by Frank J. Lieberman (who later said he received a fee of $50 for creating it), wore eyeglasses and read a book; she was called Gertrude. "For one reason or another," says Lieberman, "I named her after my mother-in-law."

The first 10 Pocket Book covers were created by Isador N. Steinberg (numbers 1-3, 5, 7 and 8) and Frank Lieberman (numbers 4, 6, 9 and 10).

The price—25 cents—was at first printed in a circle on the front cover. But by the end of 1939 that price was so well known that it could be eliminated, and Gertrude moved into the circle which had held it.

Before the war, Barbara Glitten was art director. Her husband was an artists' agent, and many Pocket Book covers of that time featured art samples to which Glitten had bought reproduction rights, rather than specially-commissioned work. These illustrations often had nothing whatsoever to do with the subject matter of the books they illustrated.

World War II began in 1939; two years later, after Pearl Harbor, America joined in. In sales terms, the war was a boon to the young paperback industry: print runs were larger than ever as thousands upon thousands of books were shipped off to American soldiers overseas, and there were few returns. The Army, the Marines and the Red Cross bought a total of 25 million Pocket Books during the war years; some editions were even prepared with the overprint "Armed Services Edition" or "Special Edition for Free Distribution by the American Red Cross." Furthermore, the reading public back home in the States was encouraged by Pocket Books to send used paperbacks on to family and friends in the services or to donate them to public libraries.

Starting in 1943, Pocket Books worked on the production of the Armed Services Editions (among others, Robert DeGraff, Richard Simon and Philip Van Doren Stern, all of Pocket Books, were responsible for the management of this series); because of that connection, the paper rationing of the later war years did not have much effect on the firm.

World War II did have an indirect influence on the appearance of the Pocket Books line. James Jacobson, head of production, was also acting as art director by that time; when he was called up, the art direction was taken over by Ed Rofheart, a designer from the advertising and magazine world. Rofheart found the cover illustrations which Pocket Books had been using "corny," and chose design-oriented artists (including poster artist E. McKnight Kauffer, calligrapher George Salter and designer Leo Manso) to provide future covers. He also used freelance designers Sol Immerman and H. L. Hoffman as cover artists. A new style quickly became visible, especially with the new basic cover concept developed by Laura Hobson in 1942: every cover illustration was framed by a rectangle with rounded-off corners, suggesting gently that the book was a window through which the reader could look to another world. Gertrude was put out to pasture, and replaced by a colophon composed of the letters "pb" in a circle. Later on, Ed Rofheart saw that such a fixed design had its disadvantages: "You find an attractive style, but after a while it starts to get boring and you begin to change it. I started letting pieces of the illustration stick out beyond the edge of that round-cor-

---

"Out here in the Pacific my pockets are stuffed with sea shells, souvenirs, and a couple of Pocket BOOKS. , . . There is no worry about what to do with them. We servicemen just naturally share all our books. I read mine, pass it on to my buddies until it finally wears out."
—CPL. G. K. E., c/o FPO, San Francisco

Ellery Queen's *Halfway House*, published in
May of 1944, featured E. McKnight Kauffer's
first cover design for Pocket Books. The oblong
format (right), with the spine at the bottom of
the page, was an experiment which was not
repeated.

Ed Rofheart in 1978 (Photo: Piet Schreuders)

nered frame, for example, things like that. Finally you've had enough of it and you just do away with it altogether." Rofheart did away with the "pb" colophon after a year and brought back Gertrude, who had apparently been busy during her brief retirement: there was a baby in her pouch when Gertrude returned, holding up a book for Mamma to read. The drawing was a product of the Walt Disney Studios.

Many wartime Pocket Book covers carry the signature "manso." They were designed by Leo Manso, who came to Pocket Books from its parent company, Simon and Schuster. Manso remembers: "You were pretty free, then. Your work was reviewed by a sort of committee—the art director, the editor of the book, a few people from sales—but I don't think they were as narrow-minded as the folks in charge these days. They were much more open to other people's ideas. If you can get 10% of your ideas approved today you're lucky; back then you could realize at least 50% of what you thought up, which was reasonable. Sometimes you had to go back and do something over."

Manso's covers were often surrealistic, and frequently suggest the

Leo Manso in 1979 (Photo: Bert Haagsman)

work of Herbert Bayer, a Bauhaus artist who drew posters and magazine covers and who has lived in the United States since 1938. Many symbolic objects appear on Manso's covers—daggers, open books, photographed hands, straight lines converging towards the horizon. "Yes," he says, "I used lots of stage props; some covers were crawling with them. I used any material at hand—I would have used xeroxes if we'd had them then! Looking back at them, I think those covers were rather banal, but at the time they were really something. There weren't many people doing that kind of work, so it seemed very exciting. But when I look at it now I think, my God, did I do that?"

FDR died on April 12, 1945. The directors of Pocket Books immediately arranged to publish a tribute to the late President, and 300,000 copies of *Franklin Delano Roosevelt: A Memorial*, the first "instant" book, went on sale on April 18, with a simple cover lettered by George Salter. Ed Rofheart remembers the Pocket Books staff all going along to the printers to watch the book roll off the presses.

A similar tour de force was carried off later the same year: *The Atomic*

Sol Immerman in 1978 (Photo: Piet Schreuders)

Age Opens (see page 178), a book on atomic energy written in layman's terms and complete with photographs and diagrams, went on sale less than three weeks after the first atom bomb was dropped on Hiroshima.

Not much later, Ed Rofheart left Pocket Books and Louise Crittenden became the firm's art director. As of January, 1946, the books again had a new general style, this time designed by Gordon Ayman. The round-cornered frame was gone, and in its place was a white stripe at the top of the cover carrying the legend "This is Pocket Book No...," with the exact number of the copy filling the blank, placed there automatically during the printing process by a "numbering box" (see page 176 for an example). Gertrude was also redesigned, and now appeared without her glasses or her baby. The story goes that some readers found the little tyke in Gertrude's pouch "unhygienic," and the spectacles were dropped so that no one would get the idea that reading Pocket Books might cause eyestrain.

Sol Immerman soon became art director, and he held that position at Pocket Books for almost 30 years. Leo Manso talks about working with Immerman: "In the war years and for a while thereafter, you were working more with individuals than with a big company, and I think that a lot of decisions depended on your relationship with the art director. Ed Rofheart always gave me a lot of room to play around in, but Sol Immerman had definite ideas about what he wanted. Some of the beginning designers, especially, had problems with that. Immerman was more commercial than Rofheart, maybe more practical but also more commercial. In my opinion, he always wanted to add a touch of sex to everything. Now, that was not my forte, and I think it was about that time that I quit. I have worked for him, but in other genres. No mystery stories or novels. I did books by Sophocles or Aristotle for Immerman, that sort of thing."

The difference between Immerman's and Rofheart's approaches can be seen from the dustjackets which, in 1948, Pocket Books began to wrap around certain titles, either to capitalize on their having recently been successfully filmed or because the books weren't selling well enough with their original covers. Leo Manso's symbolic design for *The Maltese Falcon*, for example, produced during Rofheart's tenure, was later dustjacketed with a Stanley Meltzoff illustration of a half-naked woman (see page 167). A "touch of sex," or just the spirit of the time? The management of Pocket Books didn't worry about questions like that: their only concern was what would sell the most books.

Immerman's contributions to the graphic form of Pocket Books were considerable. He would develop a new style, then replace it a few years later with something better. In 1949 he substituted a design of his own for the red inside covers which had been created by Ed Diehl only a year earlier. It was Immerman who began crediting cover artists on every volume. He came up with a new colophon in which the words "Pocket Books" were ranged in a half-circle around Gertrude, then, in 1949, moved her *between* those two words: "Every paperback is a pocket book," he has said, "but only a pocket book with Gertrude on it is a Pocket Book." In 1949 and 1950 he designed a number of luxurious releases with support color and sometimes even four-color illustrations inside. And he was responsible for several further alterations in Gertrude's appearance.

In the early '50s, Immerman organized a series of contests for Frank Reilly's students at the Art Students League of New York in West 57th Street. Immerman supplied the subject matter and more than 150 hopeful students submitted sketches, 75 of which were then fleshed out to finished drawings. The winner received $300 and his painting was used as a Pocket Book cover, while Immerman received some 150 inexpensive

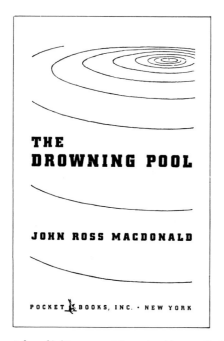

A few of Sol Immerman's inventive title pages for Pocket Books (1949-1950)

1939	1941	1942-43	1943-45	1946

1948	1949	1962	1964	1977

Gertrude the Kangaroo as drawn by Frank Lieberman, the Walt Disney Studios, Milton Charles, Sol Immerman and Milton Glaser

sketches from promising illustrators, a number of whom (Rudy Nappi, Lou Marchetti, Tom Ryan, Mel Crair, Robert Schulz, Clark Hulings, Jack Faragasso, Gerald McConnell, Robert Maguire, Stanley Borack, Verne Tossey and others) later developed into professional cover artists.

Meanwhile, the company steadily broadened its activities. Pocket Books (G.B.) Ltd. was established in August, 1949, to publish a separate series of books in Great Britain; the first titles appeared in the spring of 1950. A year later, *The News of the World* was brought in to manage this British affiliate and to run its distribution, but the series was closed down in 1953. .

The CARDINAL EDITIONS were hatched in 1951. Cardinals were originally intended as a more expensive series; they were priced at 35 cents, while Pocket Books still cost only 25 cents. Cardinal's mascot, naturally, was a bright-red cardinal. To avoid confusion, the Cardinal Editions were published with gold spines and the Pocket Books with silver spines. The CARDINAL GIANTS appeared in 1952, priced at 50 cents.

The COMET BOOKS, a children's series since November of 1948, were replaced by POCKET BOOKS, JR. in January, 1951. The standard paperback format was used, instead of the digest format of the Comets; the colophon was a drawing of a little boy kangaroo and a little girl kangaroo reading a paperback together (the girl kangaroo was the one with the long eyelashes). The series lasted 43 titles.

The first editions of the POCKET LIBRARY, "books of classic literary stature," came out in May, 1954, priced at either 35 or 50 cents. They were supposed to look serious and, therefore, their covers were offset printed and unlacquered (which was actually cheaper than the standard plastic-coated or lacquered covers). The first titles were rereleases of earlier Pocket Books and Cardinal Editions. In 1959, the Pocket Library was renamed the WASHINGTON SQUARE PRESS.

In 1954, the entire paperback industry was faced with a gigantic book surplus; Pocket Books' warehouses were so full of unsold stock and returns that it was decided to dispose of a large number of books by burying them in an abandoned canal near Buffalo, New York. According to "Doc" Lewis, 60 million paperbacks were handled in similar manner around the country. There is a rumor (as yet unverified) that cost-cutting building contractors stacked thousands of paperbacks within the walls of houses constructed around this time, as surplus books were cheaper than any other insulating material then available.

GRAPHIC DESCRIPTION—1939: The price (25 cents) is indicated in a circle on the cover. Gertrude, drawn by Frank Lieberman, is on the spine; the back cover has a yellow border and lists the titles which are "now ready." The covers are of strong paper, the endpapers are a dark red. 1941: Attractive double title pages are introduced. 1942: The number on the spine, until now hand-drawn, is typeset. In November, Gertrude is replaced by the "pb" colophon. Cover illustrations are set off within a round-cornered frame. 1943: There is a black box on the back cover with text about sending books to soldiers. Gertrude, newly-designed by the Walt Disney Studios, returns in the autumn. 1944: The Disney kangaroo replaces the "pb" colophon in the circle at the top of the cover. 1946: The round-cornered frame is elimated. Starting in January, the words "This is Pocket Book No…" and the exact number of the copy appear in a white band at the top of the cover. Gertrude has lost her glasses and her child. A new circular Pocket Books colophon appears at the top of the spine. Cover illustrations become more realistic. 1947: The use of endpapers is dropped. 1948: Sol Immerman designs a new colophon—the words "Pocket Books" in a half-circle around Gertrude—which appears at the upper-left of the cover. From now on, spine texts are set using sans serif type. Cover artists are credited on the last page of the book. The inside covers, designed by Ed Diehl, feature kangaroos and wavy lines of text, white on a red background. 1949: Diehl's inside covers are replaced by a red, white and black Immerman design. The last page carries the legend "This is a Genuine Pocket Book," with Gertrude standing between the words "Pocket" and "Book." 1951: The genre of each book is listed at the top of its spine. Tom Dunn creates many covers. 1952: A black band at the bottom of the cover carries the text, "A Genuine Pocket Book Novel/The Complete Book—Not a Word Missing." The book number appears in a white space at the top of the spine. 1953: The left side of the cover has a silver border with a milled edge. Yellow disappears from the back cover. Many front covers use photographs from Silver Studios. 1954: A silver border is added to the right side of the back cover. 1959: The milled edge of the silver border on the front cover is straightened out. The kangaroo becomes more stylized and smaller.

Avon Books, 1941-1959

If the words "American paperback" suggest to you a book with a thin cover overcrowded with too much fierce color and too many nice words praising its own contents, a book whose contents have little or nothing to do with its cover illustration, a book which falls to pieces if you page through it more than a few times, a book put together without care, consistency, taste or style... then you are the victim of a serious prejudice. AVON BOOKS, however, came closer to matching that series of stereotypes in the 1940s and 1950s than did the products of any other publisher.

Like the Popular Library, Avon Books are "in" with collectors. Their erotic, flashy covers, strongly reminiscent of the pulps, probably account for their popularity. For ordinary readers, though, their annoying lack of style and originality put old Avon Books in the category of throwaway literature, unlike Signet, Pocket Books, Bantam and even Popular Library itself.

Only a few Avons are historically interesting: because Avon was the first to release a short-story collection by Raymond Chandler, because they published pulp author A. Merritt, or because some of their covers are so kitschy that they are touching.

Avon Books were really pulps in paperback form. Even after the firm had been around for years, they still remained true to their roots by publishing at least 10 different series of novels in digest format, including the *Avon Annual* (1945-47) and, from 1947 through 1950, *Avon Detective Mysteries, Avon Fantasy Reader, Avon Monthly Novel, Avon Western Novel, Avon Bedside Novels* and *Avon Fantasy Novels*.

When Pocket Books switched from the American News Company (see page 101) to a network of independent distributors in 1941, ANC asked pulp publisher Joseph Meyers to begin a paperback series for them to distribute. The result was Avon Books.

"Meyers had terrible taste, not only in literature, but in women and even in home furnishings," according to one of his former competitors. He never made it past the fifth grade in school, but he had a firm understanding of business practices. He was the driving force behind Avon; Charles R. Byrne was his editor-in-chief, Frederick Klein was vice-president and V. Diamond took care of production and art direction. The first

Avon Books

13 Avons were published in November of 1941, and the plan was to add four or five titles each subsequent month. But only 10 new volumes were released in all of 1942, and production in 1943 averaged only $1\frac{1}{2}$ titles per month.

One of the first Avon Books proudly displayed this text: "These volumes have been designed with a two-fold purpose...to please your literary taste and to soothe your critical eye. The books, in many instances, contain frontispiece drawings, and, indeed, many are illustrated throughout by world-famous artists in the field of book illustrating. All will be strongly bound, with full-color covers, and the books protected against all weather by special lacquering which gives the book that glossy appearance, and is proof against damp, dirt and everything which makes a book soil after being handled a few times."

According to the quote, "many" Avons were to be illustrated throughout. In fact, only six such volumes appeared during the firm's first 10 years.

Shortly after their first releases hit the stands, Avon found itself embroiled in what turned out to be a lengthy lawsuit with Pocket Books. Avon was accused of having stolen Pocket Books' format and page-edge coloring ("stain"), as well as the term "pocket-size book." On January 19, 1942, a judge ruled in Avon's favor, stating that it was improbable that any consumer would be confused by the appearance of an Avon Book and would buy it thinking that it was a Pocket Book. Pocket Books appealed this decision and, on November 2, 1942, the Appellate Division of the Supreme Court of the State of New York ruled *against* Avon, finding them guilty of unfair competition because of their deliberate imitation of Pocket Books' style and format. The court decided that only Pocket Books would be allowed to sell paperbacks with a red stain and the word "pocket" on the cover, and issued an injunction to that effect. Avon immediately bought a different color ink for its page edges, made sure that the word "Avon" appeared clearly on every cover, and kept right on publishing. And in January of 1944 the Court of Appeals reversed the decision again: from that point on, it has been officially acceptable for any company to publish paperbacks using the Pocket Books format.

Raymond Chandler's novel *The Big Sleep* appeared as an Avon Book in 1944; two Chandler short-story collections followed, *Five Murderers* in 1945 and *Five Sinister Characters* in 1946. Books by A. Merritt (*Seven Footprints to Satan, Burn Witch Burn, The Ship of Ishtar*) were reprinted many times. Jerome Weidman was also a typical Avon author; his *I Can*

Get It for You Wholesale (1937) sold a million copies when Avon released its 1949 edition.

In 1946, Avon covers were bordered by a painted picture frame. This embellishment was dropped early in 1947, shortly after *New Yorker* cartoonist Richard Taylor, as a joke, used an out-of-perspective picture frame on the cover of his collection *The Better Taylors*.

The amateurish manner in which graphic design was approached by Avon can be seen from the drawings of William Shakespeare which served as their corporate colophon (Shakespeare was chosen as patron saint because of his birthplace: Stratford-upon-Avon). In 1944, Joseph Meyers began repeatedly changing the portrait ("Look for the Shakespeare-Head Imprint," the advertisements suggested), until one version seemed to catch on; this was a line drawing, with the left side of Shakespeare's head sliced off at the ear. Meyers did not commission this portrayal of the Bard of Avon—he simply clipped it out of some book or magazine and adopted it as his own, amputated head and all. The missing section of Shakespeare's head was not drawn in until 1952, and the drawing was scrapped completely in 1954.

Avon's best years were '50 and '51. Twelve new titles a month appeared and covers were more colorful, more daring and better printed than ever before. Irving Shulman's *The Amboy Dukes* and *Cry Tough!* each sold over a million copies, as did Nelson Algren's *Never Come Morning*. But production was cut back to eight titles a month in 1954 and to four a month in 1957. Charles Byrne and Frederick Klein left Avon in 1954, to found Berkley Books; when they went, art director Joe Mann was fired and his assistant, Roy Lagrone, was promoted to Mann's job.

Roy E. Lagrone, born in 1926, studied art at the University of Florence in Italy and at Pratt Institute in Brooklyn. He contributed a more modern look to Avon, a look which is clearly visible in the books published after 1955. Instead of continuing to use pulp-influenced cover art-

LOOK FOR THE *Shakespeare-Head* IMPRINT!

| 1941 | 1944 | 1944 | 1947 | 1953 | 1953 |

MYSTERIES • CRIME & DETECTIVE STORIES
ANTHOLOGIES • NOVELS • CLASSICS

The NEW *Avon* pocket-size *Books*
GOOD BOOKS *complete* IN EVERY WAY

The New Avon Books are well-printed on good paper, with large, clear type; strongly bound in colorful, glossy covers treated to resist wear and tear! In many instances the books are printed from the publishers' original $2 and $2.50 plates.

Some are illustrated throughout by renowned artists. The text of all Avon Books is exactly as published in the original higher-priced editions, and is not expurgated, cut, or condensed.

ONLY
25¢
EACH

IN U. S. A.

Because the New Avon Books are easy to open, light to hold, thrilling to read and compact to carry or store in clothing or bags, they are ideal as gifts to the boys in the Armed Forces.

Roy E. Lagrone in 1978 (Photo: Piet Schreuders)

ists, Lagrone hired people like Mitchell Hooks, Lou Marchetti, Victor Kalin, Harry Schaare, Harry Bennett, Robert McGinnis, James Bama and many other young artists. He ususally made sketches for them to work from, but sometimes skipped over the whole process of commissioning artwork and simply used art samples which happened to be lying around his office as cover illustrations.

Lagrone designed covers until the '60s, creating a style for Avon which, while not particularly original, was at least less amateurish than the style he had inherited from his predecessors.

GRAPHIC DESCRIPTION—1941: "AVON *Pocket-Size* Books" is printed on the front cover, at the bottom of the spine and in various places within each volume. A blue frame on the back cover holds a list of recently-released titles. There are endpapers with a spider-web motif. 1946: A painted picture frame borders the front cover. 1947: The picture frame is dropped. The word "Avon" appears twice in a black triangle at the upper-left of the cover. 1949: A hand-lettered "Avon" appears within concentric circles at the upper-left, replacing the black triangle. 1950: The 1949 colophon also appears at the bottom of the spine. 1951: The designer gives special attention to the back cover. 1952: The missing portion of Shakespeare's head is restored. 1954: Shakespeare's head is dropped, and replaced by the word "Avon" between two half-circles. 1959: Roy Lagrone designs yet another new colophon, this time featuring a large "A."

Penguin Books, 1941-1948

The British might disagree, but PENGUIN BOOKS can be considered the most European of all American paperback series. The firm began, in a sense, as a European colony on the American continent: Robert Jonas, Penguin's most important cover designer, was a European at heart, and Kurt Enoch, a director as of 1941, was German by birth. Penguin originally used the same format as Pocket Books and Avon, but after four years they chose a stylish "tall" format similar to that used by Albatross and British Penguin. Where the competition's covers were little more than an attack on the senses, Penguin's were more civilized, more cultured, and also more complex; most of them could be used today without seeming dated or ridiculous. With their introduction of PELICAN BOOKS (later to be renamed MENTOR BOOKS), a series of nonfiction titles, Penguin set a precedent which was not followed up by other quality-paperback publishers until after the war.

In July of 1939, a month after the first Pocket Books were distributed in New York, British Penguin opened an American branch in that same city, with offices at 3 East 17th Street. The new firm's initial stock consisted of a hundred British Penguins; the director of the enterprise was Ian Ballantine, a young American who had studied economics in London. Ballantine had a staff of two: his wife Betty and stockboy Bill Halusic.

The American Penguin branch was set up strictly as an importer: their task was to bring Penguins, Pelicans and PENGUIN SPECIALS in from England and to sell them in America for 25 cents a copy. This turned out not to be quite as simple as it sounds, though, as the books had to be transported not only from England to East 17th Street, but also from East 17th Street to booksellers throughout America. At this point, Ballantine was missing the one service to which Pocket Books owed its phenomenal success: an effective distribution network.

Ballantine learned a great deal of value about the publishing business from importing British Penguins. He learned to choose titles selectively, for example: if he wanted to, he could order 20,000 copies of a given title, or only 200.

The books were wrapped in lots of 100, and a total of 1,000 books were packed to a crate. About once a month, 10-20 such crates were shipped to New York and delivered to Penguin's American office. Ballantine and his "staff" had to cart these large crates up a flight of stairs from the sidewalk in front of the building to the warehouse space a-

Penguin Books with covers by Robert Jonas, Lester Kohs and others

Ian and Betty Ballantine at their Penguin desks in the early 1940s (Photo: Phillip Album)

bove. On delivery days, Ballantine's friends (including Walter Pitkin and Sidney Kramer) were called on to help out with the barge-toting and bale-lifting.

As Penguin grew, the available amount of warehouse space quickly became insufficient: Ballantine moved his headquarters from East 17th Street to 41 East 28th Street in 1940, to 300 Fourth Avenue in 1942 and, finally, to 245 Fifth Avenue in 1943.

Penguins and Pelicans slowly began to sell. In 1941, Ballantine began importing KING PENGUINS and PENGUIN HANSARD BOOKS as well. King Penguins, advertised as "the ideal gift," were deluxe Penguins with hard covers and color illustrations throughout; they sold for 50 cents. The Hansard series ran from August, 1940 until September, 1942, and featured books about the progress of the war; there were six Hansards altogether, beginning with *From Chamberlain to Churchill*.

Allen Lane, the man behind British Penguin, visited New York in 1941 and was not pleased with Ian Ballantine's results. At a cocktail party given by U.S. publishers in his honor, Lane spoke with one of the founders of the Albatross Modern Continental Library, Kurt Enoch, who had come to America to escape the Nazis. Soon after, Lane hired Enoch and make him vice-president of Penguin Books, Inc.

The threat of war, documented in the Penguin Specials, and the outbreak of war in Europe, reported by the Penguin Hansards, were followed, on December 7, 1941, by the Japanese attack on Pearl Harbor.

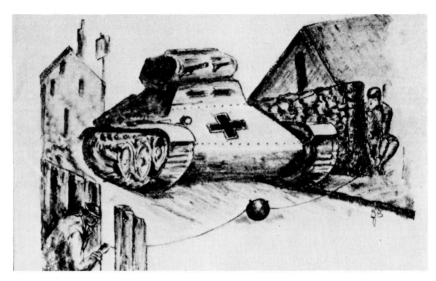

Ian Ballantine's father, actor Edward J. Ballantine, drew this cover illustration for Penguin Special S75, *New Ways of War.*

America declared war on Japan a day later, and on Germany and Italy on December 11.

For Penguin, war meant an immediate and enormous increase in the demand for modern novels and books of political exposition. Unfortunately, the war also meant that the paper used to print these books in England became increasingly worse and, tragically, that many shipments never made it across the Atlantic to America, as the vessels carrying them fell victim to submarine attacks.

Ian Ballantine was forced to switch hats, from importer to publisher.

The first step was to close a deal with Colonel Joseph E. Greene of the *Infantry Journal* and the Military Service Publishing Company. The agreement: Penguin would supply the words, *Infantry Journal* would provide the paper and the military would purchase the lion's share of the print runs. The result: Penguin began to specialize in war books.

The first titles (*The Case for the Federal Union*, *Warships at Work*, *New Ways of War*, *Russia* and *Aircraft Recognition*) had already appeared as British Penguins between 1939 and 1941 and only needed to be reprinted, but the first original American Penguin Specials (*What's That Plane?*, *New Soldier's Handbook* and *How the Jap Army Fights*) soon followed. These INFANTRY JOURNAL – PENGUIN BOOKS, printed in a somewhat smaller format than the British Penguin Specials, with an orange support color and an illustration on the cover, first appeared in March, 1942. They had been put together around the Ballantine's kitchen table. For *What's That Plane?* (numbered s201), for example, Ian designed the cover, Betty did the layout, Walter Pitkin wrote the text and his wife Suzanne traced silhouettes of airplanes from drawings provided by the British Information Service. For *New Ways of War*, the cover was created by Edward J. Ballantine, Ian's father.

Although the covers of the British Penguins were purely typographical, the British Specials were sometimes published with a modest illustration between the wide orange bands at the top and bottom of the cover; on the American editions, the illustrations were larger. The regular American Penguins, which also began to appear in March of 1942, also had illustrated covers; according to *Publishers Weekly*, type designer Lucian Bernhard created the basic cover design.

The American Penguins were reprints of popular or important novels and mysteries. In March, 1942, British Penguin 357 was released, so it seemed safe to begin the American series with number 501.

In Europe, Albatross, Penguin and Tauchnitz had used a color-coding system in which the color of each book's cover indicated its genre. American Penguin adopted the same idea: novels and dramas used maroon as a support color on their covers; Penguin Specials used orange; biographies, memoirs, historical works and other nonfiction used yellow; mysteries used green; and all other books, such as *The Penguin Book of Sonnets*, used blue.

By 1943, Kurt Enoch had hired Gobin Stair to help out with production and design, and Stair had hired illustrators like Lester Kohs and H. Lawrence Hoffman to do covers. Compared with Pocket Books and Avon Books from the same period, Penguin covers were models of good taste and modesty; they were, however, radically different from the purely typographical British Penguins, and they were not admired by Allen Lane. In *The Penguin Story*, a British publication, the American Penguins were described as "commodities with garish and sensational eye-appeal. The contents of the book...were relatively unimportant: what mattered was that its lurid exterior should ambush the customers."

This quote is representative of several differences of opinion which existed at that time, with Lane on one side and Ballantine and Enoch, who knew that their books would have little or no chance against the competition in American bookstores without illustrated covers, on the other. These differences of opinion were to result in a definitive break after the war.

An Open Letter

Dear Readers:

Ever since we first realized that Penguin Books were even more successful than we expected, we have had an urge to shake hands with every stranger we have seen reading or carrying one of our books. Of course we know we would soon develop Congressman's Cramps that way; but the urge still persists. So next time a stranger shakes hands with you unexpectedly, we suggest you check quickly on two things: (1) whether you are carrying a Penguin Book and (2) whether the stranger is himself a Penguin, or looks like one. With a trade mark like ours, it won't take long for us to acquire the jaunty, devil-may-care appearance of Penguins.

Seriously, we're very grateful for the way millions of you have taken up the Penguin Book idea. It seems that all we have to do is publish the very best books at our set price of twenty-five cents. We imagine that you do the rest, because the books do disappear from the booksellers' racks.

Frankly, we don't know the whole explanation for our startling success. Maybe you like our authors —Louis Bromfield, John Steinbeck, Christopher Morley, etc.—or perhaps you prefer our attractive type page. Our best guess, however, is that the answer lies in all the factors that make Penguin Books what they are. Anyway, we're thankful, and we're doing our level best to please you as much in the future as we seem to have done in the past. We hope you'll be checking up on us!

Penguin Books

Meanwhile, American Penguins and Specials continued to appear, with a strong slant towards subject matter of interest to America's military. Fifteen Penguins were published in 1943; in addition, the Specials released that year included *Psychology for the Fighting Man*, *Shipyard Diary of a Woman Welder* and John Steinbeck's *The Moon is Down*. When there was space available, humorously-illustrated sales pitches or letters to the reader were printed at the end of the main text. The letters would run something like this: "*An Invitation.*—The Publishers cordially invite you to submit your criticisms of this book and of any other volume that bears the Penguin name. Suggestions for new books or reprints to be added to this series are also most welcome. Please address your criticism to *The Old Man, c/o Penguin Books, Inc., 245 Fifth Avenue*, N.Y. *16*, N.Y."

In 1945 Penguin published, for the first time, a book by Erskine Caldwell, *Trouble in July*. The cover was by Robert Jonas, who had done his first cover illustration for Penguin (number 560, *Murder in Fiji*) earlier the same year.

"I needed a job fast, and I was knocking on doors everywhere," Jonas remembers. "One of the first doors I tried was at Penguin Books, Inc. I met Mr. Kurt Enoch there and it immediately clicked. He was a European and he liked my ideas.

"Bauhaus influenced me in everything. They showed me a way to do what I felt I had to do with my covers, to present a strong and effective impression of the contents of the book. I always insisted on looking for the positive side, positive with regard to the world.

"My whole life I've been balancing art and social consciousness—and that's some balancing act! I've never believed in elitist art; I believe in art for the people. That's often led to problems with my colleagues: whenever Willem de Kooning saw me he used to yell, 'So? You still believe in art for the people?' Arshile Gorky called it 'poor art for poor people.' He said, 'If you've got a message, call up the union!' But that's what I believed in, and I completely agreed with the slogan that the New American Library used to use: 'Good Reading for the Millions.'

"An enormous amount of European intellect flooded the United States between 1934 and 1939, all people fleeing the Nazis. They created a new intellectual climate in America, and I was lucky enough to be in the middle of it. Even the most important European painters, like Miró and Picasso, were fugitives from their own countries; they weren't producing French or Spanish art, but *international* art. That was exactly what I wanted to do. I didn't like the idea of American art—I was only interested in international art.

Robert Jonas in 1978 (Photo: Piet Schreuders)

"I used three different approaches for my book covers. For books in which the poetic predominated I used poetic, associative images. For books with a clear and concrete social meaning, I used related images which could be clearly understood, even by people who couldn't understand the books themselves. And for books live *Sweden: The Middle Way*, with very specific subjects, I used diagrams and suchlike."

Looking back, Jonas has most to say about his cover for Carson McCullers' *The Heart is a Lonely Hunter* (see page 71): "I can't explain it. You have to feel it, you have to understand it at a subconscious level, like poetry has to be understood or felt at a subconscious level. Certain things in the cover are obvious, like the fist, that's the militant worker, the militant people of the whole world—this was long before the '60s, when everybody walked around with a clenched fist—and the eagle,.the symbol of the freedom we were willing to fight for. At the left there's a poor boy—you know, a symbol of world poverty. The writer was actually talking about completely different things in that book, but still, that's its universal theme. But explaining this kind of thing, that goes against my grain, because if you need to explain it then it hasn't worked."

The differences between American and British Penguin did not disappear after the war; in fact, they became more serious. At issue were the appearance of the books, the selection of titles and dustribution. Ballantine and Enoch wanted to follow the example of Pocket Books, Avon and Dell, publishing only popular titles and distributing to drugstores, cigar stores, and kiosks at train stations and airports. But Allen Lane wanted to keep the existing editorial standards and limit sales to bookstores. In 1945 Ballantine left; later that year, he established Bantam Books. To Penguin's management was added Victor Weybright, who had spent some time on the staff of the American embassy in London.

As late as October of '45, readers' requests for new editions of sold-out Penguins were being sadly turned down because of insufficient supplies of paper, but in November management was able to announce: "We have long planned a companion series to Penguin Books and, with the end of paper rationing, we can now launch the Pelican Books. These will be nonfiction and on the widest variety of subjects, such as Philosophy, Anthropology, Psychology, Economics, the Arts, Sociology, Science and contemporary problems both local and international....In our selection of titles we aim to satisfy specific American requirements through the publication of books of an authoritative kind by the best-qualified authors." Fifteen titles were announced, and they were published in January, 1946. The first Pelicans were *Public Opinion* by Walter Lippmann, *Patterns of Culture* by Ruth Benedict and *You and Music* by Christian Darnton.

The format of the Penguins and Pelicans was changed in 1946: the books were made taller, about the same size as the British Penguins and the prewar Albatrosses. This "strong" format was suggested by Kurt Enoch, who wanted the books to stand out more in stores, and designed by Robert Jonas. At the same time, color-coding was eliminated; in its place, a new Penguin penguin (the dancing-to-the-right version, already in use in England) appeared at the top of each cover, and a book's genre was indicated by the shape within which the bird was printed: a square meant fiction, a triangle mystery, a diamond miscellaneous titles such as biographies and histories, a circle anthologies and poetry. New Penguins released in 1945 included John Dos Passos' *Manhattan Transfer* and James M. Cain's *Mildred Pierce*; also that year, the firm began issuing new editions of earlier successful titles. Covers were mainly illustrated by Robert Jonas, but also by George Salter, H. L. Hoffman and Miriam Woods. For the Pelican series, Elaine de Kooning (the wife of Jonas' friend Willem) drew a flying pelican as the colophon.

In the autumn of 1946, the American management wrote that Penguin Books, Inc., the publisher of Penguins in the United States, was in fact an independent firm, but that it nevertheless maintained a common editorial philosophy with Penguin Books in Engeland and that the two companies worked together on "special projects." Two new American series were announced, the King Penguins (modeled after the British series of the same name) and the American Modern Painters Series, to be edited by Alfred H. Barr. Neither of these projects ever materialized, however.

What *did* materialize, in 1947, was the first (and, as it turned out, next-to-last) volume of what was intended as a series of guidebooks; it was numbered G-1 and entitled *The Penguin Guide to California*. William Faulkner's *Sanctuary*, James T. Farrell's *Young Lonigan*, James M. Cain's *Serenade* and Erskine Caldwell's *Tobacco Road* were the year's big sellers.

The relationship with British Penguin remained relatively stable through 1947, but in 1948 Kurt Enoch and Victor Weybright, unable to agree with Allen Lane on policy matters, decided to set up a completely independent publishing company: The New American Library of World Literature, Inc. All ties with Penguin Books were broken, and Penguin's British address (Harmondsworth, Middlesex) disappeared from the product. For a few months, new releases were called "Penguin Signets" or "Pelican Mentors," but by the end of 1948 the birds had flown.

In January of 1950, British Penguin once again set up an American office to handle the import and distribution of English Penguins and Pelicans; like Ian Ballantine's original branch office, this new branch (located in Baltimore, Maryland) also eventually began producing its own books, although to a much lesser degree.

GRAPHIC DESCRIPTION—1942: Green-, yellow-, red- or blue-bordered covers feature a penguin looking off to the left, with his feet on a black band bearing the words "Penguin Books," Infantry Journal - Penguin Books carry both the *Infantry Journal* colophon and a penguin in a circle. Cover illustrations have one or more support colors, or are in black-and-white. Most of the drawings are fairly primitive and are unsigned, but next year there will also be covers by Hoffman, Triggs and Kohs. 1946: Robert Jonas provides a new format, a new graphic form and most of the year's covers, which are bordered by colored bands at top and bottom, setting the illustrations off nicely. In the upper band a penguin, facing right, is dancing within either a square, triangle, diamond or circle.

Books in Wartime, 1941-1947

One might well have expected the outbreak of World War II to deal a shattering blow to the three-year-young American paperback industry, especially as the war was accompanied by extensive paper rationing; surprisingly, though, that turned out not to be the case. In fact, the number of Americans buying paperbacks went *up* during the war years, rather than down, not only because people felt a greater need of distraction but also so that the books could be sent off to soldiers at the front. Publishers printed more paperbacks than ever before and, even though the quality of the paper that was available to them became steadily worse, there were few returns of unsold stocks—an ideal state of affairs for young and small publishers. The armed forces were soon gobbling up books faster than existing firms could print them, and special wartime publishers had to be set up just to keep America's fighting men in reading material. The total number of military editions produced was well over 100 million.

The mailing of paperbacks to family members in uniform was encouraged everywhere and directed by the Victory Book Campaign, a drive organized by the American Library Association and the Red Cross. Inside paperbacks, readers found messages such as: "*Our Boys Need and Deserve Books.*—The Victory Book Campaign asks for your cooperation. Sailors at sea, Soldiers in the Solomons, Marines in Africa, Commandos on the alert in some unrevealed jumping-off place—they all need books to read—to read for pleasure, for information, and for just plain relaxation—to take their minds off sounds and sights they're trying to stop forever. Give them books—give them this book, when you are through with it—take it to the nearest Public Library, or send it to one of the addresses below—a 3¢ stamp will do it."

A black block on the back of every Pocket Book carried text reading "Share this book with someone in uniform" or "Send this book to a boy in the armed forces anywhere in the U.S." Pocket Books even thought of the prisoners-of-war: "Americans most in need of reading matter are those now held prisoners by the Germans.... Because there are many special restrictions and conditions, Pocket Books has established a Prisoner-of-War Service for the convenience of those who want to send books to American prisoners. For complete information apply to PoW Service, Pocket Books, Inc., 18 West 48th Street, New York, N.Y."

Avon Books also issued an urgent call to mail books to family members overseas: "Because the New Avon Books are easy to hold, thrilling to read and compact to carry or store in clothing or bags, they are ideal

Philip Van Doren Stern, author and editor at Pocket Books and in charge of editorial policy for the Armed Services Editions

as gifts to the boys in the Armed Forces." It cost 25 cents to send them, though, just as much as it cost to buy them.

Reactions trickled in from soldiers, affirming that all these books were filling a real need. Pocket Books chose the most usable sentences from such letters and printed them at the back of their new releases: "If I had to choose, when making up my pack, between an extra K ration and a couple of Pocket Books, I honestly believe that I would, in most circumstances, choose the books." Or: "My division was in the invasion of

Sicily and Italy. I assure you that all concerned appreciated the Pocket Books. Many a front line infantryman has carried a Pocket Book with him when going into engagements."

This was all very useful and heartwarming, yet it was also obvious that the business side of wartime publishing could and should be enlarged. The more Americans sent off to war, the greater the demand for reading material. After a few years, that demand became so large that it could only be filled by a publishing venture aimed exclusively at the military market. For that reason, the Council on Books in Wartime was established in 1943 to control two nonprofit publishers: Overseas Editions and Armed Services Editions.

The Council represented about 70 American publishers and many libraries and distributors; there was a three-man Executive Committee, and daily operations were directed by a Managing Committee which included Richard L. Simon and Philip Van Doren Stern of Pocket Books and S. Spencer Scott. Pocket Books' Robert F. DeGraff was also heavily involved.

Van Doren Stern, who was later to become executive editor at Pocket Books, had edited several anthologies (*The Pocket Reader, The Pocket Companion, The Pocket Book of America*) before becoming a member of the Council on Books in Wartime. As general manager of the Council's publishing program, he decided which books were to be issued and maintained contact with the five branches of the military, five printers, various paper factories, 12 typesetters, and the entire membership of the Council. Other important figures were Ray Trautman, chief librarian of the Army, Isabel DuBois, chief librarian of the Navy, and H. Stanley Thompson, the graphics specialist in the Special Services Division.

OVERSEAS EDITIONS were published for foreign use only; they were not for sale in the United States or Canada. The idea was to reprint recent "representative" American books and to make them available in Europe and Asia until "Axis aggression" could be put down and normal publishing activities could again be picked up. The books were slightly larger than conventional paperbacks, and had the Statue of Liberty on their covers as a colophon.

ARMED SERVICES EDITIONS were set apart for American soldiers; they were not available to the general public. There were two standard formats: 14 cm long by 10 cm high ($5\frac{1}{2}" \times 4"$) for books up to 320 pages and 16 cm long by 11 cm high ($6\frac{1}{2}" \times 4\frac{1}{2}"$) for books up to 512 pages. Books which would require more pages were "Condensed for Wartime Reading." The oblong format was not only chosen because it fit well in the

OUR MEN NEED
★ BOOKS ★

SEND
ALL YOU CAN SPARE

THIS IS A WARTIME BOOK

THIS EDITION WHICH IS COMPLETE
AND UNABRIDGED IS PRODUCED IN FULL
COMPLIANCE WITH THE GOVERNMENT'S
REGULATIONS FOR CONSERVING PAPER
AND OTHER ESSENTIAL MATERIALS.

pockets of uniform jackets, but also because it was economical to print. The Armed Services Editions were printed on presses which had been built for magazines, pulp novels or digest-format paperbacks; they were printed and bound two at a time and then, after binding, cut apart into two separate books. The digest-format presses printed sets of two 14 × 10 cm Armed Services Editions, the pulp-novel presses printed sets of two 16 × 11 cm books.

Philip Van Doren Stern hired Sol Immerman to design the covers. Immerman's basic design was simple: a small reproduction of the hard-cover cover, a circular A.S.E. colophon, a colored band and a text. Immerman had these regular elements preprinted, then pasted the rest of the design around them. He earned $10 per cover.

In the five-year existence of the Armed Services Editions, a total of 1,322 titles were issued (it took Pocket Books 20 years to get that far—number 1322 didn't appear until 1960). The first 30 titles, numbered A1-A30 and printed in editions of 50,000 copies each—1.5 million books in all—appeared in September of 1943. Every month another 30 titles were added, with similar print runs, numbered in sequence using the next available letter of the alphabet. The books were sorted in New York City's harbor and shipped by the Army Postal Service. The Special Services Division arranged for further distribution: sometimes books were transported by plane and dropped to their destinations by parachute.

Beginning with the I series (August, 1944), the books were distributed within America as well, to the many soldiers confined to hospitals there. Meanwhile, the print run per title had gone up to 155,000 copies and the number of titles per series had risen from 30 to 40.

Most Armed Services Editions were reprints of novels or collections of short stories, poetry, political essays or war journalism, provided by the 70 participating publishers. Some collections were compiled especially for Armed Services Editions, including volumes of stories by Stephen Vincent Benét, Katherine Mansfield, Paul Gallico, Edgar Allan Poe, Thomas Mann and Ernest Hemingway. As of May, 1945, from four to six previously-printed Armed Services Editions were reprinted in each new series of 40 titles.

Publication of the Armed Services Editions continued for a while after the end of the war. Beginning with number 1179 (October, 1946), the series was printed using the standard Pocket Books format, which proved more economical for editions of "only" 25,000 copies. The last title, Ernie Pyle's *Home Country*, appeared in September, 1947.

A few other publishers active during the war years deserve mention here. The collaboration between Penguin Books and the *Infantry Journal*, a magazine which was published in Washington, D.C. for circulation to the American Army, has already been referred to: beginning in 1942 they worked together on the production and distribution of a series of paperbacks. As of June, 1944, the *Journal* also published about 75 paperbacks of its own. These were "standard military books," dealing with war-related subjects; 17 of them, the FIGHTING FORCES SERIES, were, like the Armed Services Editions, only available to military personnel.

INFANTRY JOURNAL BOOKS, established as a separate series in June of 1945, did not last very long. Only two titles were released: *Boomerang/Baby Fights Back* by William Chambliss and *The U.S. Marines on Iwo Jima*.

In November of 1944, the Military Service Publishing Company (Harrisburg, Pennsylvania) initiated a paperback series, the SUPERIOR REPRINTS, in cooperation with Penguin Books. The books, which resembled Penguins, were reprints of easily-digestible novels by, among others, Faith Baldwin, Philip Wylie, Frank Gruber and Elizabeth Daly. Because of the paper shortage and because they were not war books, the Superior Reprints could not be issued with the regular Penguin series. Six titles appeared in 1944, 15 in 1945. In September of that year, the series was discontinued.

When Ian Ballantine left Penguin, he took with him supplies of a number of war books which had been published as Penguin Specials, Infantry Journal Books and Superior Reprints. Three years later, eight Superior Reprints, one Infantry Journal Book and one Infantry Journal - Penguin Book were again offered to the reading public, this time wearing dustjackets which identified them as products of Ballantine's Bantam Books.

By the end of the war, the public had become used to buying paperbacks. The earlier idea that "real" literature could only be bought at a bookshop, and not at a supermarket or a station kiosk, had disappeared. In America and abroad, it was clear that there was indeed a mass audience for paperbacks: publishers had only to look at the enormous total of almost 123 million Armed Services Editions in circulation. A seed had most definitely been planted and, in the late '40s and throughout the '50s, paperback publishers would eagerly reap the resultant fruit.

Popular Library, 1943-1959

Popular. That one word accurately describes the contemporary reaction to POPULAR LIBRARY's paperbacks from the early 1950s, especially in America: any collector of pop culture artifacts who was, until recently, satisfied with framed original comic strip drawings or daring 1930s film posters is nowadays practically obliged to give over at least a part of his house to old Popular Library releases. They are lovely to look at, these books, with their dark-green endpapers, their covers with flamboyant lettering and gay colors (lots of greens and reds) and painted men and women in almost unbelievably provocative positions. These covers have much in common with the pulps, although they are usually a little less extreme and a little better drawn. The volumes issued from 1948 to 1952, when experienced pulp artists were delivering covers, are the most in demand; the earlier books, though, where a man in a slouch hat often lurks mysteriously in the shadows somewhere on the cover, are also attractive.

The first Popular Library, Leslie Charteris' *Saint Overboard*, was

Popular Library books with covers by H. L. Hoffman, Fiedler, Earle Bergey, Rudolph Belarski, George Rozen, Paul Kresse and others actually labeled as being a Popular Book. It was published in 1943 by Ned L. Pines and Leo Margulies.

Ned Pines' first publishing venture, in the 1920s, had been the establishment of a small newspaper, the *Post*, in Brooklyn, New York, his home town. In 1929 he started a magazine, *College Life*, and then used the profits from that publication to stake the Thrilling Group, a successful publishing house which, at its peak in the late '30s, was issuing 44 different pulp series (*Thrilling Wonder Stories*, *Thrilling Western Stories*, and so on). As of 1931, Pines' editor-in-chief and partner in both Ned Pines, Inc. and Pines Publications was Leo Margulies.

Margulies (1900-1975) had begun his career as a literary agent, later becoming an editor at Tower Magazines and ultimately winding up with Ned Pines at the Thrilling Group. Together, he and Pines were responsible for the publication of magazines like *Real*, *See*, *Screenland*, *Silver Screen* and *Your Daily Horoscope*, and digests such as *Future Science Fiction* and *Thrilling Mystery Novels*. It was Charles N. Heckelman, another Thrilling Group editor, who recommended Margulies for the editor-in-chief slot at Popular Library. In addition to that supervisory position, Margulies was also to compile Popular Library 156 *(Popular Book of Western Stories)* and 187 *(Selected Western Stories)* himself.

For its first four years, the management of Popular Library steered a fairly straight course. All releases were reprints of successful mysteries by authors like Leslie Charteris, Mignon G. Eberhart, John Dickson Carr, Craig Rice, Patricia Wentworth, Q. Patrick, Jonathan Stagge and Ray Townsend. The first Westerns appeared in 1946, and adventure stories and straight novels soon followed. At the end of the '40s came science-fiction titles and collections of jokes, cartoons and crossword puzzles.

It would have been convenient to have had artists from the Thrilling Group stable also illustrate Popular Library covers, but that did not happen for the first five years. Covers for numbers 1 through 125 were all produced by Sol Immerman's studio: H. Lawrence Hoffman did the artwork and Immerman himself provided the lettering. The repetition of the cover illustration on the title page, smaller and as a line drawing, was probably their idea; this clever custom continued through 1951.

In 1949, the Popular Library slowly began to change. The cover paper became thinner, the book paper cheaper, the cover illustrations more stimulating.

Many pulp artists began doing paperback work around this time, including two established giants of the pulp world: Earle Bergey and Rudolph Belarski. The economic position of the pulps was deteriorating,

In Popular Library releases up to 1952, cover illustrations were repeated on the title page, reduced, as line drawings.

so Bergey and Belarski moved to Popular Library, where their work completely changed the direction of that company's graphic approach.

Bergey only did 16 covers for Popular Library over a span of five years, but those 16 were critically important. The first, in 1948, was for *The Private Life of Helen of Troy* (Popular Library 147; see page 53). This cover is remembered today as "the nipple cover." Nipples were not an uncommon sight on the covers of popular novels and periodicals during the '20s and '30s, but in the '40s and '50s they disappeared from the media (except, of course, for the nudie magazines); an unusual exception was made for Bergey's Helen, perhaps because of her respected position in classical antiquity.

Rudolph Belarski contributed 50 covers to Popular Library in the same five-year period. *The Silver Forest, Duke* and *Overboard* are a few of his best; *The Yellow Overcoat, The Illustrious Corpse, The Hangman's Whip, The Old Battle Ax* and *Dark Threat* reused cover drawings he had initially produced for the pulps (see pages 170 and 171). His style, although perhaps not unique for pulps, was completely new for paperbacks and was quickly imitated. George Rozen, K. Wilson, S. Cherry and others did covers for Popular Library on which Belarski's influence can be clearly seen. It is impossible to think of Rudolph Belarski without thinking of Popular Library, and it is equally impossible to imagine Popular Library without remembering Rudolph Belarski.

In the early '50s, Popular Library began publishing more and more paperback originals, especially of the so-called "hardboiled" detective genre (John D. MacDonald and William P. McGivern are representative authors). At Ned Pines' request, a new art director was taken on in January of 1952, to give the books a simpler, clearer style; Sol Immerman recommended Ed Rofheart for the job. Rofheart, who had been art director for Pocket Books during the war years, had since then been busy developing marketing campaigns for the likes of Revlon, Maidenform and Avon cosmetics on the staff of Grey Advertising.

"I couldn't stand all that pulp stuff," he remembers. "Popular Library was hiring pulp artists to draw their covers, but I was more interested in the people then doing illustrations for magazines and ads, people who had never worked for the paperbacks before. It was difficult to get them, though, because paperback work paid less. The first thing I did design-wise was pick one set typeface, Franklin Gothic Condensed, and use it for all cover text, so they couldn't screw things up too badly."

In 1952, Rofheart's influence could be clearly seen. That year, Bergey and Belarski delivered their last covers; artists with "softer" styles (like Paul Kresse, Ralph DeSoto, James Meese and, later on, Mitchell Hooks) took their places. Responding to the spirit of the times, the *design* of Popular Library covers became more important than the drawings themselves; at the same time, as at Bantam, the back cover began to be treated as an integral part of overall cover design. Starting in 1952, Popular Library books were certainly more professionally prepared than they had been, but it's hard to argue with those fans who prefer the more personal style of the earlier years.

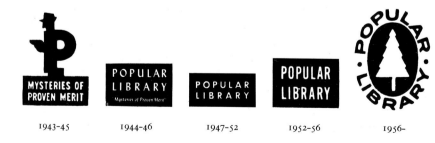

| 1943–45 | 1944–46 | 1947–52 | 1952–56 | 1956– |

GRAPHIC DESCRIPTION—1943: There are bands bordering the front cover at top and bottom. The colophon, a "P" with a slouch hat and a pistol, announces that Popular Library books are "Mysteries of Proven Merit;" it can be found on the front cover and at the base of the spine. The back cover is yellow and features a blurb about the author. H.L. Hoffman draws most covers. 1944: Titles are set within a rectangle, in Lydian typeface. There is a red rectangle on the back cover. 1945: The pistol colophon disappears. The book number is printed at the bottom of the spine. Green endpapers are introduced. 1947: A rectangle enclosing the words "Popular Library" is printed at the top-left of the cover. To the right of this rectangle is a one-line sales pitch. The book number appears in a space at the top of the spine. The back cover is still yellow; the "Popular Library" rectangle from the front appears on the back as well. The title of the book is generally hand-lettered and slants upward from left to right; this style will remain in use until Ed Rofheart's arrival in 1952. 1952: All cover text is set in Franklin Gothic Condensed. The letters in the rectangle on the front cover are thinner. The spine is white with red or black lettering. The back cover is white, with freestanding illustrations. 1954: A taller format is introduced. 1956: The green endpapers are eliminated; the inside of the cover is white. The pinetree colophon (for Pines Publications) debuts.

Dell Books, 1943-1959

The Dell "look" has little in common with that of the other paperback publishers; the differences might be explained by the fact that, while most of their competitors were based in New York, all of Dell's editorial work, production and printing through 1962 took place in Racine, Wisconsin. Like the competition, Dell developed from a reliance on expressionistic covers through a realistic phase, winding up strongly design-oriented; at Dell, however, the *manner* in which this development occurred was unique. Most paperback collectors and fans have a weak spot for the Dells of the '40s, with their "mapbacks" (see pages 82-83), their airbrushed covers and their sophisticated printing techniques.

George Delacorte, Jr., aged 28 years, founded the Dell Publishing Company as a pulp house in 1922. He borrowed the necessary funds from his father and a bank, bought publishable material cheaply overseas, and found a printer willing to extend him three months' credit while he got his new firm off the ground. His pulps (*Danger Trail, Scotland Yard, Sky Riders, Western Romances, War Birds*) were followed by magazines about radio and film stars (*Radio Stars, Modern Screen*) and, in the '30s, by comic books (*Donald Duck, Super Comics, Looney Tunes, Flash Gordon, Little Lulu*). *Popular Comics* (1936) marked the beginning of a long relationship between Dell and the Western Printing & Lithographing Company, founded in Racine in 1907 by Edward H. Wadewitz. Wadewitz

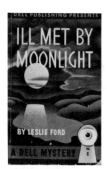

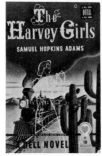

Dell Books with covers by Gerald Gregg, George Frederiksen, Earl Sherwan, Mauieri (?), Victor Kalin, Jerry Cummings and William George

was involved with much more than just printing: Western also produced children's books, playing cards, maps and jigsaw puzzles—and Dell's comic books as well. Western chose the titles and published them, Dell decided how many copies of each title to print and handled the distribution.

George Delacorte says that he was already considering publishing paperbacks by the late '30s, but that it was several years before he actually got around to beginning. He first negotiated with Allen Lane of Penguin Books, then, later, with Richard Simon, Max Schuster and Leon Shimkin, who were about to establish Pocket Books.

"They all wanted to charge 25 cents a book," Delacorte remembers, "but I didn't. I was a magazine publisher, and I believed prices should be 10 or 15 cents. They wouldn't agree to that. Finally I decided, 'Look, my whole life I've been a loner. I started up Dell Publishing all by myself, what do I want with three partners now?' So after a lot of meetings I said, let 'em go. And they went. I was very busy at that time with my comics, an enormous business grossing around 20 million dollars a year, so I didn't really *need* paperbacks. But then at one point the American News Company approached me and said, 'George, why don't you go into the paperback business? We'd like to distribute them for you!' (This was just after Pocket Books had left ANC.) So in 1940 or 1941, I don't remember which, I started publishing paperbacks."

It was more likely 1943, although the design of the books began in 1942, and Delacorte structured his paperback operation along the same lines as his existing comic book empire: Western Printing was to choose the titles, design the covers and print and bind the books, Dell was to arrange the distribution. In this way, all DELL BOOKS released through 1952 were in fact produced by the Dell Book Division of the Western Printing & Lithographing Company. These Dells were Western's first paperbacks, except for the small series of BANTAM BOOKS which had been published by their Los Angeles branch between 1939 and 1943. The Bantams were made for sale in vending machines; their spiritual father was Western's editor-in-chief, Lloyd Smith, who took over that same position in the Dell Book Division in 1943.

The first Dell titles were mysteries, featuring crime-solvers such as Ellery Queen, Kenny Kilkenny, Jane Marple, Robin Bishop, Sir Henry Merrivale, Christopher McKee and Michael Shayne. Brett Halliday and Helen McCloy were typical Dell authors.

The covers were designed in Racine by Western. Preliminary sketches were sent to New York, where a Western representative had them

George T. Delacorte in 1978 (Photo: Piet
Schreuders)

Helen Mayer in 1978, holding two old Dell
covers (Photo: Piet Schreuders)

Mapbacks   Mystery   Adventure   Western   Romance   Historical

approved by Dell's management, then the covers were produced back in Racine.

William Strohmer was the series' art director. He and his assistant, George Frederiksen, designed all of the early covers; when approved, the illustrations were drawn by Strohmer or Frederiksen or a staff artist, of whom Gerald Gregg was the most important. Bernie Salbreiter did the lettering.

The cover of Dell 1 (Philip Ketchum's *Death in the Library*) was drawn by William Strohmer. At the bottom of the front cover, in big letters, were the words "A Dell Mystery." The back cover carried the text, "This is a DELL BOOK presenting a new exciting Mystery Series selected by the Editors of America's Foremost Detective Magazines;" underneath were the words "Dell Publishing Company" and a drawing of an eye peering through a keyhole.

Dell 5, *Four Frightened Women* by George Harmon Coxe, was the first of the mapbacks: on the back cover of each of these books is, naturally, a map—a cutaway bird's-eye view of the apartment building, house, hotel or city-section in which the events of the book take place. These drawings were generally quite faithful to the books; the most careful one was probably the map sketched by author Hake Talbot for his own book, *Rim of the Pit* (Dell 173), and executed, as were most of the map-backs, by Ruth Belew.

Almost all Dell Books published until 1951 were provided with a mapback; beginning in that year, the practice was gradually abandoned. Dell's sales department hated the idea; they found the maps unnecessary and noncommercial, and felt that back covers could better be reserved for advertising blurbs.

Throughout this period, Dell Books were between 160 and 288 pages long. Lengthier novels were condensed, and the phrase "Complete and Unabridged," which most publishers proudly displayed on their covers, was dropped in such cases. The misleading "Complete with map on back cover" was used for a while in 1946, but was later changed to "With map on back cover."

In 1951, Don Ward, an editor at Western, launched the DELL 10-CENTS BOOKS: these were thin volumes (64 pages), and were staplebound rather than sewn. A total of 36 titles appeared, primarily mysteries, Westerns and straight novels. Covers were illustrated by Robert Stanley, Victor Kalin, Barye Phillips and George Mayers, all of whom were also working for the regular Dell series.

Dell's cover style was more realistic in the '50s than it had been in the

'40s, yet still lacked the emotional charge of an artist like Avati, who was very popular at that time. The most productive Dell artist of the period was Robert Stanley.

The process of sending cover designs back and forth between Racine and New York was cumbersome; in 1951, Dell decided that it was time for Western's art department to move East. Walter Brooks, a Scot who had studied art in New York at Cooper Union and at the Art Students League, and had been designing record covers and illustrating children's books for Western as a freelancer since 1950, was taken on as studio head and art director. Changes in Dell's cover style immediately followed: the keyhole colophon was dropped, sans serif lettering was introduced, and back covers (by now bearing blurbs instead of maps) were completely revamped. Brooks tried to bring back the mapbacks: a few of them, decoratively styled, were indeed released, but Dell's management was strongly opposed to them and the idea was again buried.

The relationship between Dell and Western was still complicated, and made the production of covers extremely time-consuming. To simplify the process, Brooks drew detailed sketches for each proposed cover and submitted them to Dell for approval. Approved sketches were then turned over to New York artists (or, when necessary, sent to Racine) for execution. Because of the detail of Brooks' sketches, a definite cover style was established; since most cover text was set or lettered in the studio, even that aspect of production was under the art director's personal control. He designed covers with freestanding illustrations and experimented with free graphic forms. He created a visual continuity for some of the Dell series by using one artist for all related volumes: all Mike Shayne covers, for example, were painted by Robert McGinnis, books written by Mary Roberts Rinehart were illustrated by Vic Kalin and Bill Teason did covers for the Great Mystery Library and for Agatha Christie's books, while works by classical authors were illustrated by Saul Lambert and Harold Bruder was assigned to all volumes by Evelyn Waugh.

The F SERIES, begun in 1953, initially featured classic literary works; that same year saw the introduction of the DELL FIRST EDITIONS, a series of original novels, mysteries and Westerns edited by Knox Burger.

By the end of the '50s, Dell was grossing more than any other paperback publisher. The firm's first million-seller, published in 1955, was *Bonjour Tristesse* by Françoise Sagan; their second, Grace Metalious' *Peyton Place*, followed in 1957. "*Peyton Place* was our biggest success," George Delacorte remembers. "It gave us an enormous reputation, I think it sold 14 million copies. Of course it didn't bring in as much money then as it does today, because we were selling it I think at 50 cents. Now we sell the same damned book for $2.95, so it's really big business! I always had a feeling of personal pride whenever we had a big bestseller. I used to go into stores, and if Dell Books were hidden in the back somewhere, I'd move them up front where everyone could see them."

Graphic Description—1943: Dell 5 is the first mapback. Endpapers are blue. Handlettered text appears on the front cover and the spine. The colophon is an eye peering through a keyhole. 1944: A new version of the keyhole colophon appears; it is printed on front and back covers and at the bottom of the spine. 1946: The keyhole moves to the top of the spine; at the bottom is a small square with the word "DELL" and the phrase "A Dell Book." Covers are laminated with cellophane. 1949: The inside covers are light blue, with a white space in which the colophons for the various genres are displayed. The cellophane wrapper is eliminated. 1950: Some cover text is typeset, rather than handlettered. 1951: All cover text is now typeset. The mapbacks are gradually phased out. 1952: The keyhole colophon is dropped. A new version of the "DELL" square is designed. Back covers are specially designed, and consist of blurbs and illustration. Inside covers are plain white.

Bantam Books, 1945-1959

Unlike the other paperback publishers, BANTAM BOOKS did not get off to an amateurish start: Bantams were carefully produced from the very beginning. Except for a weak period around 1952, the firm's product was of a consistently high quality in both content and form: the first two years of Bantam releases could today serve as a textbook of inexpensive yet effective production methods, although the sales figures from that period were somewhat disappointing. With the arrival of art director Leonard Leone in 1955, Bantam began its slow but steady climb to the top of the paperback world. Even now, when most paperback covers tend to be interchangeable, Bantam's are always just a little bit better than those of the competition.

Ian Ballantine left Penguin Books to set up his own paperback company early in 1945. He arranged for Grosset & Dunlap to select the titles to be published (the name Bantam Books came from Bernard Geis, an editor at Grosset & Dunlap) and for the Curtis Publishing Company to handle distribution and sales. Walter Pitkin, Jr. was Ballantine's vice-president, Sidney B. Kramer was treasurer and comptroller, and Gobin Stair, who had worked for Ballantine at Penguin, joined him at Bantam to handle production and design.

Stair, born in Staten Island in 1912, had already been head of produc-

Bantam Books with covers by Rafael Palacios, Edgard Cirlin, Lester Kohs, W. Cotton, Denver Gillen, Robert Stanley and others

tion for the traditional hardcover publishers G.P. Putnam, Coward-McCann and John Day. He was interested in literature and, in addition to planning out print runs, wanted to design books himself. It was Gobin Stair who developed Bantam's format, cover style, illustrated end-papers—even the band along the spine—all intended to emphasize the quality of the books.

A schedule of four titles per month was planned, and an initial offering of 20 titles was printed in November of 1945 and delivered to local retail outlets the following month; in January, 1946, the American News Company initiated national distribution. This first printing ran 200,000 copies per title, 20 times the impression of the first 10 Pocket Books. A text on the back cover of each copy read: "Bantam Books include novels, mysteries and anthologies, besides works of humor and information. You can recognize Bantam Books by the tasteful pictures on the covers, by their famous authors, and by the tough bantam rooster on the front of all the books. Look for the four new Bantam Books this month, next month, and every month." Also on the back cover was a reproduction of the hardcover jacket and the legend: "This low-priced Bantam edition is made possible by the large sale and effective promotion of the original edition, published by ——."

Early hits were Zane Grey's *Nevada*, John Steinbeck's *Cannery Row* and Norman Lindsay's *The Cautious Amorist*. During 1946 and 1947, Bantams remained remarkable for their tasteful covers, illustrated by artists at the top of the field; these covers, by H.L. Hoffman, David Triggs, Lester Kohs, Rafael Palacios, Edgard Cirlin, Cal Diehl and Charles Andres, created an impression of consistent quality for Bantam which was not matched even by Pocket Books.

Rafael Palacios has this to say about his work for Bantam: "In 1945, Ava Morgan, Ed Cirlin, Riki Levinson and I shared a studio together and split the rent. We each had our own work, but if one of us was pressed for time, another one would sometimes take over an assignment for him. Gobin Stair got along well with our little group. He hung out with us a lot, he used to stand around looking over our shoulders while we worked, and I guess that's why we started getting assignments from Bantam. We always made sketches for the covers, and they had to be sent in and approved. I never did that for endpapers, though—I just did the final drawing right off, because when you did a sketch first the author always either rejected it or else he liked it so much he had it framed and never sent it back. It was best just to do a 'finished' illustration right away—then if they wanted corrections you made corrections. It was al-

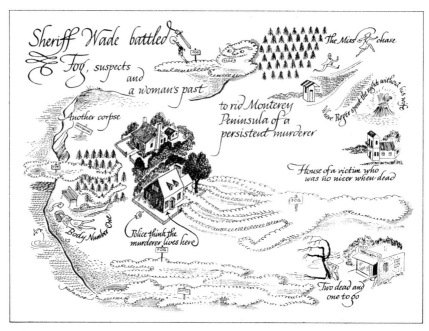

Sheriff Wade battled Fog, suspects and a woman's past

The Miss — chase

Another corpse

to rid Monterey Peninsula of a persistent murderer

Were Roger spent the night without his wife

House of a victim who was no nicer when dead

Body Number One

Police think the murderer lives here

Two dead and one to go

Rafael Palacios (Bantam 23, *The Fog Comes*)

ways fun to do endpapers for Bantam; you can tell by looking at them what a great time we had making them.

"In a sense our work was kind of rough, but you can't expect everyone to have a really refined style right at the beginning of his career. I'm not at all ashamed of that work; actually, I think some of those covers had a freshness that's not in my work anymore."

Ian Ballantine has since described these early covers as "non-newsstand." They were certainly attractive, they would sell fairly well if they were used today, but at the time they didn't do nearly as well as they were supposed to. Ben Hibbs, an editor at *The Saturday Evening Post*, advised Ballantine that Bantam Books, which after all appeared with monthly-magazine regularity, ought to have more eye-catching, magazine-like covers as well. Gobin Stair, with his artistic ideas, was quickly let go.

He was replaced by Don Gelb, who began hiring illustrators who could produce more attention-getting work; by 1948, the entire character of Bantam's covers had changed. Casey Jones, Van Kaufman and Denver Gillen produced many cartoonlike drawings around this time

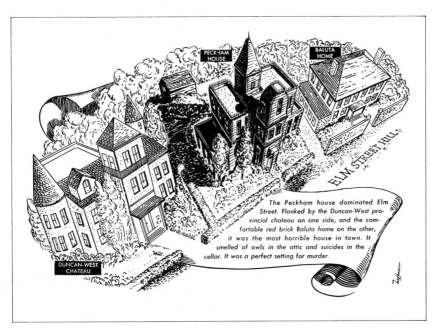

H. Lawrence Hoffman (Bantam 72, *No Bones About It*)

Edgard Cirlin (Bantam 33, *The Prisoner of Zenda*)

Isador N. Steinberg (Bantam 13, *The Last Time I Saw Paris*)

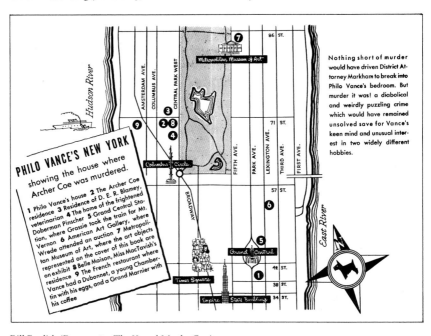

Bill English (Bantam 60, *The Kennel Murder Case*)

Boni Paper Book 1 (1929)

A Dell cover (1949)

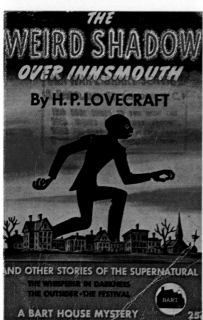

Bart House 4 (1944)

The first science-fiction paperback (1943)

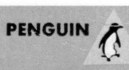

624 PENGUIN MYSTERY

THE VELVET WELL

JOHN   GEARON

Robert Jonas, 1947

70

Jonas' favorite cover, 1946

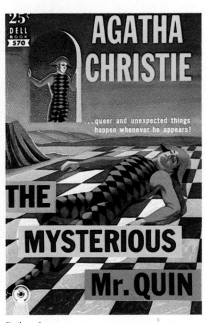

Robert Jonas, 1949 (Penguin 700)

A Jonas design from 1946, used nine years later on the cover of Mentor M109, *The World of History*.

Robert Jonas, 1952

Robert Jonas' original painting for *God's Little Acre*. Painted on wood and reproduced here slightly smaller than actual size. Facing page: 16 more peephole covers (see text for commentary).

god's little acre

ERSKINE CALDWELL

complete PENGUIN BOOKS unabridged

By the Author of "God's Little Acre"

TOBACCO ROAD

ERSKINE CALDWELL

91 LARGE PRINTINGS—OVER 1,675,000 COPIES

SIGNET BOOKS
Complete and Unabridged

A Novel by ERSKINE CALDWELL

JOURNEYMAN

A NOVEL BY THE AUTHOR OF GOD'S LITTLE ACRE

FIVE LARGE PRINTINGS—OVER 1,250,000 COPIES

Penguin SIGNET BOOKS
Complete and Unabridged

By the Author of "God's Little Acre"

ERSKINE CALDWELL

TRAGIC GROUND

12 LARGE PRINTINGS—OVER 1,680,000 COPIES

SIGNET BOOKS
Complete and Unabridged

By the Author of "God's Little Acre"

A HOUSE IN THE UPLANDS

ERSKINE CALDWELL

SIGNET BOOKS
Complete and Unabridged

ERSKINE CALDWELL

A WOMAN IN THE HOUSE
A Special Edition

ERSKINE CALDWELL'S BEST STORIES

SIGNET BOOKS
A Special Edition

ERSKINE CALDWELL

THE SURE HAND OF GOD

BY THE AUTHOR OF "GOD'S LITTLE ACRE"

SIGNET BOOKS
Complete and Unabridged

Erskine Caldwell

GEORGIA BOY

FIRST SIGNET EDITION OVER A MILLION COPIES

By the Author of "God's Little Acre"
ILLUSTRATED

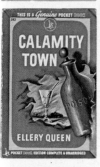

THIS IS A Genuine Pocket BOOK

CALAMITY TOWN

POISON

ELLERY QUEEN

POCKET BOOK EDITION COMPLETE & UNABRIDGED

THIS IS A Genuine Pocket BOOK

THE BISHOP MURDER CASE

S. S. VAN DINE

POCKET BOOK EDITION COMPLETE & UNABRIDGED

A PERRY MASON MYSTERY

THE CASE OF THE SUBSTITUTE FACE

ERLE STANLEY GARDNER

POCKET BOOK EDITION COMPLETE & UNABRIDGED

Pocket Book

TAPS FOR PRIVATE TUSSIE

JESSE STUART

COMPLETE & UNABRIDGED

A HENRY GAMADGE MYSTERY

EVIDENCE OF THINGS SEEN

ELIZABETH DALY

BANTAM BOOKS
COMPLETE AND UNABRIDGED

"The call came over the police tap on the Malone telephone at 11:53 P.M. an unknown girl was going to be killed."

the case of the talking bug
"THE GORDONS

Authors of CASE FILE: FBI and FBI STORY

OLIVE HIGGINS PROUTY

NOW, Voyager

A DELL ROMANCE

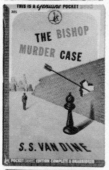

NORMAN A. FOX

THE RAWHIDE YEARS

He took to the trail as a 'scared kid'—but he rode it out to manhood

73

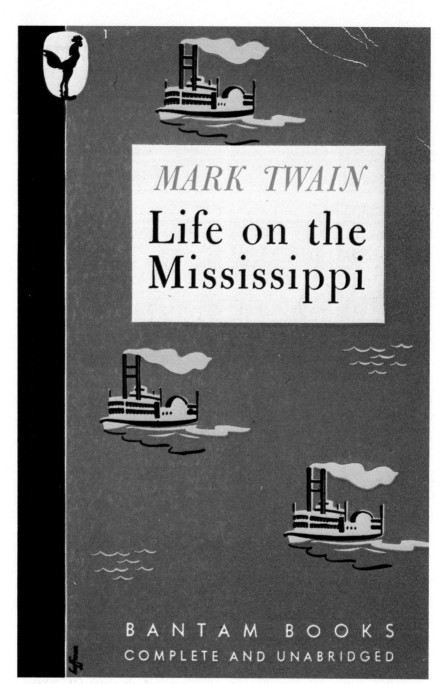

H. Lawrence Hoffman, 1945

74

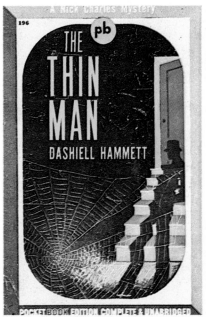

H. L. Hoffman, 1943

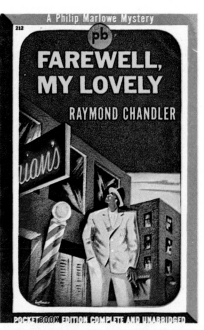

H. L. Hoffman, 1943

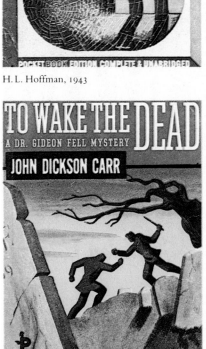

H. L. Hoffman, 1942 (Popular Library 10)

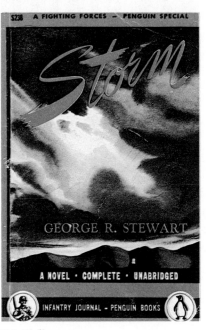

H. L. Hoffman, 1944

Gerald Gregg, 1944

76

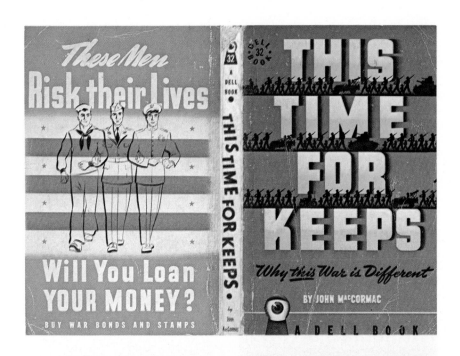

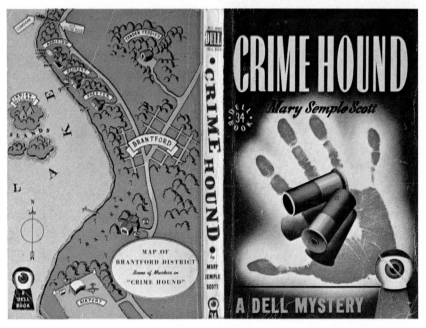

Two of Gerald Gregg's front-and-back Dell covers, from 1943 (top) and 1944 (bottom)

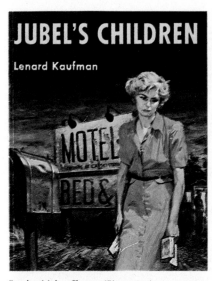

Stanley Meltzoff, 1951 (Signet 896)

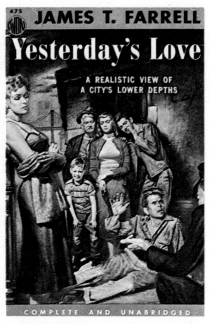

Rudy Nappi, 1952

Stanley Zuckerberg, 1952 (Signet 940)

Stanley Zuckerberg, 1954

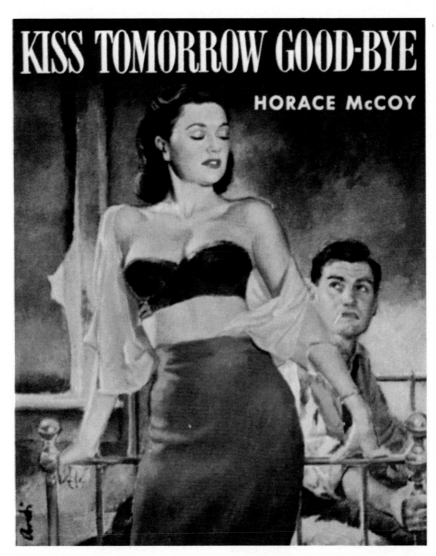

James Avati, 1949 (Signet 754)

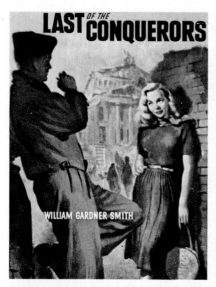

Avati's first cover, 1949 (Signet 706)

James Avati, 1952 (Signet S931)

James Avati, 1954 (Signet 1158)

James Avati, 1952 (Signet 955)

James Avati, as painted by Stanley Meltzoff. Avati and Meltzoff shared this studio, a former Masonic Temple on the top floor of an old building at the corner of Main Street and Broad Street in Red Bank, New Jersey. Models would pose on a podium at the side of the large room; Meltzoff himself often posed for Avati, and Avati for Meltzoff. A door connects the studio with a ballet school in the adjacent building, and a big neon sign outside is responsible for the bright red glow visible through the doorway. The two painters set up a cardboard wall down the middle of the room to provide each of them with a certain amount of privacy, although as they worked they would often carry on animated discussions of politics, philosophy and cosmology across the partition.

At the right of the painting Avati's wife, Jane Hamill, is helping their daughter Xan get ready for a ballet performance. The Reverend B. Goode sits at one end of the sofa, apparently engrossed in one of the theological arguments he often held with Avati; at the other end of the sofa, with toy pistol, is Ricky Avati. Baby Laurie lies on a rolled-up blanket under the easel, daughter Betsy is sitting in the doorway and, in the foreground, Margie Avati is copying one of her father's Signet covers. Stanley Meltzoff is sitting in an armchair, looking up at an exalted Avati, who is so carried away by his work that he no longer has both feet (or even one foot) on the ground. Hanging on the wall at the back of the room are Avati's original paintings for Signet 900 (*A Wind is Rising*) and Signet D926 (*A World I Never Made*).

Ruth Belew, 1946 (Dell 102)

Ruth Belew, 1944 (Dell 62)

Ruth Belew (?), 1943 (Dell 25)

Ruth Belew, 1946 (Dell 104)

Ruth Belew, 1947 (Dell 154)

Ruth Belew, 1948 (Dell 266)

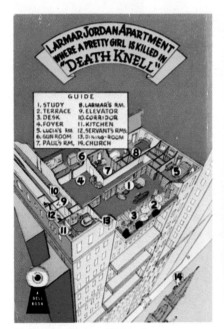

Ruth Belew (?), 1949 (Dell 273)

Ruth Belew, 1946 (Dell 113)

83

On his Dell covers, Robert Stanley often used himself and his wife Rhoda (nee Rozenzweig) as models, as can be seen in these details from books released between 1950 and 1955. Right: the face of hardboiled detective Mike Shayne is, in fact, also the face of artist Stanley.

Robert and Rhoda Stanley examining a Western Printing display of their work (Photo from *The Westerner*)

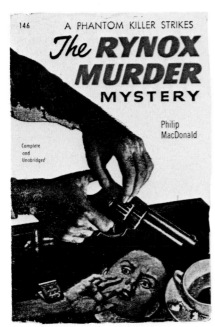

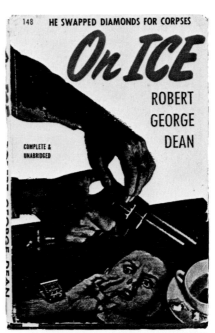

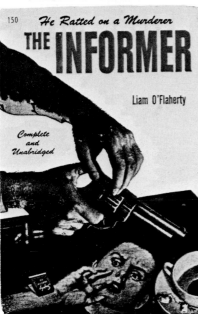

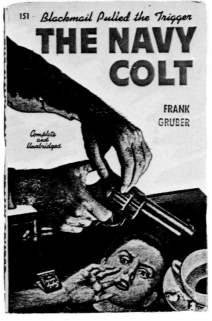

Eight Superior Reprints from 1944 and 1945 were given Bantam dustjackets and rereleased as Bantam Books in 1948. In four cases, as shown, the dustjackets used the very same cover illustration. (Photo courtesy of Paul F. Payne)

| 1945 | | | | 1950 | 1953 | 1955 |
| Robert Foster | | | | Don Gelb | | Leonard Leone |

(see page 172), and magazine illustrators whose names we know from the rubric *About the Cover* (including Bob Doares, Gilbert Fullington, Gilbert Darling, C.C. Beall, Hy Rubin, Jules Karl, Bill Shoyer, Remie Hamon and others) delivered realistic work. Even the titles became more catchy: Lewis Padgett's *The Brass Ring* was released as *Murder in Brass*, for example, and Eric Hatch's novel *Five Days* was published by Bantam as *Five Nights*.

Unsold stocks of earlier Bantam Books were given bright dustjackets and reissued. Even one Infantry Journal Book, one Infantry Journal - Penguin Book and eight Superior Reprints of which Ian Ballantine still had sufficient quantities were provided with Bantam dustjackets and remarketed. More and more Bantam Books became million-sellers; between 1948 and 1950, *The Chinese Room* by Vivian Connell, *A Stranger in Paris* (originally titled *Christmas Holiday*) by W. Somerset Maugham, *My Flag is Down* by James Maresca and *The Wayward Bus* by John Steinbeck all entered that category.

Between February of 1948 and June of 1949, Bantams were identified by an unusual numbering system in which different genres were numbered separately: Westerns began with numbers 200 and 250, mysteries with 300 and 350, novels, movie tie-ins and certain other types of books with 400 and 450, and sport, humor and miscellaneous books with 500 and 550. Thus, Bantams numbered 200, 250, 300, 400, 450, 500 and 550 were all published in February, 1948, while the following month's releases included 201, 251, 301 and so on. In July, 1949, "normal" numbering was resumed with Bantam 700.

After 1950, Bantam experienced several lean years. Few books sold well. Covers were limited to the dusky idiom which had become James Avati's trademark over at Signet, but were executed by artists who lacked Avati's mastery. This was a difficult time for all paperback publishers: an increasing number of small firms were fighting for a share of an overcrowded market, the majors were stuck with enormous surpluses, and most publishers faced escalating criticism of their lascivious cover drawings. Bantam also had internal problems: Ian Ballantine left in June of 1952 to establish Ballantine Books, and Walter Pitkin left in '54.

Pitkin was replaced by young and dynamic Oscar Dystel, who in 1955 brought young and dynamic Leonard Leone in as art director. Leone in turn brought decisive changes to Bantam and a new general design became apparent immediately. In fact, Leonard Leone was to Bantam what Walter Brooks had been to Dell and Roy Lagrone to Avon, the harbinger of a new and modern graphic approach.

The important art directors were all looking to move away from the dark Avati-style around this time; Leone also made that move, but he moved in a different direction than did his colleagues. Leone had previously worked as art director for two magazines, *True* and *Argosy*, and had been accustomed there to much better reproduction techniques than those commonly used for paperbacks. At Bantam, he began to use better, slicker paper for his covers; the slicker paper meant a finer screen could be used, and a finer screen meant more fidelity. Under Leone's close supervision, the printers were soon able to reproduce even a thin pencil line clearly; this made it possible to use pencil sketches as cover illustrations, providing exactly the light style Leone, Dystel and editor Saul David were after.

Mitchell Hooks, who had been doing cover paintings à la Avati, began to produce airy watercolors and pencil drawings for Bantam. Leone provided more appropriate typography than had previously been usual. He made a color sketch including lettering for every cover, so that his artists could plan their work accordingly. Artwork and lettering were treated as one unit, and the impact of each benefited from this closer relationship. The use of glazed paper also led to the appearance of much more white on covers, as this type of paper is at its best when it is not completely covered with ink.

James Avati himself began drawing regularly for Bantam in the early '60s, finding Leone's approach more in line with his own desires than was that of John Legakes at Signet. Other illustrators who worked frequently for Leone were Mike Ludlow, Bill Edwards, Bill Teason, Bob Abbett and James Bama.

GRAPHIC DESCRIPTION—1945: Robert Foster designs the Bantam rooster. Gobin Stair develops the cover style: a vertical band along the left side of the front cover, folding across the spine and on to the back cover; the rooster colophon at the top-left of the front and the bottom of the spine; illustrated endpapers. Leading illustrators and designers provide covers. The jacket of the hardback edition is reproduced on the back cover. 1946: As of March, all spine text is set in Futura and a small triangle appears at the top of the spine. 1947: The illustrated endpapers are dropped. Late 1949: The band at the left side of the front cover is removed. Late 1950: A new version of the Bantam rooster perches at the top-left. 1954: The triangle on the spine disappears. Books are printed in a larger format. 1955: Spines are black, with red or white text. Back covers are illustrated and are treated as an integral part of the overall design.

Signet Books, 1948-1959

SIGNET BOOKS are paperbacks with covers by Avati.

That statement is a generalization. That statement is, in fact, not completely true. And yet it is a statement which must be made.

Signet has published higher quality literature than any other paperback firm—and it has published the works of Mickey Spillane. Of all paperback series, Signet has been the most stylish—and, at times, it has been the drabbest.

But always, Signet's most noticeable, most memorable feature has been those dusky, realistic cover paintings by James Avati and his disciples: Stanley Zuckerberg, Stanley Meltzoff, Alan Harmon, Carl Bobertz and many others.

Signet Books appeared for the first time in the summer of 1948. Under the general banner of the New American Library, "Signet" was the new name for Penguin Books and "MENTOR" the new name for Pelicans. From March through August of '48, either "Penguin Signet" or "Pelican Mentor" appeared on all covers, but as of August the break with Penguin was complete, and Signet and Mentor were left to stand on their own.

William Faulkner, James T. Farrell, Ann Petry and Theodora Keogh were all Signet authors. The most successful has been Spillane, whose Mike Hammer novels have always sold from three to four million copies in Signet editions. *I, the Jury* (1948) was followed by *My Gun is Quick*, *The Big Kill*, *One Lonely Night*, *Vengeance is Mine*, *The Long Wait*, *Kiss Me Deadly* and other titles. The straightforward prose of these books—in his first five adventures, Hammer killed a total of 48 people!—was mirrored by Lou Kimmel's rough cover illustrations.

Erskine Caldwell also sold well for Signet, especially *A House in the Uplands* (1948) and *Georgia Boy* (1950); Caldwell's peak period was pre-1948, though, in the Penguin era. Penguin referred to him as "the world's bestselling author," a title Signet later bestowed on Spillane in the '50s and on Ian Fleming in the '60s.

Signet Books with covers by, among others, Robert Jonas, Lou Kimmel, James Avati, Stanley Meltzoff, Stanley Zuckerberg and Barye Phillips

The beginning of the Signet years marked an increase in the number of Westerns and other minor-league fiction being published by NAL. Paul Evan Lehman, Will Ermine, William Colt MacDonald, William MacLeod Raine and Charles N. Heckelman wrote hard-as-nails horse operas for Signet with titles like *Lobo Law*, *Clattering Hoofs* and *Blood of the West*. The covers for these books were at first signed "Rob-Jon," a pseudonym for Robert Jonas, who was ashamed of himself for producing this sort of highly realistic work. Later, a whole school of Western artists developed.

Although Jonas stopped illustrating Westerns, he continued making covers for the New American Library, usually limiting himself to works of nonfiction. More than 95% of all Mentor Books released through the mid-'50s carried Jonas covers—and he was also responsible for the cover typography for the Signet series until, in February of 1949, John Legakes became NAL's first official art director.

A month after Legakes took on that position, Signet 706, *Last of the Conquerors*, a book about the racial problems encountered by a black man in the ruins of postwar Berlin, appeared. Its cover was illustrated by James Avati, and was his first paperback assignment.

"I liked Jim Avati at first meeting," Legakes says. "He was his own man. He was creative, with an innate ability to master a given cover problem. He improved with time; his work was honest, thorough and convincing." (Interestingly, it is not at all clear from Avati's first cover painting that the protagonist of *Last of the Conquerors* is black. At that time, to show a black man on a book cover was to guarantee poor sales in the American South.)

In *Literaire Lichtbeelden*, a 1978 magazine article, Dutch writer Ed Schilders discussed Avati's approach. "If we compare Avati's work with that of other artists," Schilders wrote, "we see that he frequently selected a small but dramatic fragment of the story line to paint, while the others went for more general statements. Almost all of the covers which show 'only' a beautiful woman fall into this general category. They may be quite attractive covers, but I for one always want to know if that lady is the main character's wife, or his lover, or what. It is his precise choice of subject matter, I think, that gives Avati's covers their incredible excitement. After reading the books, you realize that Avati's paintings are entirely true—they are painted quotations." Schilders added that Avati's women are more than the standard "silicone-stuffed versions of every American boy's favorite dream.... Their charms, even their weaknesses, are visible in their faces. Avati usually captures them in moments when

James Avati, 1948. The old man who posed for this painting was not a professional model. Avati met him in a small village and wound up painting him into a number of his Erskine Caldwell covers; on *Trouble in July*, he appears four times! "He always took his false teeth out before I painted him," Avati says. "He was my standard old man."

James Avati (left) and Stanley Meltzoff in December, 1980. The photo was taken at Meltzoff's home in Fair Haven, New Jersey. Meltzoff's painting "Avati at easel" (see page 81) is visible in the background. (Photo: Piet Schreuders)

92   HISTORY OF THE PAPERBACK

they are hurt, sad or embarrassed—or in moments when they have hurt or embarrassed themselves."

James Avati's work is inseparably tied to the small-town milieu, to the torrid slum atmosphere which he could portray like no one else.

Avati was himself at home in the America he painted for books by Caldwell, Farrell and Faulkner. His father was an immigrant from Italy who found success in New York as a photographer; his mother was a Scot. Orphaned in childhood, Avati was raised by a Scots-American aunt and her wealthy husband, who sent him to fine schools where he found it impossible to fit in; the other children, looking at his background, nicknamed him "Wopscotch." Throughout his life, Avati has always felt himself an outsider, without class, uncertain about his heritage and his place in society. The only area in which he has found it possible to manifest his talent is in his work for the paperbacks.

"When I look back at that time," he has said, "I realize where all my early covers came from. They were a mixture of my despair and my naiveté. I had had no formal training in art, but I wanted to be an artist. I had the idea: if I can't do this, then I'll never be able to do *anything*. I did some very beautiful work back then, I can say that without exaggerating, but some of it was awful. I was the first to bring certain visual elements together, and I can see how good that was. Not that those covers could ever complete with *real* art, the way I used to hope! I always thought that I'd failed, then, although the publishers were constantly congratulating me because my covers sold so well. But I thought it was tiresome that my work caused so much of an uproar and that they were fighting over me. Why did I have to go out with those people? Why did they invite me to their parties? That's not my field of interest at all...."

Not the best, but certainly one of the best-known of Avati's covers was created for an edition of J. D. Salinger's *Catcher in the Rye* (Signet 1001). A young man in a red hunting cap stands with a suitcase in his hand at the left of the cover; it is night, and the young man's face is lit by the glow from a theater's entrance. "That was a mess, that cover," he says, "from beginning to end. I did it against Salinger's express wishes. Salinger, Victor Weybright, the original publishers (Little, Brown) and I sat down in a little room together and went back and forth about it for half an hour before I finally decided I was going to squeeze Salinger's permission out of him. 'Look,' I told him, 'you want your book to sell, don't you? Well, Signet is supposed to know *how* to sell books, aren't they? So, screw it, let's do it!' And we did it.

"Salinger and Little, Brown *dictated* that cover to me, right down to the block of text in the middle of the image. That was supposed to be pretty terrific, the idea of putting text in the middle of the drawing.... Letting people like that decide what stays and what goes is incredible. All those publishers are really just a bunch of hopeless amateurs. A publisher's first instinct is to copy something that's already been tried out and found to be successful. If a book called *Lolita* sold a lot of copies, somebody would come out with a book called *Lola*. But when all a publisher will do is imitate himself and everybody else, he loses any chance he might have had to come up with something that, even though it might not look marketable on the surface, might really turn out to be something important and new.

"Other publishers started telling their artists to imitate *me*, and pretty soon the Avati-look was everywhere. It got to the point where I had to stop doing Avati covers. I was estranged from my own style, I had to start doing something else. Then I made a cover for Bantam Books and I got into another school of thinking altogether. Leonard Leone was in charge of their art direction, and he was a man who thought the way I did. When he felt he had to, he would go against what the publisher wanted. He got me started doing smaller illustrations; if you just show *one* clear scene on a cover, which is what I'd been doing up till then, you imply that that's all the book is about; the mood you establish with that painting makes any other mood impossible. Leone believed that the art *direction* was more important than any one big effect. He made the book's title larger and the illustration relatively smaller and freer in form."

More recently, Avati has worked for almost all of the paperback publishers; today he does covers largely for Dell and Avon.

Another typical Signet artist was T.V., who illustrated, for example, Signets 668 (*The Dim View*) and 690 (*No Pockets in a Shroud*; see page 226); his specialty was closeups of faces. The initials T.V. may stand for Tony Varady, a cover artist active around that time, but not even art director John Legakes can satisfactorily settle the question of T.V.'s identity: Legakes did not work directly with his artists during the relevant period, but through art agencies.

Throughout the 1940s, many important books were not published in paperback form because they were too long for it to be economically feasible to retail them for 25 cents and because breaking them up into several separate volumes was considered impractical. Kurt Enoch solved this problem in 1950, with the introduction of the SIGNET DOUBLE VOLUMES and, three years later, the TRIPLE VOLUMES. The Double Volumes were

The "double" spine of the first Signet Double Volume (1950)

priced at 35 cents and the Triple Volumes at 50 cents and, to clearly show the reader that he was getting extra value for his extra money, spine texts were printed two or three times side-by-side over contrasting backgrounds to symbolize the doubleness or tripleness of the book; sometimes even the serial number was subdivided into, for example, 802A and 802B. These new series definitively removed the price barrier against publishing longer books; once removed, it was not long before even shorter books were being sold for prices higher than 25 cents.

Signet and Mentor Books became more modern-looking in the mid-'50s. John Legakes' assistant, Bill Gregory, who would replace Legakes in 1961, stripped away the horizontal bands which Robert Jonas had designed for Penguin in 1946. He also produced new colophons, modernized the typography and hired new artists.

Through 1960, the phrase "Complete and Unabridged" appeared at the bottom of most Signet covers. Some titles were condensed, though, and in such cases this legend was replaced with "Authorized Abridgement," "With Minor Abridgements," "A Special Edition," "A Popular Condensation," or something of the kind.

GRAPHIC DESCRIPTION—1948: Penguin Signet Books become Signet Books, Pelican Mentor Books become Mentor Books. There is a line or two of blurb in a horizontal band at the top of the front cover. Robert Jonas supplies realistic illustrations. 1949: The blurb on the back cover no longer refers exclusively to the author, but to the contents of the book as well. James Avati begins work as a cover artist. 1950: The spine, until now white, is colored. 1954: The horizontal bands at top and bottom of the cover become broader. A new colophon is introduced. 1956: The bands on the cover are dropped. The back cover receives added attention from the art director.

1948

1953

1954

Graphic, Checker, Pyramid, Lion, Fawcett, Ballantine, Ace and Berkley

The publishers so far discussed were all founded before the end of the war; even Signet, which didn't begin using that name until 1948, had operated as Penguin Books since 1941. These half-dozen firms, by the way, are still the most important paperback publishers in America.

A fairly large number of additional publishers first saw the light of day at the end of the '40s and during the '50s, though; not all of these newcomers were equally successful, but many of them continue to operate today.

So many were active during the relevant period, 1939-1959, that I have decided to limit this chapter to only eight of them; others are discussed in Part Three of this book, in the appendix titled *Overview of American Paperback Publishers.*

GRAPHIC BOOKS—Sam Tankel and Zane Bouregy founded the Graphic Publishing Company in 1948. They published a total of 147 paperbacks: mostly mysteries, but also a number of straight and historical novels. The technical quality of the covers was, for the time, extremely good, perhaps because both Tankel and Bouregy were particularly concerned with color reproduction: they had written a book about two-color reproduction together, and Tankel was president of a lithography firm. The Graphic Books colophon was a reproduction camera shaped like a G. All books carried the legend "A Graphic Mystery," "A Graphic Western," "A Graphic Original," or whatever.

The firm went out of business in 1957.

CHECKERBOOKS—Lyle Kenyon Engel set up Checkerbooks, Inc. in 1949; his idea was to publish 16 paperback titles a year. The series did not last through its *first* year, though, and only 12 titles were ever released. A probable cause for this quick failure was that the retail price of the books, 15 cents, was too low.

PYRAMID BOOKS—The Almat Publishing Company was established by Alfred R. Plaine and Matthew Huttner. Although their original purpose was to publish exclusively paperbacks, they also wound up issuing several magazines, such as *Challenge, Men's Magazine* and *Mechanics Today*. In their paperback series, PYRAMID BOOKS, four titles were published every month, except in 1954 when, like many other firms, Pyramid slowed down production in response to a glutted market. Most of the Pyramids were Westerns, mysteries and straight novels. Rolf Ericson was art director; he worked with illustrators including, among others, Harry Schaare.

LION BOOKS—Martin Goodman, owner of the magazine house Magazine Management Company, founded Lion Books in November of 1949. Early releases carried the imprint RED CIRCLE BOOKS (numbers 1-7, 12 and 13); later volumes were LION BOOKS (numbers 8-11 and 14-233). Most Lions were reprints, but occasional originals were also published: in such cases, editor-in-chief Arnold Hano developed a plot and commissioned an author to work it up into a book. Writers David Karp (*Hardman* and *Cry, Flesh*) and Jim Thompson (*Recoil, The Criminal, Roughneck, A Hell of a Woman*) worked for Hano in that manner. The LION LIBRARY began in 1954, and included reprints of earlier Lion Books; the Lion Books themselves were discontinued in 1955. In the summer of 1957, the New American Library bought the name Lion Books, Inc. and the rights to most of the Lion titles. A number of Lions which had been planned but never released, and a number of reprints of the earlier Lions, were eventually issued as Signet Books.

FAWCETT—Fawcett Publications was founded by Wilford H. Fawcett and his brother Roscoe, and published the magazines *True Confessions* and *Mechanix Illustrated* during the '20s. Fawcett's headquarters and distribution center was established in Greenwich, Connecticut in 1935, while the editorial offices were located in New York City. By 1942, with 60 different magazines in production, business was so strong that the company was able to buy a 21-story office building in New York. The best-known Fawcett publications of the '40s were *True, True Confessions* and *True Police Cases*; the most important Fawcett comic books were ·*Slam Bang, Wow Comics, Captain Marvel* and *Holiday Comics*.

An anthology, *The Best from True*, was published as a paperback in 1949, along with *What Today's Woman Should Know About Marriage and Sex*. These two volumes can be considered the forerunners of the Fawcett GOLD MEDAL BOOKS. The first official Gold Medal, which appeared

Gold Medal Books

in 1950, was number 101, *We Are the Public Enemies*, a collection of stories about famous gangsters.

The idea behind the Gold Medal series was to bring out originals; that idea was not completely adhered to—it was not *half* adhered to—but Gold Medal was in fact the first paperback series to release really important original work. It was Gold Medal editor William C. Lengel, for example, who discovered author Richard S. Prather; other typical Gold Medal writers included Richard Himmel, Vin Packer and John Flagg. Theodore Pratt's *The Tormented* and Bruno Fischer's *House of Flesh* were the first Gold Medal million-sellers.

Art director from the beginning was Al Allard. Allard was born in Minneapolis in 1904; at school he was interested in anything having to do with the theater, and he seemed to have a talent for set design. Leaving school, he steeped himself further in that field at a stage design studio in Minneapolis. From 1921 through 1928 he worked in the advertising and publicity department of a large theater chain, and in 1928 he became involved with Fawcett Publications. In 1950, when Fawcett began its paperback series, Allard was named art director. He put together a stable of artists for Gold Medal covers: Barye Phillips was certainly the most important and most productive member of that stable, which also included James Meese, Mike Hooks, Louis Glanzman, Frank Tinsley and John Floherty, Jr.

In addition to the Gold Medals, Fawcett also published RED SEAL BOOKS from February, 1952 through March, 1953, and has released both CREST BOOKS and PREMIER BOOKS since the autumn of 1955.

Ballantine Books

BALLANTINE BOOKS—Ian Ballantine, the economist who published the first American Penguins in 1942 and founded Bantam Books in 1945, decided in 1952 to establish his own firm, so that his talents as an editor could be more fully utilized. The result was BALLANTINE BOOKS, with former Bantam editor Stanley Kaufman as editor-in-chief. Ballantine's idea was to release paperbacks simultaneously with their hardcover release by other publishers; his books would thus not exactly be reprints, but they would not exactly be originals either. This system had one major advantage for authors: they would receive, from first publication of their books, 8% royalties instead of 4%. Hardcover publishers Houghton Mifflin and Farrar, Straus participated with Ballantine from the beginning, and each had a representative in the management of Ballantine Books. The first Ballantine Book, Cameron Hawley's *Executive Suite*, was published in cooperation with Houghton Mifflin; both publishers' names were listed on the cover.

Bob Blanchard was art director at Ballantine. He worked with illustrators Harry Bennett (who provided the cover for *Executive Suite*), Norman Saunders, Verne Tossey, Robert Maguire, Charles Binger, Robert Schulz, Mel Crair and, especially, Richard Powers (who, early in 1953, did the cover for Ballantine's first science-fiction title, *Star Science Fiction Stories*).

Science fiction quickly became a Ballantine specialty, and Powers' covers—wild, almost abstract images of strange space creatures—became a Ballantine trademark (although he did work for other publishers as well). Powers also created the cover and the illustrations for *Ballantine Star Science Fiction*, a digest which appeared in January of 1958. The popularity of science fiction slacked off a bit in the late '50s.

GRAPHIC CHECKER, ETC. 99

Ace Books

ACE BOOKS—A. A. Wyn and his family already owned and operated
A. A. Wyn, Inc., a magazine publisher, when they set up Ace Books, Inc.
in 1952. The idea, developed by Wyn in collaboration with Donald A.
Wollheim, was to produce a series of paperbacks, each volume of which
would contain *two* complete novels. Each ACE DOUBLE NOVEL was to include one reprint and one original, bound back to back, each with its
own front cover. At the top of both front covers would be the text:
"Turn over Book for 2nd Novel."

Wyn was president and editor-in-chief of Ace Books, Wollheim led
the editorial staff and handled daily management. The first titles appeared
in September, 1952: Ace D-1 included *The Grinning Gismo* by Samuel W.
Taylor, a reprint, and *Too Hot for Hell* by Keith Vining, an original; both
covers were drawn by Norman Saunders.

At first, two Double Novels per month were released: a pair of mysteries and a pair of Westerns. Later, production was upped to four volumes
a month: the extra two books contained a pair of science-fiction novels
and a pair of adventure stories.

Ace Books are quite highly valued by collectors today, probably because of the charming double-cover idea. The "original" half of number
D-15, *Junkie*, marked the print debut of William Burroughs, writing then
under the pseudonym "William Lee;" today, a copy of this book in good
condition sells for $100.

As of 1954, single-novel Ace Books also began to appear. The first
"single" was numbered S-54 (the S or D indicated whether the book was
a single or double novel, the numbering was consecutive and included
both types of release), Carl Offord's *The Naked Fear*.

After 1955, Ace specialized in the science-fiction genre.

BERKLEY BOOKS—The Berkley Publishing Corporation was founded in September, 1954, by Frederick Klein and Charles R. Byrne, both of whom had originally been at Avon Books. Their first publications were *Chic* and *News*, both magazines in paperback format, both quickly abandoned. The first BERKLEY BOOKS appeared early in 1955; Klein and Byrne actually wanted to call the series "Merit Books," but it turned out that there was already a publisher using that name in Chicago.

The editorial formula, at first, was that each group of 17 books released would include eight novels, three thrillers, two Westerns, two anthologies, one mystery and one humorous work.

From the beginning, Tom Dardis served as art director. Among others, he worked with Harry Bennett, David Attie, Rudy Nappi, Mel Crair and the Silver Studios.

The BERKLEY GIANTS were introduced in 1955, the BERKLEY DIAMONDS in 1959.

The Distribution of Paperbacks in America

In New York City, 2,000 paperback books are sold every day *underground*, from bookstalls at a number of the city's subway stations. These stalls comprise only one tiny part of America's massive network of over 100,000 retail outlets for paperbacks, a network which includes not only ordinary bookstores, but specialty bookstores (university, medical, government and so), drugstores, department stores, supermarkets, and newsstands on street corners and at airports and bus and train stations as well.

Publishers not only need to choose a strong list of titles and select effective covers—another important task is to move the stacks of finished product from printer or warehouse to all relevant retail locations. For the publisher himself to tool merrily around America in a delivery van is obviously not the answer. And so, for as long as there have been books and magazines, there have been organizations concerned with distributing them efficiently.

In the latter half of the 19th century, distribution in the United States was largely controlled by the American News Company. ANC had a network of about 400 local branches, which transported dime novels and other paperbacks from printers to retailers. A number of "independent" distributors were also nominally active; these independents were originally of little importance and had few clients, but that situation began to change in the early years of the 20th century.

Street & Smith, a major publisher of pulps, switched from ANC to independents shortly after 1900, and other publishers followed their example. Distribution wars broke out in many cities during the Roaring '20s, and it was not unusual for the driver of a delivery truck to keep a loaded gun available under his front seat. Most of these independents began by distributing horse-racing papers from one or two small vans or wagons; today there are over 500 of them, each with its own fleet of trucks and its own working territory.

When Pocket Books began publishing paperbacks in 1939, its distribution was handled by ANC; soon, though, some of the work was farmed out to independents. In 1941, four magazine distributors were taking care of most of Pocket Books' distribution; by 1943, the firm had 600 independents under contract. Like the pulp publishers had followed Street & Smith away from ANC 40 years earlier, many paperback publishers followed Pocket Books away from ANC during the World War II years. Shortly after 1945, publishers were obliged either to let ANC exclusively manage their distribution or not to use them at all: Avon, Dell and Popular Library stuck with ANC, while Pocket Books, NAL and Bantam switched completely over to independents.

A standard system was for the publishers themselves to set up and own a national distributor, which would handle the distribution of its parent company's product to a number of independent local distributors. Thus Fawcett, a magazine publisher, distributed the books of the New American Library until the early 1950s, while Affiliated Publishers, a subsidiary of Pocket Books, distributed, promoted and sold all Pocket Books publications. (In 1957, Affiliated was taken over by Select-Magazines, Inc., which distributed the *Reader's Digest* and other periodicals.)

Between 1952 and 1956, a series of mysterious symbols appeared on the spines of Gold Medal Books: an s lying on its side, a green heart, a five-pointed star, an arrow pointing downwards. These signs were probably introduced to make it easier for distributors to sort books: each volume in an offering of 10 to 12 titles would carry the same symbol. Pocket Books introduced its own set of signs in 1953, Popular Library and Avon followed in 1954. In 1955, perhaps because they were running out of new symbols, Pocket Books began printing the last digit of the book number on the spine instead (so different titles from one offering now had different, rather than identical, identifying marks); Bantam Books also switched to this system.

Meanwhile, where the American News Company had had some 400 warehouses scattered around the United States in 1945, by 1955 only 35

Mysterious symbols...

of these warehouses were left. ANC's importance dissipated quickly, and the firm ceased distributing magazines and paperbacks in 1957.

The role of the jobber in paperback distribution became increasingly important in the late '50s. Jobbers are paperback wholesalers; they do not own their own delivery fleets, but work through the mails or with delivery services and are not bound to any one geographical area. Jobbers supplied many books to chain stores (another development of the late '50s), although chains may also receive books directly from publishers and, in fact, some chains have ownership ties to particular publishing houses.

During the '40s and '50s, a few publishers experimented with the idea of paperback vending machines at stations and airports, making it possible for book sales to go on 24 hours a day. Bantam Books of Los Angeles was a perback series sold *only* from such machines. Vending machines for Pocket Books cropped up in a number of locations in 1947 and 1948; these contraptions were, for some reason, named "Dadsons." In 1952, a "Vendavon" sold Avon Books at LaGuardia Airport in New York.

Sale from racks easily triumphed over sale from machines, though. Pocket Books, Dell and Bantam were delivering special paperback racks to their distributors as early as 1941. These racks were wooden at first, and their bulky construction concealed the bottom halves of the books they held; cover designers had to make sure that all titles and other important attention-getting matter appeared at the top of a cover, so that it would remain visible if the book was displayed in a rack. Later, racks were made of the thin iron-rod construction still in use today, and the entire book cover could be seen.

In a shop, books from a variety of publishers are generally displayed in the same rack, although books from a single publisher may well be grouped together within the rack. The number of books displayed per publisher is usually determined by sales figures: if New American Library sells better than Dell, more NAL books will be displayed.

With an eye to the way their product will look in the rack, art directors (especially since the late 1950s) make sure that there is contrast between the covers of different titles of an offering: half of the books released in January may have light covers, for example, while the other half may be darker. This practive is known as "dressing the rack." Today, one edition of a particular book may be outfitted with six or seven differently-colored covers, sometimes even with six or seven differently-*illustrated* covers, to encourage retailers to display more copies than they otherwise might. And if this year's style at Signet features dark covers, then it's a good bet that Bantam will be using lighter colors to ensure contrast within the rack.

The shelf life or rack life of a paperback is relatively short. If a book isn't selling well after a month on the stands, its place will be given over to some newer release; unsold stocks will be returned to the publisher for refund or credit. Because of the huge numbers involved, sending returns back to publishers can be quite expensive; since about 1955, it has become customary for independent distributors to return only the front covers of unsold books and to destroy the rest. Special machines tear off and stack the covers, then grind the remainder of the book to confetti. From time to time distributors have been caught returning thousands of counterfeit covers, which were never attached to paperbacks in the first place: it is a simple matter to print up exact replicas of real book covers, and it can take months before the discrepancy between books sent out, books sold and books returned reveals the fraud.

If you have ever seen coverless paperbacks on sale at a secondhand bookstore, or magazines with half their cover ripped off, you may have witnessed another example of distributor fraud. After returning the paperback cover, or that section of the magazine cover including the title and date of issue, the distributor will receive a refund or credit for the full wholesale price from the publisher; additional money can then be made by selling the remainder of the book or magazine, cheap, to a retailer.

Paperback Covers

A Few Generalizations

MERICAN PAPERBACK COVERS have, like movies and television, mirrored public taste down the years. The various stylistic periods through which paperback cover art has progressed are so clearly defined that it is only logical to discuss them here. During the 1940s and '50s, five separate periods of roughly three to four years each can be identified, periods in which, generally speaking, one particular graphic style or fashion dominated amongst most paperback publishers.

It is no coincidence that, from the very beginning and with the possible exception of the earliest Pocket Books and Bantams, American paperbacks have had a close relationship with the Hollywood film, a relationship which is especially noticeable when the characteristics of these two mass media are compared. The first paperback period, during the war years, was a time of thin, dull cover paper printed with surreal images suggestive of modern art, of the *film noir* and the psychological thriller; even straightforward mysteries by authors like Erle Stanley Gardner wore covers whose designs might have been inspired by Salvador Dali's dream sequence for Hitchcock's *Spellbound* (see Leo Manso's Gardner covers on pages 168 and 169). In the period shortly after the war, covers were more colorful and cheerful; there is often a feel reminiscent of film comedies in these covers, while their lettering bears a certain relationship to the titles and credits of animated cartoons (see page 172). The sex era began around 1948, and many publishers returned to the steamy pulp style of the '30s (see, for example, Rudolph Belarski's buxom ladies on pages 170 and 171, and Robert Stanley's first *Fools Die on Friday* cover on page 110). Signet introduced the fourth stylistic period at the beginning of the '50s: dark, somber covers were painted in a style that seems influenced by the films of the great metropolis like *Naked City* (see pages 78-80). The last period, which may be called the "modern" era, began around 1955, and was a time when the influence of the art director was more clearly seen (see page 173 for several examples).

The years before 1941, back when Pocket Books stood basically alone as a mass producer of paperbacks, can be considered the prehistory of the softcovered book. Pocket Books' first titles were reprints of serious novels and genteel mysteries by writers with established reputations. Like hardcover dustjackets, their covers were civilized, sober, conservative, culturally responsible; compared with the hardcovers, though, these first paperback illustrations were somewhat primitive. Frank Lieberman's kangaroo, the Pocket Books trademark since 1939, was constantly being redrawn, one example of the lack of a truly coherent style characteristic of this time.

Stylistic consistency began in 1942, when Ed Rofheart became art director at Pocket Books and Laura Hobson designed the standard round-cornered-frame motif, also known as the "medallion format." Gertrude the Kangaroo was replaced by a strong typographical symbol and artists recruited from respectable design circles created strange, surreal covers with frequently-recurring elements: holes in walls, silhouetted men wearing trenchcoats and slouch hats, big disembodied eyes, horizons, arrows, curtains, bloodstains, tombstones, bony hands, skulls....

Noteworthy during this period were the fiercely-colored, theatrical illustrations on the early Dell Books, which were produced by Western Printing and painted by experienced artists like Gerald Gregg.

Like Pocket Books, Avon (established in 1941) at first released primarily classic novels and mysteries; they were wrapped in striking, lively, but amateurishly-executed covers.

The end of the war marked the beginning of a period of great productivity for all paperback publishers. Covers, which could again be printed on strong paper, became colorful and extravagant, while the high artistic level which had already been reached was maintained. The surrealists kept working for Pocket Books, but realistic magazine and advertising illustratiors and cartoonists also received assignments and the medallion format was discarded. A new publisher, Bantam Books, arrived on the scene and, under Gobin Stair's graphic supervision, created true jewels of paperback art: tasteful designs and well-produced books, complete with illustrated endpapers and covers by respected calligraphers and designers. At Penguin Books the picture was similar: Robert Jonas, who worked with colorful, symbolic imagery, was responsible for the appearance of almost all releases. Jonas created a personal style at Penguin which was, and remains, unique in paperback history.

After 1948, though, Jonas at Penguin, Manso at Pocket Books and the aesthetic artists at Bantam were faced with serious competition from a realistic school of illustrators who provided covers for a growing number of novels which were, if not great literature, at least commercially successful. Publishers noticed that more blatant sex meant more impressive sales, and sex became a key element on more and more covers regardless of the contents of the books in question. Pulp artists like Bergey and Belarski produced a large number of Popular Library covers on which magnificent women could be admired in varying stages of undress.

During this period, realistic illustrator Robert Stanley was extremely productive for Dell Books and James Avati, the finest representative of a stream of artists sharing an "emotional realistic" style, began making covers for Signet. Paperback covers became paintings, although primarily paintings of one particular genre: dusky, sweltering scenes representing the lower reaches of the American class structure.

In 1947 a group of cover designers, recognizing the sexual morass into which their field threatened to sink, established the Book Jacket Designers Guild. The first governing board, which called itself the Cultural Committee, included George Salter (chairman), Leo Manso, Meyer Miller, Jeanyee Wong and Miriam Woods; H. Lawrence Hoffman and John O'Hara Cosgrave II joined in later years. The Guild began holding annual exhibitions of the best paperback and hardbound book covers in 1948; they advocated the production of covers with Quality.

What that word "Quality" meant can perhaps best be explained by quoting what the Guild was *against*: "...the stunt jacket that screams for your attention, and then dares you to guess what the book is about... the burlap backgrounds, the airbrush doilies and similar clichés as well as the all-too-many good illustrations that [are] stretched, squeezed, tortured and mutilated to fit a jacket with just enough room for an unrelated title."

The Guild felt that covers should not be judged solely on their artistic or technical merit, but also by their relationship to the books they were designed for. Books were to be considered as literature, the Guild said, and not simply as one more commercial product, to be sold by sensational covers alone. As Leo Manso put it: "That's plain bad taste; you just *can't* put a sexy cover on *Magic Mountain* or *The Brothers Karamazov*, can you? But, hell, some publishers actually tried. They'd find *one* steamy passage halfway through a book and, sure enough, that's the scene that turned up on the cover. Not only does that give the wrong idea of what the book's about, it lowers the whole level you're dealing on."

The Book Jacket Designers Guild was also involved with promoting other artists' concerns. They tried to set up standards for the relationship between publisher and illustrator, for example, and to determine precisely the responsibilities of each. Their dominant concern, though, was the overuse of sex on book covers. In 1952, John O'Hara Cosgrave wrote: "The sleaziest form of sex appeal, the 'peekaboo' jacket, is definitely not included [in this year's Guild exhibition]. The BJDG members feel that comparative anatomy is a field entirely unrelated to the task of coordinating author's idea, publisher's hopes, manufacturing possibilities and jacket designer's creativeness." A year later, Cosgrave continued: "Rejected [is] the jacket that is born of the assumption that if the book has a heroine, or if the author is a woman or the author's mother a female, then the cover must say: *SEX!*"

On May 12, 1952, the BJDG received unexpected assistance in its crusade with the publication of the report of the *Gathings Committee on Current Pornographic Materials in Pursuance of House Resolution 596, Eighty-Second Congress, Second Session*. The Gathings Committee concluded that it was time for Congress to legislate an end to the interstate and international transportation of "immoral, offensive, and other undesirable matter," that the Postmaster Genral should have the power to prevent the American mails from being used for the transportation of such matter, and that the publishing industry should immediately begin to censor itself against obscenity. The Committee's report included a list of works which they considered to be pornographic, although a minority of the members disagreed with the inclusion of such books as Erskine Caldwell's *God's Little Acre* on the forbidden list. Even this minority, however, agreed with the conclusion that cover illustrations ought to accurately reflect the contents of the books they covered.

Victor Weybright spoke out against the Gathings Committee report in a 1953 document titled *Complete and Unabridged Statement to the Gathings Committee by the New American Library of World Literature, Inc.* "At the point where one group seeks to impose its own private standards upon members of the general public," he wrote, "the activity of such a group becomes vicious."

Despite Weybright's comments, however, much self-censorship did occur in the industry between 1952 and 1955. The amount of visible flesh

A lecture at New York's The Composing Room, held during the 1940s under the auspices of Robert "Doc" Leslie. Jeanyee Wong is in the center of the front row, with George Salter beside her. Riki Levinson, Sam Fischer and Miriam Woods are in the second row, and Meyer Miller, with glasses and necktie, is in the third row. (Photo: A. Burton Carnes)

decreased, and even the blurbs, those often-provocative advertising texts, became somewhat less stimulating. A Popular Library book which had, in 1950, carried the line "Death, Dope and Sex Betray a Harlem Youth" on its cover was later toned down to read "Death, Dope and Passion Betray a Harlem Youth." The words "Violent Young Love," which appeared on a 1952 Popular Library cover, were changed to simply "Young Love" on a subsequent edition. Robert Stanley's 1951 and 1953 covers for A. A. Fair's *Fools Die on Friday* provide a classic example of self-censorship: on the first cover, Stanley's wife and model Rhoda is getting dressed; her blouse is unbuttoned and her breasts and white panties are seen. Two years later, the publisher had Stanley zip up Rhoda's skirt and button her blouse; after she fastens just one more button at her cuff, she will be completely clothed (see next page).

In the mid-1950s, after eight years of life, the Book Jacket Designers Guild was disbanded. Perhaps the Guild had somewhat improved the position of the cover artist, but in spite of its fulminations against "top-heavy ladies draped in undress" and a few brief years of industry self-discipline, the number of stimulating book covers being produced at the time the Guild passed out of existence had actually gone *up* rather than down.

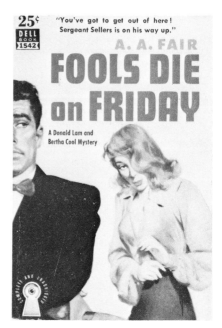

Robert Stanley's 1951 cover for *Fools Die on Friday* was toned down two years later, probably at the request of the hardcover publisher.

Meanwhile, Avati's influence had also broadened. Zuckerberg, Erickson, Phillips, Maguire, Nappi, Cardiff, Meese, Meltzoff and Dunn all used Avati-like styles, and every self-respecting paperback publisher employed at least a few of them.

At the same time, art directors began to play a more important role. Through the '40s it had not been unusual for a publisher to operate without any art director at all; Gobin Stair, who laid down stylistic guidelines at Bantam since that firm's infancy, was a rarity. In 1949, John Legakes became the New American Library's first art director, after the firm had already been around for over four years. Publishing houses generally had no studios of their own, no rooms teeming with drafting tables, nothing of the kind. Cover illustrations were obtained through art agencies; any attempt at consistency in the handing out of assignments was unusual, and the development of a true corporate style was practically unheard of.

This all changed between 1952 and 1955. Sol Immerman, who had been art director at Pocket Books since 1947, slowly became more of a creator than a coordinator; Joe Mann and his assistant Roy Lagrone handled art direction at Avon, John Legakes at Signet, Ed Rofheart at Popular Library, Walter Brooks at Dell and Al Allard at Fawcett (Gold Medal). Their growing influence was at first visible only on title pages and back covers; with Leonard Leone's appointment as art director of Bantam Books in 1955, this influence extended to front covers as well.

Leone brought a modern, breezy, dynamic style to the paperback industry. Many publishers abandoned long-standing graphic characteristics and adopted new ones: Bantam introduced a new rooster colophon, Dell scrapped the mapbacks, Signet dropped the horizontal bands bordering the illustrations, all houses devoted more attention to their cover lettering. The color and form of lettering was increasingly emphasized (as was background color), the standard rectangular format of most illustrations was less rigidly adhered to, and sketches, pen drawings and photographic covers were used in addition to paintings. Although the total amount of cover space taken up by the illustration was often smaller, the quality of reproduction improved significantly: Bantam was the first to print covers by offset, using a finer screen and making more faithful reproduction possible; since most other publishers held back from switching to offset until the mid-'60s, there was a rush of artists who suddenly wanted to work for Bantam. James Avati modernized his own Avati style; his imitators either disappeared or themselves adjusted to the New Airiness. Mike Hooks, Bob Abbett, James Bama, Clark Hulings, Bob Maguire, Charles Binger, Harry Schaare, Lou Marchetti, Robert McGinnis and Richard Powers were the most important representatives of this late-'50s change in direction.

Ultimately, realistic art won the battle for stylistic dominance. Art directors reached the height of their power, although in practice the commercial insights of sales departments have decided which genres are and are not acceptable. The situation today is stable: capable professionals have a certain amount of freedom within which they can often produce quite good work, but there is little room for eccentric, strange, or truly striking achievement. Along with film and television, paperback covers became largely predictable assembly-line products in the '60s and '70s, and they remain so today—we may breathlessly admire their outstanding degree of technical excellence, but we miss the touching naïveté and the enthusiastic originality of the earlier years.

A Few Particulars

In 1946, Penguin Books published an edition of Erskine Caldwell's successful novel, *God's Little Acre*. Six printings were needed to meet the demand for this book during its first year of paperback release, and there were *14* more printings in the autumn of 1947 alone, totaling 3,008,379 copies! Obviously, the book's cover became quite well-known: through a hole in a wooden fence, you see a house with a beat-up old car out front and an outhouse out back, a water pump, some scraggly trees and a patch of otherwise barren land (see page 72). Robert Jonas created the cover, using poster paints on a real piece of wood: "When *God's Little Acre* came out and was a hit," he remembers, "Kurt Enoch at Penguin decided there had to be a peephole on every one of Caldwell's other books, too. And then he had to have a peephole on *every* book he published, whether it was about anthropology or the rise of Protestantism. Enoch was a businessman, just like the Hollywood gang. They figure once they have a success on their hands, the best way to guarantee more successes is to copy the first one as closely as possible."

So all new Penguin editions of Erskine Caldwell's books came out with peepholes on their covers (see page 73 for numerous examples). *Tobacco Road* was issued in 1947: the cover showed a wooden fence with a hole shaped like a house cut through it. *Journeyman*, released the same year, once again had a wooden fence on its cover: a man in a black frock coat and hat gazes through an arched opening in the fence at a blonde in a red dress. In 1948, *Tragic Ground* featured another blonde, this one sitting in front of a curtain with a rip in it, while *A House in the Uplands* showed a brunette leaning against a wooden doorway. Although this was Jonas' last cover for a Caldwell novel, other artists continued putting peepholes on subsequent volumes: on *A Woman in the House* (1949) we look through a keyhole at, naturally, a woman in a house; also naturally, considering the state of paperback art that year, this particular woman is undressing herself. For *The Sure Hand of God* (also released in 1949), James Avati, who had taken over Jonas' position of importance at Signet, painted a man peeking through a window at an airily-dressed girl; Avati himself describes this painting as "a Jonas cover done in an Avati way."

With a little effort, Signet managed to continue equipping Caldwell novels with peephole covers on into the '50s, and Avati stuck with the early wood motif as well: every Caldwell cover he drew somehow involved either a wooden fence, a wooden veranda, or both.

Around 1946, other publishers jumped on the peephole bandwagon (see page 73). An illustrator named Gressley, whose first name is not known, put a group of hillbillies behind a hole in a fence on the cover of Pocket Books' *Taps For Private Tussie*. Gerald Gregg drew a ship at sea for a Dell edition of *Now, Voyager*; the ship is visible through a heart-shaped opening in a rose. Avon's 1946 releases all featured covers bordered by painted wooden picture frames, a peephole-like feature through which the reader could see a variety of beautiful women threatened by a variety of horrible monsters and/or vicious criminals. As late as 1955, Robert Stanley used a peephole on Dell's *The Rawhide Years*, and Lou Kimmel did something similar for Gold Medal on a book called *Hell Strip*.

It is certain that Jonas' cover for *God's Little Acre* turned peepholes into big business—although that was surely not his intention when painting it—but whether or not Jonas actually *created* the peephole genre is open to question. Combining several images by letting the viewer see one through a hole in another, with the hole itself often having a special or particular shape, is a trick well-known to the surrealists. Pocket Books' "artistic" wartime covers, especially those executed by Leo Manso, provide many examples. On Ellery Queen's *Calamity Town*, for instance (released in February of 1945, a year before *God's Little Acre*), a bare field and a house in the distance can be seen through a rip in a red curtain. For *The Case of the Substitute Face*, Manso painted a ship at sea, seen through a hole cut out of a black plane; the hole is shaped like a woman's head. There is a small heart-shaped hole through a fence on the 1945 Pocket Books edition of *The Bishop Murder Case*, while the fourth Bantam Book, *Evidence of Things Seen* (also from 1945), shows, through a leaf-shaped cutout, a woman running past a cemetery and into a forest.

In fact, Robert Jonas' own cover for *Trouble in July*, an Erskine Caldwell novel first released by Penguin in October of 1945, could also be considered a forerunner of the peephole era (see page 38).

Another image which often appears on paperback covers is the beautiful young woman with a look of unspeakable terror on her face, running downhill towards the reader and away from an old Victorian mansion or a castle, which is preferably located atop a rocky hill or, better yet, a mountain; on an upper story of this threatening structure, a light burns evilly behind a single window. This standard picture—the only variables seem to be the colors of the beautiful young woman's hair (usually blond) and dress (often red or white)—appears exclusively on a certain type of novel, the "Gothic" or "historical romance," which is devoured in droves by American schoolgirls, housewives and elderly women alike.

The Gothic rage began in 1960, when Fawcett published Mary Stewart's *Thunder on the Right* and Ace released Phyllis A. Whitney's *Thunder Heights*. According to artist Harry Bennett, "I was in Al Allard's office at Fawcett Publications, and he asked me to do the cover for *Thunder on the Right*. I did a drawing of a running girl and a castle, and it was an immediate success. The minute that book hit the stands, America's female population suddenly spawned this massive audience for Gothics. Back then an edition of 75,000 copies was still impressive, but these days, even though the books cost four times as much, they sometimes sell two or three million of them! The women out there just keep on buying them—it looks like they've found the answer to boredom."

In artist Lou Marchetti's *Thunder Heights* castle, no upstairs light burns. Marchetti, who estimates that he has since produced 500-700 Gothic covers, says that "that standard element was introduced a short time later by Donald A. Wollheim, editor-in-chief at Ace—his was 'the hand that lit the mysterious lamp.'" Wollheim is said to have discovered that simply lighting that one upstairs window can mean 5% more sales for a Gothic.

Long before 1960, however, this Gothic style was already a cliché on paperback covers. H. L. Hoffman's illustration for Pocket Books' 1943 edition of Daphne du Maurier's *Rebecca* showed a somber house in an inhospitable environment, where the trees have barren branches bending away from the violence of the weather—the only element missing was the running girl in the foreground. She first appeared in 1946, with her face in closeup, on the cover of du Maurier's *Jamaica Inn* (see page 176). Also in '46, Robert Jonas did a cover for Penguin's *Put Out the Light*: no horrified woman, but a man's face in the foreground and an old-fashioned house in which a light burns behind one window. And Robert Stanley brought all these elements together in his 1951 cover for Dell's *The Web of Evil* (again, see page 176), almost a decade ahead of Bennett and Marchetti.

One popular Gothic author tells a wonderful story about the immutability of the Gothic cover: "Once, just to see what would happen, I wrote a story set in a suburban ranch house in a densely-populated valley, with every single scene taking place in broad daylight; the heroine was a short-haired redhead who wore jeans throughout the entire book. But when the paperback came out, sure enough, there on the cover was a long-haired blonde in a flowing white dress, haring away from some frightening mansion at the top of a lonely hill in the dead of night!"

As graphic styles have changed, it has often been considered necessary to provide books with new and different covers. Countless covers from 1945 and 1946, many of them quite well done and effective, fell victim to the stylistic changes of 1947 and 1948. Some covers were changed two or three times within the space of a few short years; looking back at these changes today, we can see the paperback industry's progression from an abstract and even surreal "artistic" approach to the steaming realism of Avati and his followers.

The fall from grace of Robert Jonas' symbolic covers at Penguin and Signet can be followed from various editions of several titles released during the period 1946-1949 (see page 175). At first, Jonas was asked to change with the times and draw more realistically, but when that met with little success he was simply replaced by other artists. In 1946, two novels by James M. Cain appeared as Penguins: *Mildred Pierce* (Penguin 591) and *Serenade* (Penguin 621). Jonas' covers were among the most beautiful he ever produced. Still, he was assigned to do a new illustration for the second printing of *Mildred Pierce* only a year later: although the dusky blonde who resulted was certainly more realistic, the cover was equally less impressive. A third printing, released nine months later (in February, 1948), offered a gauzy, inexpressive picture by an anonymous artist; this design did not last very long, either. *Serenade* was also redrawn numerous times; the 1949 version was one of James Avati's first assignments.

Like Pocket Books, Bantam also wrapped new dustjackets around unsold stocks with oldfashioned or unpopular covers in an (often successful) attempt to remarket them. It is interesting to note that many covers which at the time proved commercially ineffective come across today as striking, interesting and strongly human: *One More Spring* (Bantam 19, issued in 1945) and *Valiant is the Word for Carrie* (Bantam 24, issued in 1946) featured extraordinarily original illustrations and lettering in their first paperback editions, but were later covered over with dustjackets which now seem stiff and lifeless. The original covers featured much green, brown and black, however, and it has been proven that those are colors which do not sell well.

Dustjackets were also used when a publisher wanted to capitalize quickly on a book's having been successfully filmed. In 1948, *Chicken Every Sunday* (Pocket Book 321, originally published in 1945) was given a dustjacket featuring photographs of Dan Dailey and Celeste Holm from the film of the same name. *The Great Gatsby*, published in 1945 as a Bantam Book with an attractive cover by Edgard Cirlin (see page 167), received an ugly dustjacket in 1949 when the Alan Ladd film hit the theaters. Such movie tie-ins were quite common: the covers were easy to design, consisting usually of a few still photos from the film, some text, and the standard phrase "Read the book—see the movie." These, incidentally, were the first purely photographic covers, in a period when paintings and drawings were still the rule.

Some collectors now specialize in these film covers, perhaps because they represent a slice of the American culture of their time. In any case, their rather forced combination of unrelated graphic elements made most of them rather unattractive.

In the 1981 paperback exhibit at the Gemeentemuseum in The Hague, we displayed groups of paperbacks arranged according to visual elements held in common: peepholes, Gothics, skulls and skeletons, large hands, disembodied eyes, bare legs, naked and partially-naked women, swamp girls, dead women lying on the ground, women on beds with men standing next to them, women in red dresses, women being carried by men, bound women, women being slapped in the face and, on a lighter note, an extremely popular motif: embraces and kisses. If I wanted to make an exhaustive list of *all* popular cover themes which have been used down the years, it would probably take months to compile and many pages to print—and anyway, it's much more fun for the fan or collector to discover them for himself.

Happy hunting!

Art Directors

A paperback cover ought to have some connection with the contents of the book it illustrates; it must attract or intrigue the potential buyer; it may need to make a book recognizable as one of a series by a particular author or about a particular subject; it must in all cases be recognizable as coming from a particular publisher, a publisher proud of the appearance of its product; it must be better than the covers of the books around it in the shop window or the display rack; it must, at least to a certain extent, meet with the approval of the book's author; it must be neither too complicated nor too costly to print; finally, it must, if possible, stand on its own as a beautiful, witty, or unique work of art.

It is the art director's task to deal with these considerations.

Most paperback covers reflect their art direction clearly. Ed Rofheart,

art director first at Pocket Books, then at Popular Library and then at Fawcett, says, "If you do it long enough, your work takes on its own personality. My covers are always recognizable. I do things with letters, for example, that nobody else does, and others do things that I don't do."

According to Sol Immerman, art director at Pocket Books for almost 30 years: "My starting point has always been, 'What you see is what you get.' The cover has to say, 'I am such-and-such a sort of book; if that's the sort of book you want to read, then buy me!'" However, Immerman admits that covers may also be used like some film posters: "If a book is weak, it needs help. So if a cover is loud, it's usually because the book's contents aren't loud enough. Somebody's just helped it out a little."

Before the revolution in art direction occurred in the mid-1950s, the paperback field offered only one possible forum for designers to express themselves creatively. Roy Lagrone remembers: "Walter Brooks and I always fought to get our books to look like something, but the only place they would let us be free was on the back covers. We got to be friends in the first place because I used to study his back covers and he used to study mine." According to Brooks, "We always had a lot of fun with those back covers."

Although there were good art directors before 1952, and although quality covers have been produced without them since, it was in that year that the art director's role was first seen as being of true importance. When Walter Brooks, Ed Rofheart and Leonard Leone became art directors at Dell, Popular Library and Bantam, the use of lettering began to be approached more consciously, illustration and text began to be considered a single graphic unit, and back covers began to be treated as an integral part of the overall cover design.

Art directors found it possible and desirable to exchange ideas in those days. As late as 1963, Leonard Leone, Roy Lagrone, Sol Immerman, Bill Gregory and Walter Brooks lunched regularly together at the Society of Illustrators in New York. Recalls Ed Rofheart: "The competition wasn't as murderous as it is today. If we liked another house's cover, we called up their art director and asked him who'd painted it, and then we'd use the same artist, too. But now that's all top-secret information. Book publishing used to have a kind of gentleness about it, but that's long gone now."

On the other hand, Al Allard of Fawcett Books tells a different story: "I was usually too busy keeping things rolling at Fawcett to pay much attention to what the competition was up to, but I do know that sometimes they went to a lot of trouble to steal a few of our illustrators."

How Are Covers Produced?

The cover of an American paperback usually consists of a color reproduction of a drawing or painting, some text (the book's title, a price, a corporate colophon and possibly a line or two of plot description or sales blurb) and, occasionally, further design elements such as bands or other areas of color. This chapter is a discussion of the production of such covers.

It needs to be noted at the beginning, however, that not all covers are produced in exactly the same way. Is the sales department's influence great or small? Does the illustrator develop the cover concept himself, or is it provided by someone else? Does the art director enter the process before or after the original drawing is made? Different answers to these and similar questions may result in significant differences in production procedure.

These differences operate not only between publishers, but between time periods as well: as noted earlier, artists tended to have more freedom during the '40s than they had during the '50s, while the art director's role became much more prominent around 1955; during the '60s and '70s, commercial considerations were the decisive factor.

Especially during the early paperback years, designers had to work within certain limits imposed by the state of printing technology available at the time; offset printing, for example, which offers better color reproduction than does letterpress, did not become the rule for paperback covers until the '60s.

Generally speaking, the production of a paperback cover involves the following steps: reading the book, sketching, cover meetings, execution of the finished illustration, lettering, preparation for the printer and printing. In the process of putting the complete book together, covers may sometimes be given a protective layer of either cellophane or varnish; afterwards, the cover is glued to the book and the pages are cut.

READING AND DOCUMENTATION—When asked, most cover artists will say that they always read a book before beginning on an illustration for its cover. In practice, however, that is not always what happens. In the early years, leftover art samples were often used as book covers, if they had only the slightest of connections with the contents of the book (and sometimes even when there was absolutely *no* connection).

At Dell Books, artists frequently received sketches on which their illustrations had to be based. An editor chose three different scenes from the book, three sketches were made by the art director and the artist then selected the sketch most appropriate to his style to work from.

Charles Andres says that he always read the books he was to illustrate, for their content, atmosphere and ideas. In addition, he sometimes read other books or stories from the same historical period or covering the same subject, and examined relevant paintings or objects to check certain details.

Robert Jonas speedread books; he learned that skill from his wife, who had been a censor during the war. He did not, however, read mysteries, he says, because "they're all the same anyway;" instead, he would leaf through them, looking for the page on which the body was discovered. If the victim had been poisoned, he would draw a bottle somewhere on the cover; if the victim had been shot, Jonas drew a revolver.

James Avati read all books he worked on, at least during his Signet period. "I'd read the book, set it aside and go to bed," he says. "Then I'd think over all the possibilities and eliminate the ones which wouldn't sell or which had some other negative aspect. Usually I'd be left with just a few ideas, maybe only one. So I'd call the art director up to talk it over, and we'd work something out." Avati found this process unnecessary when he worked for Bantam Books, as art director Leonard Leone provided all cover artists with detailed sketches, complete down to the lettering.

Leo Manso also always read the book: "I had to read a lot of lousy books," he remembers, "but it was the only way to come up with good ideas."

Today, with the production process having been thoroughly streamlined, an artist almost always receives extensive visual suggestions from the art director and editorial leads and reader's reports from the editor, which not only include concise plot summaries, but information about locations, costumes and historical background as well. As Avati found when working for Bantam, reading the book is no longer necessary.

SKETCHING—An artist usually first presents his ideas in one or more rough sketches, which must be approved by the publisher before the actual illustration can be drawn or painted.

Harry Bennett makes as many as 12 black-and-white sketches illustrating the most important aspects of a book. "I have to find the essence of the story," he says. "This is the most important stage in the creation of a good cover, so I work hard at it. I do my homework, so I know what kind of clothing the figures have to be wearing, what facial expressions

The best sketch idea is chosen by the art director

are appropriate, what colors to use. After that it's just sketching, sketching, and more sketching!"

Robert Jonas found this phase of cover production the most difficult: "For example, I'd get an assignment on Monday, 'Make a cover for Walter Lippmann's *Public Opinion*; we want to see a sketch a week from today.' What they wanted was a 'comp,' a color sketch the actual size of a paperback cover, with the lettering roughly indicated. So I'd sit down and think, 'Public opinion, Jesus....How am I ever going to show *that*?' After a while I'd start doodling, little scrawls the size of a postage stamp; gradually my doodles would get bigger, and eventually I'd start noticing certain images cropping up again and again. That's the great thing for me about the creative process; that's where my ideas come from. Thinking about public opinion, I came up with the thundering of printing presses, trucks delivering newspapers, radio, telegraph, telephone, everything dynamic. At last I knew exactly what I wanted, so I asked myself, 'What are you waiting for? Why don't you get started?' Because there was always some article I figured I had to read first, some film, some museum.... I'd use any excuse not to have to start drawing. So then it was Saturday, and then it was Sunday, and then it was Sunday night and I'd finally get to work. I'd go until two or three in the morning, until I was shaking from the tension—and then I would finish, and it would be good."

COVER MEETING—As a rule, the president and vice-president of the publishing house, several editors, the art director, the artist and sometimes a representative of the sales department would all be present at an official cover meeting during the '40s and '50s. The art director showed the proposed sketch, perhaps using a slide projector to blow it up quite large. The participants offered their opinions: that lady there needs to be smaller, she needs to be larger, she doesn't have enough clothing on, she has too *much* clothing on, she's not showing enough bosom, and so on.

James Avati: "It was always a battle, all the way! I have mainly negative things to say about those meetings. It was always, 'No, no, you can't do that!'" Nowadays, Avati usually discusses his ideas by phone, simply in order to avoid cover meetings.

Robert Jonas had a different approach: "I would walk in there like I'd just dashed off the most wonderful cover in the world. You had to have that attitude, because otherwise they would see the uncertainty in your face before they saw your sketch. Mr. Enoch used to look at what I'd come up with first, and then he'd say, 'Hmmmm.... Could you wait just a moment, please, Mr. Jonas?' And then buzz buzz buzz, the editors would trickle in. If I couldn't bear to stick around for the dissection, I'd just go for a walk."

Eventually, with or without changes, a sketch is approved for development.

EXECUTION—Robert Jonas remembers: "Once the sketch was approved, there were no more problems. It took me three days or so to get the thing done: I'd go home, grab a pencil and whistle while I worked, because at least now I knew for sure I was going to get paid!"

Realistic cover paintings are usually made from posed photographs; Norman Saunders, Robert Stanley, Stanley Meltzoff and Van Kaufman almost always used their own wives as models. James Avati had a regular group of models; he walked into a session with a detailed image of the finished cover in mind and discussed the effect he wanted to capture with the models before photographing them. Barye Phillips also did his own photography; if a cover had to be completed especially quickly (some-

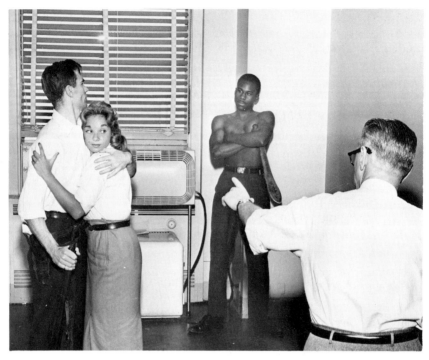

Directed by the artist, models are photographed

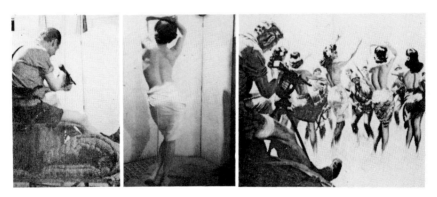

Norman Saunders and his wife posing for photographs, which Saunders then used in creating the paperback cover painting shown at right

times he was only given *one* day to work), he might deliver the photograph instead of a painting. Today, the publisher will provide costumes, models, equipment and photographers when these are necessary, in order to speed up the process.

Most paintings are done two or three times cover size. It is easier for the artist to work that way, and reduction adds sharpness to the image. Robert Jonas, however, nearly always worked at actual size.

Harry Bennett takes from three to five days to complete a cover, and has spent up to 10 days on an illustration for a front-and-back cover. "I like painting to be fun," he says. "If it isn't, I wind up doing mediocre work. So I do my best to be in a good mood for painting, to be delighted about getting started."

Cover painting may be limited by size, typographical considerations, demands from the art director and public expectations. Although Popular Library covers from the '50s suggest exactly the opposite, it is today an unwritten law that green on a cover does not sell. On the other hand, it is always a good idea to work some red in somewhere: "They love red!" Harry Bennett exclaims.

Bob Abbett says he enjoyed working within the medium's limitations, even enjoyed the continuous fighting against the ideas of certain art directors ("arbitrary and amateurish," he calls them). According to Jack Faragasso, "There are always limits. The color, the amount of sex, whether they want it hard or soft, or if they want it to look like a Bama, a McCarthy, a McGinnis, an Avati, whoever happens to be fashionable at the moment."

Covers may be executed in watercolor, poster paint, tempera, oil, acrylic, pencil, pen-and-ink, or with an airbrush.

Watercolors, or designer colors, are pigments mixed with a water-soluble base; when thinned with water, they provide a thin, transparent layer of color. Darker colors can be obtained by painting several layers deep—the first layer must be allowed to dry before the next can be applied. Standard watercolor technique is to use the paper itself, whether white or tinted, as the lightest color of the painting; some artists add accents with poster paints or by scratching the paper with a knife. Sam Savitt, Earl Sherwan, Cal Diehl, Norman Saunders, Gerald Gregg, Frederick Banbery, Paul Kresse, Gerald McConnell and Charles Andres, among others, have done watercolor covers; many of them use the artist's colors manufactured by Winsor & Newton.

Poster paints (also called gouache or body paint) are watercolors mixed

James Avati's original painting for *Scalpel* (Signet 1017, 1953)

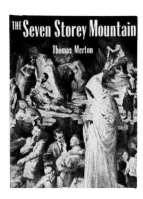

Avati only painted covers filled with many people when he had a lot of money on hand, as he had to pay the models himself. Sometimes he would use one model for multiple figures within a single painting.

Stanley Meltzoff's original painting for *The Green Hills of Earth* (Signet 943, 1952)

George T. Erickson's original painting for *Old Hell* (Perma Books)

with a glue (like gum arabic); they are opaque, and the colors tend to lighten somewhat as they dry. Pigment quality is generally not as good as it is with most ordinary watercolors; the quality difference is particularly noticeable when colors are mixed. Sam Savitt, Bill Teason, Robert Jonas and others have worked with poster paints.

Tempera (sometimes called casein or egg tempera) is a type of paint made with egg yolks; it may be mixed by the artist or purchased readymade. It dries quickly and, like poster paint, tends to lighten in color as it dries. It is often used in combination with oils; the oils are added to make changes and provide accents, the oil itself adding depth to the tempera colors. Before painting with tempera, surfaces must be prepared with gesso, a plaster-like white powder made of chalk, oil and a filler (such as zinc-white); the gesso forms a hard white undercoat which reflects up through the tempera and adds brilliance to the colors. Harry Bennett, Harry Schaare, Earl Sherwan, Robert McGinnis, Cal Diehl and Bob Abbett have worked with tempera.

Oils are pigments mixed with oil, usually linseed oil or poppy oil. The most effective technique for working with oils, as practiced by masters like Rembrandt and Rubens, is to first draw the image onto the surface to be painted (generally canvas), then roughly paint over it with grey, then add layers of color, each layer thicker ("pastier") than the one before it. Some layers may also be thin enough to allow the layer beneath

The artist does his final sketch, then executes the painting

them to remain visible; this process is called "glazing." James Avati, Harry Bennett, Frank McCarthy, Sam Savitt, Harry Schaare, Robert McGinnis, Stanley Zuckerberg, Cal Diehl, James Bama, Charles Andres, Bob Abbett (sometimes), Norman Saunders, George Erickson and Stanley Meltzoff have all used oils, generally over gouache or tempera on gesso panels.

Acrylics are synthetic, water-soluble paints. They may be applied layer by layer, like watercolors and oils, or in a single, thick layer. Walter Brooks, Harry Bennett, Harry Schaare, Charles Andres, Bob Abbett, George Erickson and Stanley Meltzoff regularly used acrylics for underpainting.

Sam Savitt and Mike Hooks, among others, often worked in *pencil*, which did not become technically feasible until, at the end of the '50s, offset printing made it possible to reproduce pencil lines with sufficient fidelity. It was Leonard Leone who first used a pencil sketch (by Mike Hooks, incidentally) as a paperback cover.

Pen-and-ink was used for endpaper illustrations at Bantam Books.

Last-minute corrections and changes are made

Combined with painting, it has also been used on covers by Harry Bennett, Sam Savitt and Barye Phillips.

George Salter has combined pen-and-ink with *airbrush* painting; an airbrush is, as its name suggests, an apparatus which shoots an extremely fine spray of paint onto a wide range of possible surfaces (even porous cloth, such as T-shirts). Masks may be used to cover off certain areas of the paper or canvas (or shirt!), so that they remain untouched by the spray of paint. Much of the effectiveness of the old Dell covers is owed to Gerald Gregg's airbrush virtuosity.

Many cover artists sign their work, although there have been publishers who insisted that illustrations be unsigned. Rafael Palacios, whose covers are always signed, remembers that many artists preferred paperback work to advertising work, even though advertising paid better, because they were allowed to sign their paperback covers, a form of self-publicity not offered by the ad agencies.

Robert Jonas, who at first signed his work by hand and later had his name typeset in lower-case Ultra Bodoni italic letters, saw another side to the publicity value of a signature: "There were times, if I thought one of my covers was no good, when I really didn't want to put my name on it, but I realized that the thing worked both ways. If I *didn't* sign a cover, then the publisher would know I was ashamed of it, so to protect myself I wound up signing everything."

Stanley Zuckerberg, Barye Phillips (who used his first name only) and James Avati were also well-known as cover signers. Avati even signed his first cover, *Last of the Conquerors*, a Signet Book from 1949; his signature did not change noticeably until the '60s, although he sometimes presented it in humorous ways: on three 1951 Signets by Erskine Caldwell, *This Very Earth* (Signet 838), *Kneel to the Rising Sun* (869) and *The Humorous Side of Erskine Caldwell* (899), Avati's last name has been "whittled" into the wood of either a fence or a veranda on each cover. Stanley Meltzoff, an Avati fan, did something similar on a number of covers for Signet and Gold Medal: you may need to search quite closely before you finally discover Meltzoff's name on a fence or scrawled graffiti-style on a poster, or his initials carelessly lettered on a mailbox.

Signatures may often vanish in the process of converting a signed illustration into a published cover, as portions of the illustration are cropped away, as colored borders and cover text are added, or as the pages are cut. James Avati was once asked to sign a cover painting a second time, when art director John Legakes realized that his original signature would have to be cropped away—which shows how proud Signet was to have Avati's name appear on their books.

The normal fee for a single cover was $100-125 around 1945. In the '50s, prices ranged from $200 to $250, although the really big names (Avati at Signet, Tom Dunn at Pocket Books, Ben Stahl at Bantam) received $500-1,000. In 1980, a $1,000 fee was about average for a paperback cover, while Avati today gets between $2,000 and $4,000 plus expenses.

LETTERING—When the artist has finished his illustration, the art director must then arrange for cover text to be lettered or typeset. In the '40s and '50s, art directors often crammed that text into whatever "holes" the artist happened to have left in his work.

"I thought that brutal," says Leonard Leone, "a kind of unprofessionalism that was just completely uncalled for." Leone and his contemporaries put an end to the practice: as of 1955, a layout in which the location, size, shape and even color of all cover text was precisely indicated was

Bernie Salbreiter (sitting), the lettering specialist at Dell, with artist Gerald Gregg. Right: Salbreiter's lettering for Dell spines; *The Harvey Girls* was lettered by Marguerite Sherwan.

A DELL WAR BOOK • **THE RAFT** • GEORGE TRUMBULL

• **THIS TIME FOR KEEPS** • Jim McConaughy

• **DANCE OF DEATH** • HELEN McCLOY

•**CRIME HOUND**• MARY SEMPLE SCOTT

• **THE CAT SAW MURDER** • D.B. OLSEN

• **THE BODY THAT WASN'T UNCLE** • PAT McGERR

• MADE UP TO KILL *By Kelley Roos* •

•**The Harvey Girls** • *by* SAMUEL HOPKINS ADAMS

The Innocent Mrs. Duff *Elisabeth Sanxay Holding*

Death Knell *Baynard Kendrick*

MR. PINKERTON GROWS A BEARD DAVID FROME

NIGHT FLIGHT ANTOINE DE ST. EXUPÉRY

AN ENEMY OF THE PEOPLE: ANTISEMITISM JAMES PARKES

TOMBSTONE WALTER NOBLE BURNS

THE GOOD SOLDIER SCHWEIK JAROSLAV HASEK

GOD'S LITTLE ACRE ERSKINE CALDWELL

THUNDER ON THE LEFT CHRISTOPHER MORLEY

WINESBURG, OHIO SHERWOOD ANDERSON

BACK STREET FANNIE HURST

MILDRED PIERCE JAMES M. CAIN

THE HEART IS A LONELY HUNTER CARSON McCULLERS

PUT OUT THE LIGHT ETHEL LINA WHITE

JURGEN JAMES BRANCH CABELL

JAMES T. FARRELL • SHORT STORIES

MESSER MARCO POLO DONN BYRNE

SARATOGA TRUNK EDNA FERBER

THE PERENNIAL BOARDER PHOEBE ATWOOD TAYLOR

SERENADE JAMES M. CAIN

GOOD READING

THE SILVER JACKASS FRANK GRUBER

THE PURPLE ONION MYSTERY H. ASHBROOK

THE KING IS DEAD ON QUEEN STREET FRANCIS BONNAMY

MOTHER WORE TIGHTS MIRIAM YOUNG

GREAT SON EDNA FERBER

THE UNBEARABLE BASSINGTON "SAKI"

John Legakes, art director for the New American Library from 1949 through 1961. The photo was taken in 1954. Left: spine lettering for Penguins and Signets, 1942-55.

The assistant art director prepares a mechanical

designed and given to the artist before he ever began working, so that the illustration could be planned out accordingly.

Even in the '40s, though, many covers balanced illustration and text wonderfully, especially in cases where the artists themselves provided the lettering for their covers, as did George Salter (at Mercury Publications, Penguin and Pocket Books), Leo Manso, Miriam Woods and others. Robert Jonas also lettered his own covers, but in his case the results were less wonderful.

Dell Books released from the company's inception through 1950 are a model of excellent hand-lettering. Bernie Salbreiter of Western Printing was Dell's lettering specialist and handled most of the work; covers illustrated by Earl Sherwan (*The Harvey Girls*, for example) were an exception—they were lettered by Marguerite Sherwan, the artist's wife.

The consistent use of a particular lettering style can provide a publishing house with a recognizable "look," but not all publishers have taken equal advantage of that opportunity. While Penguin used bold sans-serif letters on cover and spine from its first releases in 1942 through the '60s,

Avon seemed to change typography, colophon and other design characteristics practically every month. Not until the mid-'50s did Avon introduce a certain amount of consistency to its graphic style.

Robert Jonas either accidentally or purposely served as the graphic director of Penguin/Signet between 1945 and 1948. He drew most covers during that period, was responsible for the tall format of the books and, as type director, handled all typography. He did not draw the lettering himself, but cut letters out of type catalogs. In 1949, John Legakes became Signet's art director and took over this work. James Avati, Signet's most important cover artist at the time, says he was rarely satisfied with the lettering of his covers; he found the procedure used unprofessional. Only about Barbara Bertoli, art director at Avon in the '60s, does Avati have a positive reaction when the subject under discussion is cover lettering.

The quality of cover typography at Bantam, especially early on in that firm's existence, when Gobin Stair was art director, was rather high. It is obvious that the intention was to deliver a product which could compete successfully with hardcovered books—obvious from the choice of cover illustrators, the format of the books, the use of endpapers and the typography.

Typographically, Popular Library went through an early, a middle and a late phase. The first covers were all designed by the Immerman studio, with lettering by Sol Immerman himself; the lettertype employed was Lydian, which Immerman would also use, eight years later, on the Cardinal Editions. In the middle phase, book titles and authors' names were often hand-drawn. When Ed Rofheart became art director, he decided that all cover text was to be typeset using Franklin Gothic Condensed; he considered the use of many different typefaces and styles of hand-lettering "too pulpy."

PREPARATION FOR THE PRINTER—The cover illustration, the lettering and the other design elements (colophon, numbers, areas of color, etc.) are combined in the art studio into a working drawing, or "mechanical." On a translucent sheet of paper, the art director can indicate sections of the drawing to be eliminated, the edge along which the pages will be cut, and places where letters and other elements will appear over the drawing, concealing parts of it from view; if the drawing is not of the correct size, the necessary percentage of reduction or enlargement must also be indicated. On a second translucent sheet, all letters, numbers, colophons and other elements which are to appear as outlined areas in the

The manufacturing chief checks proofs against the original (This photo, and those on pages 120, 122, 126, 127 and 130, originally appeared in the March, 1957 issue of *Newsdealer Magazine*. *Something of Value*, by Robert Ruark, was published as Cardinal GC-753. The cover was painted by Charles Binger, who was unable to attend this photo session; the name of his stand-in is not known. The art director is Sol Immerman.)

four-color photo are sketched. And on a third sheet, the colors in which these elements are to be printed is indicated: full colors (such as black, red or blue) or a color mix (composed of varying percentages of two or more full colors) may be used, or white may be obtained by not printing *any* color in a given area.

WHERE ARE THE ORIGINALS?—Once a color photograph of a cover illustration has been made and the proof has been approved, the original painting or drawing is no longer needed for the production process. What happens to that original is rather painful: it usually disappears. It is rare today to find an artist who still owns his own originals from 1945; most of them say that their work was never returned to them after it was used. "A lot of nonsense goes on about that," one artist has complained. "We ought to be able to get our work back without having to threaten to go to court."

What happens to original artwork? Does it just go up in smoke?

No. A man from the sales department walks into the art director's studio, sees a painting by James Avati and thinks, "Hey, that'd look pretty good in my living room." An editor has a bare bit of wall in his office, just right for one of Richard Powers' outer-space scenes. A Robert McGinnis oil is offered to the company president at a business meeting, without McGinnis himself knowing anything about it.

Art directors, printers and artists all blame each other for having mislaid original cover art. One illustrator says that a number of his originals were actually "stolen"—by two of his own agents.

Gobin Stair, on the other hand, asserts that all artwork done for Bantam Books was returned after use, but adds that that work had no real value, because it was not real art. "It was commercial art," he says, "and the same thing happens to that kind of stuff as is happening these days to the dollar: it just disappears."

Artistic Influences

If a cover illustrator is very good, he may be able to succeed as a "fine" artist. Most illustrators are *not* fine artists, though—which is not to say anything at all about the quality of their work: an excellent illustrator may be an average artist, and an excellent artist may only be an average illustrator. Actually, commercial art and fine art have never been all that far apart in 19th and 20th century America anyway. There is an important realistic tradition in American painting, which began in the 1800s and which is still blooming today. The landscapes, seascapes and portraits of major realists such as Harvey Dunn, Norman Rockwell and Harold Von Schmidt are highly respected, and those men all began their careers as book and magazine illustrators. Landscapes by Stanley Zuckerberg, Frank C. McCarthy and James Bama, all successful paperback artists, are currently greatly in demand as works of fine art.

Howard Pyle (1853-1911) is often considered to have been the father of American illustration. He drew dramatic images, lively and strongly composed—and he was also an author of short stories and adventure novels. He taught at the Drexel Institute in Philadelphia, at the Art Students League of New York, and in Wilmington, Delaware; his students included Harvey Dunn and N.C. Wyeth. Many contemporary paperback illustrators, among them Charles Andres, Verne Tossey and George Erickson, name Pyle as an important influence; when Louis

Glanzman is asked to list the artists who have had an impact on his style, he is likely to answer, "Howard Pyle, Howard Pyle, and Howard Pyle."

Harvey Dunn (1884-1952) was born in South Dakota and studied at the Art Institute in Chicago. He was an illustrator and painter; during World War 1 he made journalistic sketches and bird's-eye-view battlefield perspectives from the trenches. As a teacher, he hammered into his classes that the essence of illustration was to "convey the spirit;" students including Norman Rockwell, Harold Von Schmidt, Dean Cornwell and Norman Saunders all seemed to take the point. Stanley Zuckerberg, Cal Diehl and Charles Andres mention Dunn as an important influence.

George Erickson names Newell Convers Wyeth (1882-1945), student of Howard Pyle and father of famed painter Andrew Wyeth, as a great inspiration. Wyeth illustrated books for Charles Scribner's Sons and other publishers, and also provided drawings for dozens of magazines.

Dean Cornwell (1892-1960), who studied with Harvey Dunn, worked as an illustrator for many years. He later was noted as a muralist; a classic example of his work was done for the Los Angeles City Library. Cornwell was a perfectionist: every secondary figure, every decorative detail was carefully studied and sketched before he began to paint. Stanley Zuckerberg, Verne Tossey and Charles Andres speak highly of his impact on their work.

Harold Von Schmidt, born in California in 1893, is today a major painter of Western landscapes, much admired by Bob Abbett, Charles Andres and Stanley Zuckerberg. After studying art in San Francisco, Von Schmidt worked as an illustrator for the magazine *Sunset*; after winning a poster contest, he turned to poster work for a while and studied further with Harvey Dunn. From 1938 until 1941, he was the president of the Society of Illustrators in New York.

Norman Rockwell (1894-1979) has been internationally acclaimed for his anecdotal, homey cover illustrations for *The Saturday Evening Post*, which he began drawing in 1915. Gerald Gregg, George Erickson, James Bama and Stanley Zuckerberg all talk of having learned much from Rockwell's technique.

Younger paperback illustrators, including Robert McGinnis, James Bama and Harry Bennett, rank Andrew Wyeth and Coby Whitmore as their most important influences. Whitmore, born in 1913, studied at the Art Institute in Dayton, Ohio and learned his trade at the Sunblom-Henry Art Studio in Chicago. He later worked for a time at the Charles E. Cooper Studio in New York, where his assignments included illustrations for *McCall's*, *Ladies' Home Journal*, *Redbook*, *Good Housekeeping* and

Cosmopolitan. Although the stories he illustrated tended to revolve around practically-interchangeable plots, Whitmore consistently managed to inject something different and new into his work. His women were always stylishly dressed, even though he often had to deliver his drawings months before they were published.

Paperback artists who more designed than illustrated covers, such as Robert Jonas, Walter Brooks and Leo Manso, are more likely to name Europeans than Americans as having exerted the greatest influence on their approach to cover art. Manso says, "We thought that the European work being done at that time was much better than what was going on here. I was very interested in Cassandre [the French poster designer] and E. McKnight Kauffer, who came from England and was very good." Kauffer (who, incidentally, was born in the United States) is also highly praised by Jonas and Brooks.

Recognition of Cover Artists

Through the end of the 1950s, the images on American paperback covers were ignored by most students, lovers and critics of art. Paperback illustrators were the art world's stepchildren, who had to work themselves up to "fine" artists or, at least, to hardcover designers before anyone would pay any attention to them; many of them worked anonymously, and it was only a limited number of big names who signed their work and were well paid.

That state of affairs changed around 1960. The American Institute of Graphic Arts organized its first annual exhibition of paperback covers that year in New York, galleries began to hang original cover art, and even the exclusive Society of Illustrators opened its membership to include certain paperback cover artists.

Even before 1960, though, scattered attempts were made at giving paperback artists some of the recognition they deserved. From 1947 through 1950, during Don Gelb's tenure as art director, Bantam Books irregularly published a rubric titled *About the Cover* on one of the first left-hand pages of its books. In a few lines, the name of the artist was given, along with some information about his technique and his treatment of the subject in question; often, catchy language explained a special connection between artist and subject matter. In 1949, though, the content of *About the Cover* changed, and the episode depicted on the cover was discussed instead of the illustrator. A fragment of text referring

From *Midnight Lace*, Bantam 753 (1950)

to the cover scene was often printed; the artist's name was no longer necessarily mentioned and, when it was, the reference was quite brief. Even that token credit was soon dropped and, except for a few stars such as Ben Stahl, artists' names were no longer provided. The rubric itself was scrapped in 1950.

In 1948, Pocket Books began naming their artists in small letters at the bottom of the back cover; this practice was continued until the '60s. During the '50s, Avon and Gold Medal occasionally credited cover artists somewhere on an inside page or on the inside of the cover; Dell began mentioning artists' names on the title page or the copyright page in 1950, then moved that credit to the back cover in 1959.

Some publishers briefly made reproductions of cover illustrations available. In 1950, Bantam readers could buy copies of Ben Stahl's cover paintings for $2 each. In 1952, Pocket Books offered free enlargements of one of the drawings from *Tiger Roan*, a Junior Pocket; the artist, Sam Savitt, says the firm was so swamped with requests for that reproduction that they never repeated the experiment.

The Book Jacket Designers Guild, founded in 1947, strove for a "high artistic level and technical perfection," and organized yearly exhibitions of hardcover and paperback covers from 1948 until 1955.

In 1954, James Avati, James Meese, Stanley Zuckerberg, Stanley Meltzoff and art director John Legakes attended the opening of an exhibit of Signet covers at the Cartoonist and Illustrators School in New York. A year later, in April and May of 1955, Columbia University's School of Library Service sponsored an exhibition titled *The Evolution of American Publishing in Paperbacks*. Representative covers from 32 publishers were displayed, and 16 original cover paintings by Jim Meese and Ray Johnson (Avon), Stanley Meltzoff, James Avati and Stanley Zuckerberg (Signet), Verne Tossey, Robert Schulz and Tom Dunn (Pocket Books), A. Leslie Ross, Owen Kampen and George Mayers (Popular Library) and other artists were hung in the school's Butler Library. The exhibit was later transferred to the New York State Library and, eventually, visited libraries throughout America.

The Artists Speak

STANLEY MELTZOFF: "The paperback field is less imaginative than comic strips, less strong than *imagerie populaire* or any other folk art, less vivid than movie posters—but it does have a certain charm. Paperbacks were a common evening amusement during the years before television, and they gave visual form to certain kinds of American wishes, myths, dreams, forebodings and pretensions. They were neither the most powerful nor the most determinative medium—but they were always there.

"The place of paperback cover illustration is and was as a training field for illustrators: the demands were low, the turnover rapid and the subjects varied. Paperbacks took the place of pulp magazines, which had trained the previous generation of illustrators. The use of color and the complexity of subjects was stimulating, while the tiny reproductions hid poor execution and the type and art direction concealed bad design. As soon as anyone got better (always with the exception of Avati), he or she moved on to more ample fields. It was a great place for beginners, but a penance and a shame for older workers. But on the other hand, old illustrators often reverted to the paperback field as a means of sustenance when times got tough."

BOB ABBETT: "The moust important thing about my years as an illustrator was the experience it gave me in the physical practice of painting—

the research and drawing and, of course, the conceiving and designing of a picture. Illustration served fine art the way vaudeville served the theater, as a marvelous and well-paying school which was both inspiring and practical. When I reached the stage of maturity at which I desired to do paintings of a more personal and lasting nature, my experience was sufficient for me to do so in a way that freed my mind creatively; it was not necessary any longer for me to worry about 'what style' to use. When I reached that stage, I realized that my works were honest and my own. No, although the 'craft' aspect of being an artist has often been played down in both practice and education, in the realistic school of painting it is in fact a necessity."

GOBIN STAIR (art director at Penguin until 1945, then at Bantam until 1948): "The paperback industry very quickly fell into the big pit of successful business, and salesmen rather than artists determined the appearance and the content of the product. In the '50s and '60s, quality paperbacks were only published by the trade houses, like Anchor, Vintage, Beacon and Torchbooks."

GEORGE ERICKSON: "I don't think books are sold because of that commercial approach. Rather, they are sold in spite of it. My approach to a cover is to show that quality especially relevant to that particular book, so that the reader wants to become involved in its content. A good cover needs to look 'real.' Real people in a real situation that is exciting to the reader."

ROBERT JONAS: "I couldn't have made realistic covers if my life had depended on it. That kind of work is regressive, it's only done because it appeals. It may have snob appeal or some other sort of appeal, but it has no other *meaning* of any kind. The illustrators aimed at the lowest violent and pornographic human instincts. I don't want to insult illustrators—some of my best friends are illustrators, I admire James Avati's and Stanley Meltzoff's technique enormously. But if you look at it carefully, a realistic cover is much more misleading than anything I ever did. You can't express the true meaning of a book in a realistic cover."

JAMES AVATI: "Contemporary covers all look so much alike. It's always the same pretty people, painted in the same pretty way. But how could you possibly believe that human beings are *always* beautiful?"

Appendices

Year by Year

1929-1938

The St. Valentine's Day Massacre and the Stock Market Crash slam the door on the Roaring '20s and usher in the Great Depression. The Empire State Building opens, the U.S. goes off the gold standard and Prohibition is repealed. Franklin Delano Roosevelt is twice elected President while, in England, King Edward VIII abdicates his throne for the woman he loves. The National Socialist movement becomes more aggressive towards Jews in Germany and civil war breaks out in Spain. The Social Security Act is passed, *Gone With the Wind* is published, the Dionne quintuplets are born and Charles Lindbergh's son is kidnapped. The Hindenburg catches fire in Lakehurst, New Jersey. Jesse Owens wins four gold medals at the Berlin Olympics and is snubbed by Adolph Hitler. Germany annexes Austria, and Orson Welles shocks America with his radio dramatization of an invasion by Martians.

The Boni brothers begin to publish their **Boni Paper Books** in 1929, proving that it is possible to produce tasteful paperbacks. In 1930, Emanuel Haldeman-Julius introduces the **Little Blue Books**, which will survive until the '50s.

In 1932, the same year in which the **Albatross** series first appears in Germany, the National Home Library Foundation brings out the first volumes of its **Jacket Library** in Washington, D.C. The series is abandoned in 1935, as the first 10 **Penguins** are published in England.

Modern Age Books, Inc., publishers of the **Blue Seal**, **Red Seal** and **Gold Seal Books**, is founded in 1937, and American Mercury Books prints James M. Cain's *The Postman Always Rings Twice* as the first of its **Mercury Publications**.

In the autumn of 1938, Robert F. DeGraff markets 2,000 copies of a test edition of Pearl S. Buck's *The Good Earth*, which is about to win the Nobel Prize for Literature; the sales figures are encouraging, and he plans to release the first **Pocket Books** next year.

1939

The New York World's Fair opens. Frank Sinatra makes his first record, and John Steinbeck's *The Grapes of Wrath* is a bestseller in hardcover. The Soviet Union invades Finland, the German Army marches into Poland and war breaks out in Europe; the United States declares itself neutral.

German publisher Kurt Enoch leaves Europe for New York, where the British firm, **Penguin Books**, sets up an American branch office headed by Ian Ballantine.

The first 10 **Pocket Books** are published, all but one in editions of 10,000 copies; 24 more titles are released by the end of the year.

The Los Angeles branch of the Western Printing & Lithographing Company begins issuing a series of paperbacks intended for sale from vending machines, the **Bantam Books**.

The **Red Arrow Books** are born and, after 12 releases, die in Milwaukee, Wisconsin.

In this first year of the paperback "revolution," paperback covers are generally purely typographic and uninteresting. Pocket Books, however, carry illustrated covers from the very beginning, although the illustrations themselves (by Isador Steinberg, Frank Lieberman and Eve Rockwell) are rather primitive, as is the original drawing of Gertrude the Kangaroo by Lieberman.

1940

As Germany launches its Blitzkrieg, with troops goosestepping across Holland, Belgium, Luxemburg and France and the Luftwaffe terrorizing England by air, America introduces its first peacetime draft. FDR wins an unprecedented third term as President. Alfred Hitchcock films *Rebecca*, Donald Duck stars in *The Riveter*, John Lennon is born, and nylon stockings make their first appearance on American legs.

Pocket Books releases 49 new titles, with cover illustrations by Steinberg,

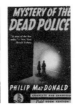 

Rockwell, Allen Pope, Van Doren and Frye; number 68, Dale Carnegie's *How to Win Friends and Influence People*, is the bestselling paperback of the year.

Penguin Books, Inc. imports and sells British **Penguins**; the **Penguin Specials**, which first appeared in England in 1937 and which deal with war-related subjects, are especially popular.

American Mercury Books introduces their **Bestseller Mysteries** and **Mercury Mysteries**, digests with covers and typography by George Salter.

1941

Orson Welles films *Citizen Kane* and W. C. Fields stars in *Never Give a Sucker an Even Break*. FDR makes his Four Freedoms speech and signs the Lend-Lease Act. Germany attacks Russia. On December 7, "a day that will live in infamy," Japanese planes attack Pearl Harbor; America declares war on Japan the following day, and on Germany and Italy on December 11.

German submarine activity in the Atlantic Ocean interferes with the transportation of **Penguin Books** to the United States, so Ian Ballantine decides to publish American Penguins himself; the first titles will appear in 1942.

Avon Books is founded by Joseph Meyers, and is immediately sued for imitating the format of **Pocket Books**. Twelve titles are released by Avon, including *Elmer Gantry*, *The Big Four* and *Ill Wind*.

Pierre Martinot, Miriam Woods, Silten and Immerman/Hoffman illustrate covers for Pocket Books. When that firm's production leader is drafted, Ed Rofheart takes over. *The Pocket Book of Short Stories* is the year's bestselling paperback.

The first **Handi-Books** appear.

1942

American fighter planes bomb Tokyo, Guadalcanal is attacked and North Africa is invaded. In the United States, gasoline is rationed, the first nuclear chain reaction is set off and 110,000 Japanese-Americans are interned in detention camps on the

West Coast. Spencer Tracy and Katherine Hepburn make their first film to-gether, *Woman of the Year*; Walt Disney's *Bambi* is released, Irving Berlin writes "White Christmas" and Edward Hopper paints *Nighthawks*.

Ned Pines and Leo Margulies establish **Popular Library** and David McKay founds **The American Library**.

The first American Penguins are published: 10 **Infantry Journal - Penguin Books**, which deal with current war subjects, and 14 **Penguin Books**, which are classic mysteries and novels. The covers are illustrated (by Busoni, Ethel-bert White and others), which will later lead to problems with the British par-ent company.

Elizabeth Moody's *The Pocket Cook Book* is a bestseller. Laura Hobson de-signs a general style for **Pocket Books**, the round-cornered frame, which makes its appearance on this autumn's releases. Gertrude the Kangaroo is temporarily retired, and replaced by a typographic colophon. Immerman/Hoff-man, Salter, John Allen Maxwell, Troop and Harve Stein are the most impor-tant cover artists.

Avon publishes 10 titles, and introduces the *Murder Mystery Monthly*.

1943

As Allied ships hit the beaches of North Africa, American troops attack Sicily and mainland Italy and the U.S. Navy establishes strongholds on more and more islands in the At-lantic Ocean, war correspondent Richard Tregaskis publishes his *Guadalca-nal Diary* and journalist Ernie Pyle describes the life of a soldier in *Here is*

Your War. Donald Duck stars in *Der Fuehrer's Face* and Humphrey Bogart does not tell Dooley Wilson to "Play it again, Sam," in *Casablanca*.

Paper is rationed, and the paperback industry feels the crunch. Few books are published; those that do come out use small type and thin paper.

Pocket Books and **Penguin** are less affected by the rationing: Pocket Books because of their connection with the new **Armed Services Editions** and Penguin because Ian Ballantine is working in close cooperation with *The Infantry Journal*. The Pocket Book edition of Marion Hargrove's *See Here, Private Hargrove* sells a million copies, and the firm also publishes the first book to make use of the term "science fiction." H. Lawrence Hoffman and Leo Manso provide many covers and the Walt Disney Studios designs a new Gertrude.

The first **Popular Library** titles appear (with covers by Hoffman), along with the first **Dell** releases and a single **Hillman Detective Novel**. Dell publishes 32 books this year, mostly mysteries and mostly with covers by Gerald Gregg.

Beginning in September, 30 titles in the Armed Services Editions series appear each month; they have covers by Sol Immerman and are shipped to soldiers fighting overseas.

Avon Books releases 17 titles.

1944 On June 6, the Allied Forces invade Normandy. Ernie Pyle wins the Pulitzer Prize for his journalistic coverage of the war. Franklin Delano Roosevelt is reelected to a fourth term, and Ingrid Bergman receives her first Oscar.

The paper shortage worsens: **Pocket Books, Avon, Penguin** and **Popular Library** publish less than 20 new titles each; **Dell** releases 35 titles.

Perhaps inspired by the **Armed Services Editions**, Pocket Books experiments with an oblong format, but only uses it for one book.

Through June, 30 new titles are added to the Armed Services Editions per month; afterwards, the monthly figure goes up to 40 titles. The **Mercury Library** also works for the Army.

The American Library is discontinued, but a number of new, small paperback houses are established (such as **Bart House**, **Green Dragon Books** and **Quick-Reader Books**), and **Bestseller Mysteries**, **Mercury Mysteries** and **Handi-Books** continue to appear.

H.L. Hoffman is the year's dominant cover artist, working for Pocket Books, Penguin and Popular Library. E. McKnight Kauffer makes his first covers for Pocket Books.

1945

Roosevelt, Churchill and Stalin meet in Yalta; not long afterwards, FDR dies of a cerebral hemorrhage in Warm Springs, Georgia and Harry S Truman becomes President. Germany surrenders, Hitler commits suicide in his bunker and, after atomic bombs are dropped on Hiroshima and Nagasaki, Japan surrenders as well. In America, the United Nations is founded and 31 flavors of Baskin & Robbins ice cream go on the market.

Pocket Books publishes a record 70 titles, more than **Popular Library** (with 25) and **Dell** (with 27) put together; number 300, *Franklin Delano Roosevelt: A Memorial*, hits the stands only six days after the President's death, while number 340, *The Atomic Age Opens*, follows the Hiroshima explosion by a few weeks. Salter, Kauffer and Bill Gillies provide many covers.

Troubles continue between Allen Lane, director of British **Penguin**, and Ian Ballantine; Ballantine leaves Penguin (where covers are being drawn by Edgard Cirlin, David Triggs, Lester Kohs and Robert Jonas) to found **Bantam Books**, whose first titles appear in November with covers by Hoffman, Triggs, Cirlin, Clement, Rafael Palacios, Cal Diehl and Ava Morgan. Gobin Stair, who had also worked at Penguin until this year, is art director.

Popular Library covers are by Hoffman and Fiedler, Dell covers by Gregg, Ben Hallam and others.

Avon publishes 18 titles.

Newly-established small houses include **Keep-Worthy Books** and **Pony Books**.

1946

With the signing of peace treaties, World War II is now officially over. Americans are able to listen to an atomic explosion on the Bikini Atoll over their radios and to see Frank Capra's *It's A Wonderful Life* at their neighborhood cinemas. Hungary becomes a republic, the Phillipines gain their independence and Truman establishes the CIA. In their first major political campaigns, both Richard M. Nixon and John F. Kennedy are elected to seats in the House of Representatives.

The demand for paperbacks lessens, and many publishers are left with unexpected surpluses. Some of the smaller firms, including **Pony Books** and **Keep-Worthy Books**, go broke, but others (such as **Bonded Mysteries**, **Hangman's House**, **Hip Books**, **Black Knight Mysteries** and **Trophy Books**) are founded.

Several paperback series undergo changes this year. **Pocket Books** abandons the round-cornered frame and begins using more realistic cover illustrations. **Penguin** debuts a taller format and introduces the **Pelican Books**. **Dell** first uses the word DELL as a colophon and **Bantam** first prints a triangle on its spines. The **Armed Services Editions** adopt the Pocket Books format.

Robert Jonas is an important cover artist for Penguin and Pelican; Penguin covers are also illustrated by Cirlin, Salter, Woods, Kohs, Hoffman, Arthur J. Hawkins, Michael Loew and Arthur Getz. At Bantam, Hoffman, Alexander, Diehl, Morgan, Palacios, Triggs, Steinberg, Kohs, Charles Andres and Bill English are active. Earl Sherwan begins to do covers for Dell.

Dr. Benjamin Spock's *Baby and Child Care* is published by Pocket Books; it is to become the world's bestselling paperback. Other bestsellers this year are *Duel in the Sun* (**Popular Library**), *Mister Roberts* (Armed Services Editions and Pocket Books), *Butterfield 8* (**Avon**) and *God's Little Acre* (Penguin). Robert Jonas' cover for *God's Little Acre* ushers in the age of the peephole.

1947

The Marshall Plan is announced, India and Pakistan become independent states, the Dead Sea Scrolls are discovered and flying saucers are sighted across America. *A Streetcar Named Desire* opens on Broadway and Danny Kaye stars in *The Secret Life of Walter Mitty*. Jackie Robinson becomes the first black to play major-league baseball.

Many paperback publishers replace sewn bindings with a process called "perfect binding," which is in fact far from perfect and which no longer provides for the use of endpapers.

After publishing more than 100 titles in its "postwar" series this year alone, the **Armed Services Editions** are discontinued. Also in 1947, **Green Dragon Books** is slain and **Hangman's House** gives up the ghost. **Eagle Books** lifts off but, after three releases, takes a nose dive.

Sol Immerman becomes art director at **Pocket Books** and covers are illustrated by Barye Phillips, Roswell Keller, William Wirtz, Troop and Reynold Brown. Jonas, Hawkins, Strobel, Woods, Getz and Loew draw for **Penguin**; Maxwell and Walt Killam for **Avon**; Gregg, Sherwan and W.G. Jacobson for **Dell**; Andres, Kohs, Alexander, Paul Galdone, Stevan Dohanos, Geoffrey Biggs, David Attie, Van Kaufman, Bernie D'Andrea and Hy Rubin for **Bantam**, where Don Gelb replaces Gobin Stair as art director.

1948

Underdog Harry S Truman defeats Governor Thomas E. Dewey and is reelected President. Israel becomes a state. The U.S.S.R. blockades West Berlin, but a massive airlift by the U.S. and the U.K. delivers over 2 million tons of food and coal to the beleaguered city. The *Kinsey Report on Sexuality in the Human Male* is published, as is Norman Mailer's *The Naked and the Dead*. The Alger Hiss case breaks. Milton Berle, "Mr. Television," begins his first network series, and D.W. Griffith, "The Man Who Made the Movies," dies.

Cover artists George Salter, Leo Manso, Edgard Cirlin, H.L. Hoffman, Miriam Woods and Jeanyee Wong found the Book Jacket Designers Guild.

Victor Weybright and Kurt Enoch break their connection with **Penguin**

Books to establish the New American Library of World Literature, Inc. After a brief period in which new releases are called **Penguin Signets** and **Pelican Mentors**, the **Signet Books** and **Mentor Books** take over; Mentors are priced at 35 cents. Signet covers are more realistic than Penguin covers had been.

The first of a long series of hardboiled Mickey Spillane novels, *I, the Jury*, appears as a Signet Book; it is an instant bestseller, and Spillane soon takes over Erskine Caldwell's position as "the world's bestselling author."

Rudolph Belarski, noted pulp illustrator, delivers his first cover for **Popular Library**. Phillips, Keller, Wirtz, Frederick Banbery, Milton Wolsky, Harvey Kidder, Curt Witt and Halleck Finley do covers for **Pocket Books**. Wolsky, Wirtz, Ben Barton, C.C. Beall, Bob Doares, Gilbert Fullington, Jules Karl, Casimer Norwaish, Van Swearingen, Cliff Young, A. Leslie Ross, Gilbert Darling, Ed Grant, Robert Harris, Casey Jones, William Shoyer, Leon Gregori, Al Brulé, Ben Stahl and Norman Saunders all make their first covers for **Bantam**. Saunders also works for **Handi-Books**.

Perma Books begins publishing a series of paperbacks-in-hard-covers.

1949

New York City suffers a serious water shortage. NATO is established. Tokyo Rose goes to jail. In China, President Chiang Kai-shek is forced to resign and Mao Tse-tung proclaims the People's Republic. William Faulkner wins the Nobel Prize for Literature.

W. Somerset Maugham's *Stranger in Paris* is a bestseller for **Bantam**, as is Jerome Weidman's *I Can Get it For You Wholesale* for **Avon**.

The export of paperbacks to Europe becomes more important, and a change in public taste becomes apparent: less mysteries are being published, but more science fiction.

James Avati paints his first cover for **Signet**, and his realistic style is quickly imitated by other artists. Also working for Signet are Jonas, Loew and T.V.

Kidder, Keller, McCarthy, Phillips, Young, Stanley Meltzoff, Charles

Skaggs, Jon Nielsen, Louis Glanzman and Victor Kalin provide covers for **Pocket Books**; Belarski, Ray Johnson and Paul Kresse for **Popular Library**; Avati, Barton, Johnson, Shoyer, Harry Schaare, Robert Stanley, H. E. Bischoff, Ed Paulsen, Tom Lovell, Remie Hamon, Robert Skemp, Ken Riley, Bernard Safran and Stanley Zuckerberg begin working for **Bantam**. *My Flag is Down*, with a cover by Casey Jones, is one of Bantam's bestsellers.

Five new paperback series spring up: **Gold Medal Books**, **Pyramid Books**, **Graphic Books**, **Lion Books/Red Circle Books** and **Checkerbooks**.

1950 Anton Karas' theme from *The Third Man* is the number one song throughout America. The Brink's Robbery gang walks off with $2.8 million. Senator Joe McCarthy begins gunning for Communists. The United States sends troops to South Korea and 35 military advisers to South Vietnam.

This year's paperback bestsellers are Mickey Spillane's *My Gun is Quick* **(Signet)**, *Duke* **(Popular Library)**, *Cry Tough!* **(Avon)** and *The Wayward*

Bus (**Bantam**).

Pocket Books introduces the first **Collector's Editions**; in England, **Pocket Books** (G.B.) releases its first titles. Bantam inaugurates the **Bantam Giants** and Signet the **Signet Giants** and **Signet Double Volumes**, all simply excuses for charging more than 25 cents per book.

Dell publishes a record 100 new titles. Covers are illustrated by Griffith Foxley, Robert Hilbert, Bob Meyers, Ric Grasso, W. G. Jacobson, George Mayers and, especially, Robert Stanley.

Kalin, McCarthy, Skaggs, Glanzman, Meltzoff, Barton, Phillips, Kidder, Mike Ludlow, Simon Greco, Lew Keller, Wayne Blickenstaff, Sam Savitt, Raymond Pease and Harry Bennett all work for Pocket Books; Riley, James Bama, George Erickson and Verne Tossey for Avon; Tom Lovell, Bob Fink and Earl Mayan begin drawing for Bantam.

Perma Books switches over to a paperback format; Chuck Gabriel becomes art director and hires artists such as Tom Dunn and George Erickson.

The first 40 **Gold Medal** titles are released, including one comic strip in paperback format; *House of Flesh* is a bestseller.

Checkerbooks does not make it through the year.

1951

General Douglas MacArthur is removed from his Korean command. Color television is introduced to the United States and the first hydrogen bomb is exploded. Humphrey Bogart and Katharine Hepburn play together in *The African Queen*, and Abbott and Costello meet the Invisible Man. The first episode of *I Love Lucy* is broadcast.

Mickey Spillane's *The Big Kill* (**Signet**) is the year's bestselling paperback. Other popular titles are *Hill Girl* (**Gold Medal**), *Jailbait* (**Popular Library**), *The Sex Habits of American Women* (**Eton**) and *The Greatest Story Ever Told* (**Perma Books**).

Pocket Books introduces the **Cardinal Editions**, which retail for 35 cents, and the **Pocket Books, Jr.** Tom Dunn becomes the house Avati, and other artists include Erickson, Kalin, Meltzoff, McCarthy, Savitt, Kresse, Ludlow, Mayers, Carl Bobertz, Don Neiser and Ed Vebell.

Trumpets West! is the first **Dell 10-cents Book**; Stanley, Foxley, Hilbert, Jacobson, Mayers, Bobertz, Kalin and H.W. Scott all do covers for Dell.

Barye Phillips is extremely productive at Gold Medal, along with Frank Tinsley and John Floherty, Jr.; Johnson, Belarski, Ross, Earle Bergey and George Rozen are active at Popular Library.

James Avati continues to be Signet's star illustrator; his colleagues include Dunn, Phillips, Meltzoff, Kalin, Pease, Schaare, Lou Kimmel, Warren King, Alan Harmon and Mike Hooks. Skemp, Zuckerberg, Mayan, Carl Rose and others work for **Bantam**.

Handi-Books goes gently into that good night.

1952

Playwright Lillian Hellman tells the House Committee on Un-American Activities, "I cannot and will not cut my conscience to fit this year's fashions." Ernest Hemingway wins the Pulitzer Prize for *The Old Man and the Sea*. Charlie Chaplin and Buster Keaton appear together for the first and only time, in *Limelight*, and the first Cinerama films are released. King Farouk of Egypt abdicates amid charges of corruption, Elizabeth II becomes Queen of England and Dwight David Eisenhower defeats Adlai Stevenson for the Presidency of the United States.

The Gathings Committee comes out against sexy covers and covers which have little or no relationship to the contents of the books they appear on. An atmosphere of censorship descends on the publishing industry, and many publishers begin to feature less stimulating covers.

Earle Bergey and Rudolph Belarski draw their last illustrations for **Popular Library**.

The art department of the **Dell** Book Division of Western Printing moves from Racine, Wisconsin to New York, and Walter Brooks becomes art director. The keyhole colophon is scrapped, and sans-serif letters are used in the DELL block.

Pocket Books introduces the **Cardinal Giants** and Popular Library the **Popular Giants**, **Signet** brings out *New World Writing*, a magazine in paperback format, **Perma Books** issues the first **Perma Stars** and **Perma Spe-**

cials, and two new paperback houses are launched: **Ballantine Books** and **Ace Books**. Ballantine issues paperback titles simultaneously with their hardcover release, while Ace publishes sets of one reprint and one original bound together as a "double novel."

James Meese is a productive cover artist, supplying illustrations to Pocket Books, Signet and Dell; Stanley Meltzoff works for Pocket Books and Signet, while Harry Schaare makes covers for Ballantine and Signet. Norman Saunders paints the first Ace covers, and Cardiff, an Avati disciple, does realistic work for Perma Books and Signet.

The year's bestsellers include *Spring Fire* (**Gold Medal**), *Never Come Morning* (**Avon**), *Rawhide Range* (Popular Library) and *The Long Wait* (Signet).

1953 The Korean Conflict ends. Joseph Stalin dies. Julius and Ethel Rosenberg are executed, having been convicted of conspiracy to commit sabotage in wartime. Edmund Hillary and Tenzing Norkay conquer Mount Everest, the first issue of *Playboy* is published and Marilyn Monroe stars in *Gentlemen Prefer Blondes*. Frank Sinatra makes a comeback with a dramatic role in *From Here to Eternity*.

A **Pocket Books** edition of *Facts of Life and Love for Teen-Agers* quickly sells a million and a half copies, and Mickey Spillane's *Kiss Me Deadly* (**Signet**) sells twice that many.

Regardless of these phenomenal sales figures, a surplus threatens the industry; by autumn, more than 175 million books are stored in warehouses around the country.

A silver spine appears on Pocket Books and a gold spine on **Cardinal Editions**. Covers are drawn by Bennett, Meese, Meltzoff, Mayers, Savitt, Tossey, Zuckerberg, Robert Maguire and Robert Schulz.

Barye Phillips makes covers for **Gold Medal**, **Bantam** and Signet; Stanley Borack, William George and George Gross begin to work for **Dell**.

Popular Library inaugurates the **Popular Library Eagles**, Signet debuts its **Triple Volumes**, Dell offers **Dell First Editions** and Bantam introduces the **Pennant Books**.

1954

Senator McCarthy's Army hearings are televised, France pulls out of Indochina, Alfred Hitchcock films *Rear Window* and Marlon Brando, after three earlier nominations, finally wins an Oscar for *On the Waterfront*.

A bad year for paperbacks. The book surplus is so severe that **Pocket Books** dumps thousands of volumes in an abandoned canal near Buffalo, New York and **Lion Books** announces that it is temporarily suspending its publishing activities.

Many changes are made throughout the industry. Oscar Dystel becomes president of **Bantam Books** and the format of that company's product becomes larger, as does that of **Popular Library** releases. Both **Signet** and **Avon** receive new colophons, and for the first time Avon's back covers are "designed."

Pocket Books introduces the **Pocket Library** and buys out **Perma Books**; more and more Pocket Books with photographic covers appear, courtesy of Silver Studios.

Richard Powers paints covers for **Ballantine** and **Dell**; Gerald McConnell does the same for Dell, **Gold Medal**, Pocket Books, **Pyramid** and Signet.

The year's bestsellers are *A House is Not a Home* (Popular Library) and *Battle Cry* (Bantam); also popular are *More Dennis the Menace* (Avon) and *Cartoon Fun From True Magazine* (Gold Medal).

1955

The Mickey Mouse Club makes its television debut and McDonald's opens its first stand in Des Plaines, Illinois. America's two largest labor unions merge, resulting in the 15-million member AFL-CIO. Bill Haley and the Comets sing "Rock Around the Clock."

I'll Cry Tomorrow, released by **Popular Library**, is a major bestseller.

As the industry continues to censor itself, covers become more sober. The major houses publish fewer titles, but **Berkley Books** and a number of small firms are established. Fawcett introduces two new series, **Crest Books** and **Premier Books**, but **Bantam** discontinues its **Pennant Books**.

Leonard Leone becomes art director at Bantam, and typography and background color begin to play a more important role on Bantam covers; the spines are black.

Roy Lagrone, who had been art director Joe Mann's assistant at **Avon**, becomes art director himself and gives cover assignments to Binger, Kalin, Meese, McConnell, Lou Marchetti and David Stone Martin.

1956

Russian troops put down an uprising in Hungary. Israel invades the Sinai Peninsula; Egypt closes the Suez Canal and France and Britain bomb Egyptian targets. Ike is re-elected President and JFK wins the Pulitzer Prize for *Profiles in Courage*. Brigitte Bardot plays one of the title roles in *And God Created Woman*, Doris Day sings "Que Sera, Sera" and Elvis Presley appears (from the waist up) on *The Ed Sullivan Show*.

More movie tie-ins are published, such as *Baby Doll* (**Signet**) and *The Man in the Grey Flannel Suit* (**Pocket Books**).

Pyramid introduces the **Pyramid Royals**.

Bantam Books feature modern covers by Bama, Hooks, Ludlow, Phillips, Schaare and Bill Edwards; the back covers are now "designed."

A modern approach is also visible at Pocket Books, with Marchetti, Bennett and Paul Bacon providing covers.

Back covers receive more attention at Signet, too. The bands are dropped from the front cover, and James Avati changes his style, concentrating more on design. Maguire, McConnell and Phillips also do Signet covers this year. The firm's bestseller is *The Meaning of the Dead Sea Scrolls*, a **Signet Key Book**.

Popular Library adopts a new colophon, a pine tree, inspired of course by the name of the firm's founder, Ned Pines, and designed by Ed Rofheart. Rafael DeSoto and Mike Hooks are active cover artists.

Dell has its first million seller: Françoise Sagan's *Bonjour Tristesse*, which it released in 1955.

1957

Congress passes America's first civil rights bill and Ford manufactures the first Edsel. *West Side Story* opens on Broadway and *The Bridge on the River Kwai* wins an Oscar as best picture of the year. The first artificial satellite, Sputnik-1, is launched into space by the Russians. Nikita Khrushchev is named *Time's* "Man of the Year." Oliver Hardy dies.

The 25-cent paperback is by now an exception; most softcovered books retail for 35, 50, or 75 cents.

Dell issues its first **Dell Laurel Editions** and publishes its all-time bestseller, Grace Metalious' *Peyton Place*.

Graphic Books goes out of business and **Lion Books** is bought by the New American Library.

Avati, Bennett, Binger, Borack, Dunn, Edwards, Hooks, Kalin, Maguire, Marchetti, McConnell, Meese, Meltzoff, Phillips, Powers, Ross, Savitt, Schaare, Schulz, Bob Abbett, Clark Hulings, Sanford Kossin, William Rose, Daniel Schwartz and Arthur Sussman are active cover artists.

1958

America puts its first artificial satellite, Explorer-1, into orbit. Charles de Gaulle becomes president of France. Six European nations form the Common Market. Boris Pasternak is awarded the Nobel Prize for Literature for *Doctor Zhivago*. Elvis Presley sings "Jailhouse Rock" and is drafted.

Monarch Books and **Zenith Books** begin publication, while the **Popular Library Eagle** series is discontinued.

Pocket Books covers are illustrated by Hooks, Marchetti, McConnell, Savitt, Schulz, Zuckerberg and Jerry Powell; McConnell, Hulings, Phillips and Maguire work for **Signet**; McConnell, Hulings and William Teason do illustrations for **Avon**; Teason, Marchetti and Schaare supply covers for **Popular Library**; **Dell** commissions illustrations from Marchetti, Schaare, Maguire, Powers and Darcy, and also gives Robert McGinnis his first paperback assignments; Schaare, Hooks, Phillips, Bama, Ludlow, Abbett, Kossin and Edwards all work for **Bantam**; and Phillips and Milton Charles do covers for **Gold Medal**.

The first **Bantam Classics** are released.

1959

Fidel Castro and his socialist revolutionaries take over Cuba from the Batista government, Khrushchev becomes the first Soviet premier to visit America and Alaska and Hawaii become the 49th and 50th states. Marilyn Monroe and Tony Curtis star in *Some Like it Hot*, and Cary Grant and Eva Marie Saint romp through Hitchcock's *North by Northwest*. Buddy Holly, Ritchie Valens and the Big Bopper are killed in a plane crash.

Avon adopts a larger format and a new colophon, a large A.

The first **Signet Classics** are designed by Bill Gregory.

Robert McGinnis works for **Dell** and **Gold Medal**, and other active cover artists include: Bob Abbett, James Bama, Harry Bennett, Darcy, Freeman Elliot, Ric Grasso, James Hill, Victor Kalin, Robert Maguire, Lou Marchetti, Barye Phillips, Richard Powers, Alex Ross, Sam Savitt and Harry Schaare.

Overview of American Paperback Publishers

ACE BOOKS
A.A. Wyn, Inc.; Ace Books, Inc., New York

Began, in 1952, by publishing so-called "double novels"—two novels in one volume, generally a reprint and an original. Later, in addition to the double novels, single novels were also released.

D-1. *The Grinning Gismo* – Samuel W. Taylor
Too Hot for Hell – Keith Vining
D-2. *Bloody Hoofs* – J. Edward Leithead
Bad Man's Return –
William Colt MacDonald
D-3. *Twist the Knife Slowly* – Kate Clungston
The Big Fix – Mel Colton
D-4. *Massacre at White River* – Lewis B. Patten
Rimrock Rider – Walker A. Thompson
D-5. *The Scarlet Spade* –
Eaton K. Goldthwaite
Drawn to Evil – Harry Whittington

AMERICAN LIBRARY, THE
David McKay Company

Published from 1942 to 1944 at 35 cents.

1. *Silent Witness* – John Stephen Strange
2. *Acts of Black Night* –
Kathleen Moore Knight
3. *Dead Man Control* – Helen Reilly
4. *The Case of the Constant God* –
Rufus King

ARMED SERVICES EDITIONS
Armed Services Editions, Inc., New York

Founded by the Council on Books in Wartime. Each month from September, 1943 through June, 1944, a series of 30 titles was published; at that time, the monthly series was raised to 32 titles and, as of January, 1945, it was raised again, to 40 titles per month. The titles were numbered 1-30 and each monthly release was lettered, beginning with A. Beginning with the K series, however, each release was numbered 1-32 (through P-32) and then 1-40 (through T-40). After the T series, the letters were dropped and the numbering sequence picked up with 655, which was the total number of titles published up to that point. From 655 until 1322, only numbers in sequence were used.

The original format was horizontal (oblong), rather than vertical: ASE books had the same width as a standard digest but half the height. Later, though, from October, 1946 through the dissolution of the series in October, 1947, the Pocket Books format was used. A total of 1,322 titles were published.

A-1. *The Education of H★Y★M★N*
K★A★P★L★A★N – Leonard Q. Ross
A-2. *Report from Tokyo* – J.C. Grew
A-3. *Good Intentions* – Ogden Nash
A-4. *Mama's Bank Account* – Kathryn Forbes
A-5. *There Go the Ships* – Robert Carse

AVON BOOKS
Avon Book Company; Avon Publishing Company, Inc.; Avon Publications, Inc.; Avon Book Division, Hearst Company, New York

Founded in 1941 by Joseph Meyers. At first, four or five titles a month were published; in 1945 this was raised to eight a month and in 1950 to a dozen a month, but in 1954 production was cut back again to eight titles monthly and in 1947 to four monthly.

(1) *Elmer Gantry* – Sinclair Lewis
(2) *The Rubáiyát of Omar Khayyam* –
Edward Fitzgerald
(3) *The Big Four* – Agatha Christie

(4) *Ill Wind* – James Hilton
(5) *Dr. Priestly Investigates* – John Rhode
The numbers just listed are in parentheses because the first 40 Avon Books were, in fact, released unnumbered; numbering began with W. Somerset Maugham's *The Narrow Corner*, which was thus number 41. See *The First Hundred* for titles 1-100. Numbers 36, 361, 386, 388, 409 and 840 were not issued.

The first 16 Avons had, in their original printings, endpapers illustrated with a spiderweb motif. Numbers 2, 14, 113, 127, 246 and 262 were fully illustrated.

V. Diamond was the first art director, followed by Joe Mann and, in 1955, by Roy Lagrone. Cover artists between 1941 and 1949 included: Walter Brooks, Don Milsop, John Alan Maxwell, Ray Johnson and Strick. Between 1949 and 1955: James Bama, George Erickson, Paul Kresse, Ken Riley, Rudy Nappi and Stanley Zuckerberg. After 1955: Victor Kalin, Lou Kimmel, Charles Binger, James Meese, Gerald McConnell, Barye Phillips, Clark Hulings, James Bama, William Teason, Bob McGinnis and Walter Brooks.

Another series published by Avon was the Avon Bard Books, beginning in July, 1955.

BALLANTINE BOOKS
Ballantine Books, Inc., New York
Publishing began in November, 1952. The original plan was to release new books in paperback simultaneously with their hardcover release by other publishers.
 1. *Executive Suite* – Cameron Hawley
 2. *Saddle by Starlight* – Luke Short
 3. *The Golden Spike* – Hal Ellson
 4. *All My Enemies* – Stanley Baron
 5. *The Witch's Thorn* – Ruth Park
Bob Blanchard was art director. The following cover artists worked for him: Harry Bennett, Robert Maguire (who illustrated the dustjacket for number 10, *Concannon*), Richard Powers, Hy Rubin, Norman Saunders, Verne Tossey, Mel Crair, Robert Schulz, George Erickson, Stanley Zuckerberg, Charles Binger and Bob Abbett.

BANTAM BOOKS
Bantam Books, Inc., New York
Founded in 1945 by Ian Ballantine, who had just left Penguin. The first 20 titles were distributed locally in December of 1945 and nationally the following month. The first Bantam Giants, costing 35 cents, were released in 1950, and the first Bantam Fifties, costing 50 cents, in 1951.
 1. *Life on the Mississippi* – Mark Twain
 2. *The Gift Horse* – Frank Gruber

 3. *"Nevada"* – Zane Grey
 4. *Evidence of Things Seen* – Elizabeth Daly
 5. *Scaramouche* – Rafael Sabatini
(See *The First Hundred* for numbers 1-100.)
The following numbers were not used: 153, 157, 159-199, 215-226, 228-249, 263-299, 316, 318, 319, 321-349, 367-399, 424, 428-449, 457, 468, 472, 475, 478-499, 508-549, 558-699 and 719. Numbers 7-9, 19, 22, 24, 26, 44, 67, 75, 315, 355, 360, 421 and 462 were rereleased with dustjackets. Dustjackets were also used on numbers 143-146, 148-151, 155 and 156; the first eight of these numbers were rereleased Superior Reprints, while the last two were rereleases of Infantry Journal – Penguin Book S238 and Infantry Journal Book J101.

Gobin Stair was art director during the early years; he was replaced by Don Gelb, who was himself replaced, in 1955, by Leonard Leone, who still holds the position today. The following artists provided covers between 1945 and 1948: Rafael Palacios, Robert Jonas, Alexander, Charles Andres, Edgard Cirlin, Clement, Cal Diehl, Bill English, H. L. Hoffman, Lester Kohs, Ava Morgan and David Triggs. Between 1948 and 1955: Ben Barton, C. C. Beall, Al Brulé, R. Doares, Griffith Foxley, Gilbert Fullington, Denver Gillen, Leon Gregori, Remie Hamon, Raymond Johnson, Casey Jones, Jules Karl, Van Kaufman, Norbert J. Lannon, Cass Norwaish, Ed Paulsen, Ken Riley, Hy Rubin, Norman Saunders, Harry Schaare, William Shoyer, Robert Skemp and Ben Stahl. After 1955: Mike Hooks, Stanley Meltzoff, Barye Phillips, Stanley Zuckerberg, James Avati, Bob Abbett, James Bama and Robert McGinnis.

Five nonfiction titles numbered A1-A5 appeared between June, 1948 and February, 1952. Bantam also published Bantam Biographies beginning in January of 1956, Bantam Classics beginning in September of 1958 (AC1 was *Brave New World* by Aldous Huxley) and Pennant Books beginning in June of 1953 (see separate listing).

BANTAM BOOKS
Western Printing & Lithographing Company, Los Angeles
Published from 1939 through 1943 by the West Coast branch of Western Printing, the firm which was later to produce Dell Books. The books in this series were exclusively sold from vending machines. The first 20 of a probable total of 33 titles were soberly executed in blue, black and green, with a red rooster-head as colophon. Number 21 was the first with an illustrated cover.
 1. *The Spanish Cape Mystery* – Ellery Queen
 2. *Little Known Facts About Well Known Peo-*

ple – Dale Carnegie
3. *Your Health Questions* – Morris Fishbein, M.D.
4. *Everybody's Dream Book: Your Dreams Explained*
5. *How to Make Friends Easily* –
   S. Currie, M.A., D.SC.

Western's Bantam Books had no connection with the series of the same name later published by Bantam Books, Inc. in New York (see above).

BART HOUSE
Bartholomew House, Inc., New York
This series, published between 1944 and 1946, consisted primarily of novelizations of film scripts.
1. *The Hand in the Cobbler's Safe* – Seth Bailey
2. *The Delinquent Ghost* – Eric Hatch
3. *The Spy Trap* – William Gilman
4. *Weird Shadow Over Innsmouth* –
   H.P. Lovecraft
5. *John Smith Hears Death Walking* –
   Wyatt Blassingame
Numbers 1-36, 39 and 101-103 were released.

BEACON BOOKS
Universal Publishing and Distributing Corporation, New York
Established in 1954; numbering began with B101.
B101. *She Got What She Wanted* – Orrie Hitt
B102. *Pawn* – Fan Nichols
B103. *Rooming House* – Fred Malloy
B104. *Shabby Street* – Orrie Hitt
B105. *King of Khyber Rifles* – Talbot Mundi

BERKLEY BOOKS
Berkley Publishing Corporation, New York
Publication began in March, 1955; by the end of 1959, numbers 101-112, 313-386, G1-G294, G299 and G300 had been released.
101. *The Pleasures of the Jazz Age* –
   William Hodapp
102. *Loveliest of Friends* –
   G. Sheila Donisthorpe
103. *S.S. San Pedro* – James Gould Cozzens
104. *Fever Pitch* – Frank Waters
105. *Death of an Ad Man* –
   James Wakefield Burke and Edward Grace

BLACK KNIGHT MYSTERIES
Allied Graphic Arts; Ideal Distributing Company, New York
A series of mysteries issued in 1946 and 1947. The first volumes (numbered 15-18) were digests; seven paperback titles (numbered 25-30 and 32) followed, for a total of only 11 known releases.

25. *Come Dwell With Death* – M.W. Glidden
26. *Death Is No Lady* – M.E. Corne
27. *The Psychiatric Murders* – M. Scott Michel
28. *The Kidnappers* – Albert E. Ullman
29 *Green for a Grave* – Manning Lee Stokes

BLEAK HOUSE
Parsee Publications, New York
Ten titles are known: first, two digests numbered 12 and 13, followed by eight paperbacks numbered 14-21. All titles were published in 1947 and 1948.
14. *The Case of the Blood-Stained Dime* –
   Minna Barton
15. *The Case of the Missing Corpse* –
   Joan Langar
16. *The Corpse in the Guest Room* –
   Clement Wood
17. *The Skyscraper Murder* – Samuel Spewack
18. *Murder Menagerie* – Jeremy Lane

BLUE SEAL BOOKS
Modern Age Books, Inc., New York
Paperbacks priced at 25 cents and published around 1937; all titles were original fiction. Modern Age also issued Gold Seal Books and Red Seal Books at the same time (see separate listings).
1. *Babies Without Tails* – Walter Duranty
2. *All's Fair* – Richard Wormser
3. *Murder Strikes Three* – David MacDuff
4. *Old Hell* – Emmett Gowen
5. *Red Feather* – Marjorie Fischer
Robert Josephy was in charge of typography. In 1938, the three Modern Age series were combined under the imprint Seal Books (see separate listing).

BONDED MYSTERIES
Anson Bond Publications, Inc., Hollywood
A series of digests and paperbacks published in 1946 and 1947. A total of 16 titles are known.
1. *The Goose is Cooked* – Emmett Hogarth
2. *Murder of a Novelist* – Sally Wood
3. *The Hungry House* – Lilian Laufery
4. *Murder Strikes Thrice* – Charles C. Booth
5. *I'll Eat You Last* – H.C. Branson

BONI PAPER BOOKS
Charles Boni, New York
A paperback series published from 1929 to 1931; originally, one title per month was released and books were sold on a membership basis. A test volume, *The Bridge of San Luis Rey*, was issued in May, 1929.
1. *The Golden Wind* –
   Takashi Ohta and Margaret Sperry
2. *Frederick the Great* – Margaret Goldsmith
3. *Dewer Rides* – L.A.G. Strong

4. *Prosperity: Fact or Myth* – Stuart Chase
5. *Commando* – Deneys Reitz

The membership system was dropped after 16 titles, and the Boni Paper Books were reissued as unnumbered Bonibooks; the first new titles were:

(17) *The History of Mr. Polly* – H.G. Wells
(18) *Tar* – Sherwood Anderson
(19) *Michelangelo* – Romain Rolland
(20) *The Lost Girl* – D.H. Lawrence
(21) *The Captain's Doll* – D.H. Lawrence

Rockwell Kent's covers and endpapers were extremely attractive, as was the typography. The books were quarto-sized (roughly 5″ × 7½″).

CARDINAL EDITIONS
Pocket Books, Inc., New York

A paperback series first marketed in 1951, priced then at 35 cents. The colophon was naturally, a bright-red cardinal.

C-1. *Four Great Historical Plays* –
   William Shakespeare
C-2. *Kings Row* – Harry Bellamann
C-3. *In Tragic Life* – Vardis Fischer
C-4. *Cutlass Empire* – F. Van Wyck Mason
C-5. *The Merriam-Webster Pocket Dictionary*

Number C-31, *The Man with the Golden Arm*, was published with a dustjacket illustrated by Stanley Meltzoff. Numbers C-354, C-366, C-369, C-374 and C-377 through C-390 were not used.

The Cardinal Giants, costing 50 or 75 cents, first appeared in 1952. The first title (GC-1) was *The Cardinal* by Henry Morton Robinson. Numbers GC-63, GC-64 and GC-754 were not used.

CENTURY BOOKS
Century Publications

Originally a series of digests; later, both digests and paperbacks were published. Numbering ran from 10 to 136, and the first five paperbacks, issued in the late 1940s, were:

17. *As Good As Murdered* – James O'Hanlon
19. *Fair Warning* – Mignon G. Eberhart
25. *Time Off for Murder* – Zelda Popkin
26. *Fallen Angel* – Marty Holland
28. *Bad for Business* – Rex Stout

CHECKERBOOKS
Checkerbooks, Inc., New York

Founded by Lyle Kenyon Engel in 1949; the first four titles appeared in October of that year. Eight more books were later released, and the series disappeared in November, 1950.

1. *Terry and the Pirates: The Jewels of Jade* –
   Edward J. Boylan, Jr.
2. *The Broadway Butterfly Murders* – Tip Bliss

3. *Make Mine Murder* – Robert Bowen
4. *Lost River Buckaroos* – Charles M. Martin
5. *Horror and Homicide* – an anthology of short stories

COMET BOOKS
Pocket Books, Inc., New York

A series of paperbacks for young readers, first appearing in 1948 in a slightly larger format than the standard Pocket Books. The series was renamed Pocket Books, Jr. in January of 1950, and the standard Pocket Books format was then adopted.

1. *Wagons Westward* – Armstrong Sperry
2. *Batter Up* – Jackson Scholz
3. *Star-Spangled Summer* – Janet Lambert
4. *Tawny* – Thomas C. Hinkle
5. *300 Tricks You Can Do* – Howard Thurston

CONTINENTAL BOOKS
Horace Liveright, New York

A paperback series published in 1932.

DELL BOOKS
Dell Publishing Company, Inc., New York

Dell, founded in 1922 by George T. Delacorte, Jr., was at first a publisher of magazines (*Talking Screen, Modern Screen, Modern Romances*) and pulps (*I Confess, Cupid's Diary*), then began issuing paperbacks in 1943. Editorial work, cover design and printing and binding were handled by the Western Printing & Lithographing Company, which moved its paperback art department to New York in late 1951. In 1962, Dell took over all editorial and production functions itself, using Western only as a printer and binder.

1. *Death in the Library* – Philip Ketchum
2. *Dead or Alive* – Patricia Wentworth
3. *Murder-on-Hudson* – Jennifer Jones
4. *The American Gun Mystery* – Ellery Queen
5. *Four Frightened Women* –
   George Harmon Coxe

(See *The First Hundred* for numbers 1-100.)

Dell covers drew attention in the early years because they were extremely clearly printed in brilliant four-color. The cover designs were also noteworthy, and were provided by art director William Strohmer and his assistant, George Frederiksen. Most covers were executed by Gerald Gregg, who put the airbrush to excellent use. Other cover artists included W.G. Jacobson, F. Kenwood Giles, Robert Stanley, Bob Meyers, John Alan Maxwell, Harry Barton, Griffith Foxley, Robert Hilbert and Carl Bobertz. Dell D114, *Go Down to Glory*, was published with a dustjacket.

After 1952, when Walter Brooks became art director, covers became more experimental.

Brooks actively shaped the look of Dell Books, and gave assignments to artists such as Harry Bennett, Stanley Borack, Rafael DeSoto, William George, Mike Hooks, George Erickson, Victor Kalin, Mike Ludlow, Robert Maguire, James Meese, Gerald McConnell, Clark Hulings, Robert Abbett, Barye Phillips, Richard Powers, Robert Schulz, Robert McGinnis, William Teason and Harry Schaare.

The Dell 10-cents Books both appeared and disappeared in 1951; they were thin (64 pages) but unabridged mysteries, novels, Westerns and so forth. A total of 36 titles were published.

1. *Trumpets West!* – Luke Short
2. *Rain* – W. Somerset Maugham
3. *Night Bus* – Samuel H. Adams
4. *Locked Doors* – Mary Roberts Rinehart
5. *Bride from Broadway* – Faith Baldwin

The Dell First Editions, a series of original novels, mysteries and Westerns edited by Knox Burger, began in September, 1953.

1E. *Down* – Walt Grove
2E. *Madball* – Frederic Brown
D3. *Women* – A.M. Krich
4. *Girl on the Beach* – George Sumner Albee
5. *The Bloody Spur* – Charles Einstein

The F Series was also initiated in 1953, and initially consisted of important literary works. The Dell Laurel Editions, mostly classic works of world literature, began in May of 1957.

LC101. *Four Plays* – George Bernard Shaw
LC102. *Great English Short Stories* – edited by Christopher Isherwood
LC103. *Great American Short Stories* – edited by Wallace and Mary Stegner
LC104. *Modern American Dictionary* – edited by Jess Stein
LC105. *Common Wild Animals and their Young* – Rita Vandivert and William Vandivert

EAGLE BOOKS
Eagle Books, New York

Only three books were published in this series, all in 1947. The first two titles had a small format and were unnumbered; the third used the same size and shape as the Signet Books and was numbered E3.

(1) *Dear Sir* – Juliet Lowell
(2) *Kitty* – Rosamond Marshall
E3. *Duchess Hotspur* – Rosamond Marshall

ETON BOOKS
Eton Books, Inc., New York

Published between 1951 and 1953, 32 titles in all. The first Etons were reprints of popular nonfiction works, but later titles were all novels and included both reprints and originals. Avon Books handled the production for this series,

and the Etons thus resembled Avons in both format and execution. The numbers used were ET51, 101-103, ET104-ET108, E109-E125 and E127-E132.

ET 51. *The Sex Habits of American Women* – Fritz Wittels, M.D.
101. *United States Book of Baby Care*
102. *The Sex Habits of American Women* – Fritz Wittels, M.D.
103. *The Hygiene of Marriage* – Millard S. Everett
ET104. *Control High Blood Pressure and Live Longer* – Herman Pomeranz

FAWCETT CREST BOOKS
Fawcett Publications, New York

Published since the autumn of 1955, under the editorial guidance of William C. Lengel; this series included reprints of novels and a few Western and suspense originals. The first volume released was number 114.

114. *Best Cartoons from True*
115. *Run, Thief, 'Run* – Frank Gruber
116. *Top Hand with a Gun* – Harry Sinclair Drago
117. *Stranger at the Door* – Gil Meynier
118. *The Best from Captain Billy's Whizbang* – Lester Grady

FAWCETT GOLD MEDAL BOOKS
Fawcett Publications, New York

Fawcett's first paperback series, started in 1949 and edited by William C. Lengel. Some titles were originals; authors including Richard S. Prather, Charles Williams and John D. MacDonald first became well-known through their Gold Medal publications.

The first two titles were unnumbered, and used different formats from that adopted consistently beginning with number 101.

(99) *The Best from True*
(100) *What Today's Woman Should Know About Marriage and Sex*
101. *We Are the Public Enemies* – Alan Hynd
102. *Man Story* – an anthology
103. *The Persian Cat* – John Flagg

Number 129, *Mansion of Evil* by Joseph Millard, was a comic strip published in book form.

Art director of the Gold Medal series was Al Allard, who had worked for Fawcett since 1928. Barye Phillips produced a very large number of covers in a variety of styles during Gold Medal's first five years; other illustrators who did covers for the series included Harry Bennett, Lou Kimmel, Stanley Zuckerberg, Stanley Meltzoff, Gerald McConnell, Clark Hulings, James Meese, Mike Hooks, Louis Glanzman, Frank Tinsley and John Floherty, Jr.

FAWCETT PREMIER BOOKS
Fawcett Publications, New York

A series of nonfiction books, priced at 50 cents, published beginning in September, 1955 under the editorial direction of William C. Lengel. The first title was numbered s12.

s12. *The Power of Positive Living* – Douglas Lurton
s13. *How to Write and Speak Effective English* – Edward Frank Allen
s14. *The Enjoyment of Love in Marriage* – LeMon Clark
s15. *Best Quotations for All Occasions* – Lewis C. Henry
s16. *The Art of Thinking* – Ernest Dimnet

GALAXY BOOKS
Galaxy Publishing Corporation; The Guinn Company, Inc., New York

Originally a series of digests which, in 1958, produced four science-fiction paperbacks before going out of business. Not to be confused with the identically-titled British series, which has been published by the Oxford University Press since 1955.

32. *Address: Centauri* – F.L. Wallace
33. *Mission of Gravity* – Hal Clement
34. *Twice in Time* – Manley Wade Wellman
35. *The Forever Machine* – Mark Clifton and Frank Riley

GOLD MEDAL BOOKS
see *Fawcett Gold Medal Books*

GOLD SEAL BOOKS
Modern Age Books, Inc., New York

A series of original titles costing more than 25 cents, published around 1937, at the same time as the Blue Seal and Red Seal Books (see separate listings). Typography was by Robert Josephy.

1. *The United States: A Graphic History* – Louis M. Hacker and others
2. *From Spanish Trenches* – edited by Marcel Acier
3. *Kaltenborn Edits the News* – H. V. Kaltenborn
4. *The Labor Spy Racket* – Leo Huberman
5. *Men Who Lead Labor* – Bruce Minton and John Stuart

In 1938, the three Modern Age series were combined under the imprint Seal Books (see separate listing).

GRAPHIC BOOKS
Graphic Publishing Company, New York

Founded in 1948 by Sam Tankel and Zane Bouregy. A total of 171 mysteries, Westerns and historical novels were released between 1949 and May, 1957. Graphic Books retailed for 25 cents, and Graphic Giants for 35 cents.

Numbering began with number 11 and ran through number 157. The Giants were numbered G101 and G201-G223.

11. *Murder—Queen High* – Bob Wade
12. *If I Live to Die* – Hillary Waugh
13. *FLACH—Hold for Murder* – James M. Fox
14. *Death Commits Bigamy* – James M. Fox
15. *Tex* – Clarence E. Mulford

GREEN DRAGON BOOKS
Ideal Distributing Company, New York

This series consisted of 33 titles, released between 1944 and 1947. The first Green Dragons were digests, but numbers 25-33 were paperbacks.

25. *She Screamed Blue Murder* – Kelliher Secrist
26. *Stone Dead* – Patrick Laing
27. *Headsman's Holiday* – Dean Hawkins
28. *The Late Lamented Lady* – Marie Blizard
29. *A Matter of Policy* – Sam Merwin, Jr.

HANDI-BOOKS
Quinn Publishing Company, Inc., New York

Staple-bound paperbacks published between 1941 and 1951. The first seven titles were unnumbered and were released in 1941 and 1942. Numbering began with number 8 and continued through number 139.

(1) *Odds on the Hot Seat* – Judson Phillips
(2) *Decoy* – Cleve F. Adams
(3) *12 Chinks and a Woman* – James Hadley Chase
(4) *Seven Men* – Theodore Roscoe
(5) *Curtains for the Copper* – Thomas Polsky

Four Handi-Book Westerns appeared in 1947.

1. *The Cow Kingdom* – Paul Evan Lehman
2. *Rio Renegade* – Leslie Ernewein
3. *The Long Noose* – Oscar J. Friend
4. *West of the Wolverine* – Paul Evan Lehman

HANGMAN'S HOUSE
Parsee Publications, New York

Published in 1946 and 1947. The first 11 titles were digests, but the remainder of the series (numbers 12 and 14-21) were all paperbacks.

12. *The Cowl of Doom* – Edward Ronns
14. *The Corpse that Spoke* – Robert H. Leitfred
15. *The Cipher of Death* – F.L. Gregory
16. *Thereby Hangs a Corpse* – Clarence Mullen
17. *The Road House Murders* – Robert Portner Koehler

HART BOOKS
Horace Hart, Inc., New York

Published paperbacks during the late 1940s; only two titles are known. Covers and interior typography were the work of W. A. Dwiggins.

K1. *The House of Creeping Horror* – George F. Worts

K2. *The Diamonds of Death* – Borden Chase

HILLMAN BOOKS
Hillman Periodicals, Inc., New York

Published beginning in 1948. The first volume to appear was unnumbered.

(1) *Let's Make Mary* – Jack Hanley

2. *Tumbling River Range* – W. C. Tuttle

3. *Casanova's Memoirs* – Giacomo Casanova

4. *Ironheart* – William MacLeod Raine

5. *Bluffer's Luck* – W. C. Tuttle

HILLMAN DETECTIVE NOVELS
Hillman Periodicals, Inc., New York

Only one title was ever released in this projected series, in 1943.

1. *The Arabian Nights Murder* – John Dickson Carr

HIP BOOKS
Hip Books, Inc., Alexandria (Virginia)

"They Fit on Your Hip" was the slogan by which Hip Books were to be advertised; however, only one title is known to have been released, in 1946.

1. *The Mystery of the Red Suitcase* – Lula M. Day

IN-CARD BOOKS
Bookem Corporation

Thin books which could be mailed as postcards. They were seen in 1958 and again in 1967.

INFANTRY JOURNAL BOOKS
The Infantry Journal, Washington, D.C.

Two titles, resembling the Superior Reprints in design and format, were published in 1945. J-*101 was provided with a Bantam dustjacket and rereleased in 1948 as Bantam 156.

J-101. *Boomerang!/Baby Fights Back* – William C. Chambliss

J-102. *The U.S. Marines on Iwo Jima*

JACKET LIBRARY
National Home Library Foundation, Washington, D.C.

A paperback series which appeared in 1932 and 1933, established by Sherman Mitchell. The first offering consisted of 12 titles and a total printing of 100,000 copies. · The series was resumed in 1935, but only hardcovers were published.

(1) *Treasure Island* – Robert Louis Stevenson

(2) *The New Testament*

(3) *Green Mansions* – W. H. Hudson

(4) *The Way of All Flesh* – Samuel Butler

(5) *The Merchant of Venice* – William Shakespeare

KEEP-WORTHY BOOKS
Keep-Worthy Books, Inc.

Heavily condensed versions of famous books, published in 1945 and 1946. Only four titles are known to have been issued.

1. *Twelve of the World's Famous Books* – edited by Julius Muller

2. *The Scarlet Letter* – Nathaniel Hawthorne

3. *Twelve of the World's Famous Adventure Books* – edited by Julius Muller

4. *Twelve of the World's Famous Love Stories* – edited by Julius Muller

LION BOOKS
Lion Books, Inc., New York

A continuation of the Red Circle Books (see separate listing), first appearing in 1949. Four or five titles per month were issued between 1949 and 1952, then six titles per month in 1953 and 1954. The final volumes appeared in 1955.

Numbers 1-7, 12 and 13 were Red Circle Books; the Lion Books were numbered 8-11 and 14-233.

8. *Hungry Men* – Edward Anderson

9. *Anniversary* – Ludwig Lewisohn

10. *Canyon Hell* – Peter Dawson

11. *The Blonde Body* – Michael Morgan

14. *The Lottery* – Shirley Jackson

The Lion Library, a separate series including a number of reprints of the original Lions, began in 1954.

LL1. *Number One* – John Dos Passos

LL2. *A Woman's Life* – Guy de Maupassant

LL3. *The Sky Block* – Steve Frazee

LL4. *The Flesh Baron* – P. J. Wolfson

LL5. *The Sin and the Flesh* – Lloyd S. Thompson

Lion Books was bought up by the New American Library in 1957.

LITTLE BLUE BOOKS
Emanuel Haldeman-Julius, Girard (Kansas)

A total of 2,000 titles, with prices ranging from 5 to 25 cents, were published in this series between 1920 and 1951, the year of founder Emanuel Haldeman-Julius' death.

1. *The Rubáiyát of Omar Khayyam*

2. *The Ballad of Reading Gaol* – Oscar Wilde

Edgard Cirlin, 1945

George Salter, dustjacket for Random House

George Salter, cover and typography

George Salter, 1952

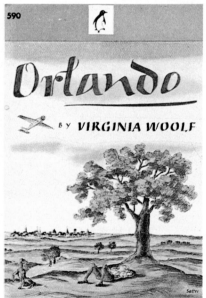

George Salter, 1946

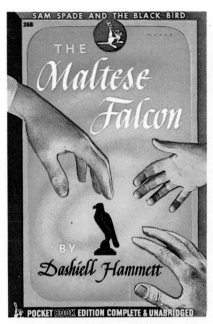

Leo Manso, 1944

Stanley Meltzoff, 1947 (dustjacket)

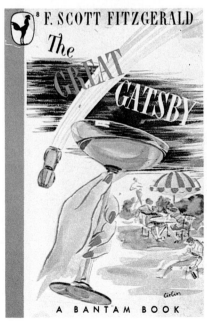

Edgard Cirlin, 1945

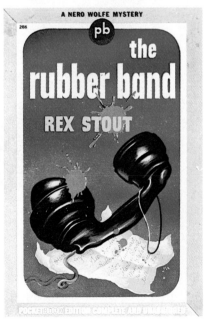

Leo Manso, 1943

Leo Manso, 1943

168

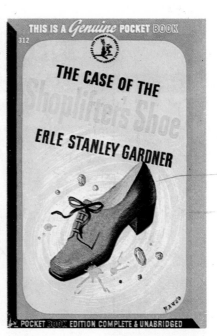

Leo Manso (dustjacket for The World)   Leo Manso, 1945

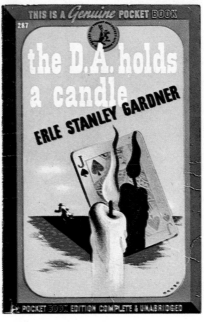

Leo Manso (dustjacket for The World)   Leo Manso, 1945

169

Rudolph Belarksi, 1950

170

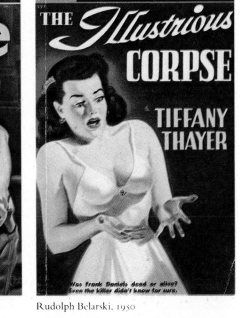

Rudolph Belarski, 1949

Rudolph Belarski, 1950

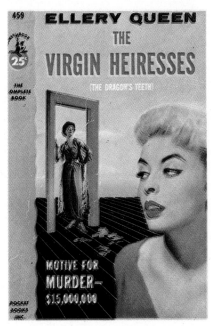

Silver Studios was a commercial photography firm headed by brothers Henry and Stanley Silver, with offices in New York's West 51st Street. During the early 1950s, the Silver brothers provided photos for many Pocket Books covers and for use by James Avati. Other cover photographers active at this time were Alfred Gescheidt, Halleck Finley, Paulus Lesser, Benn Mitchell, Lester Krauss, Frederic Lewis and the Color Graphic Studios.

Silver Studios, 1954

Denver Gillen, 1948

Van Kaufman, 1947

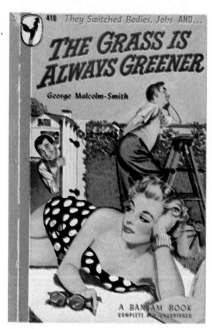

Casey Jones, 1949

Casey Jones, Van Kaufman and Denver Gillen belong to a group of artists who did humorous covers for Pocket Books and Bantam during the late '40s. Gillen was known as a cartoonist for *Esquire*, but he also did realistic work.

Kaufman's wife posed for *The Cautious Amorist*, which was one of Bantam's first humorous covers.

The story goes that Bantam's art director told Casey Jones, "This has to be an amazing cover: the grass *really* has to look greener on the other side of the fence, no matter which side you're standing on!"

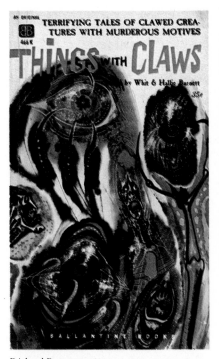

Richard Powers, 1961

Mike Hooks, 1958

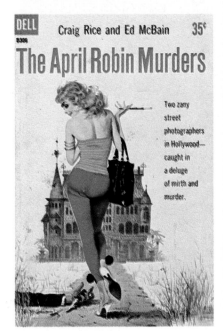

Robert McGinnis, 1959

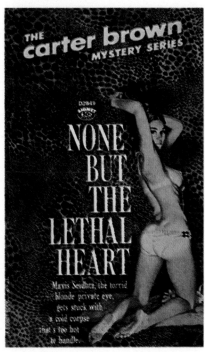

Robert McGinnis, 1965

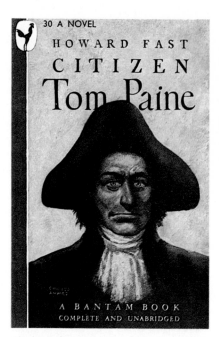

Charles Andres, 1945

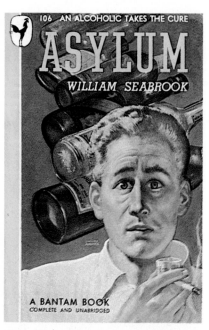

Charles Andres, 1947

David Triggs, 1945

Cal Diehl, 1946

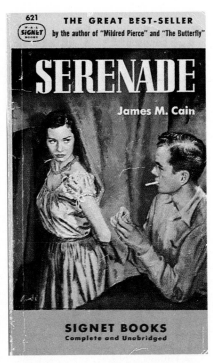

Robert Jonas, 1947…   …and James Avati, 1950

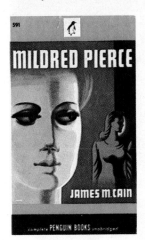

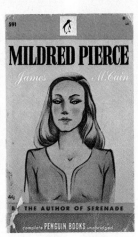

The first two of these covers, from 1946 and 1947, are by Robert Jonas; the third, from 1948, is by an unknown artist.

Barye Phillips for the Farrar, Straus hardcover

Robert Stanley for the Dell paperback

Anonymous, 1947

Robert Stanley, 1951

Barye Phillips, 1948   Barye Phillips, 1956

A paperback collection (Photo courtesy of Glenn Bray)

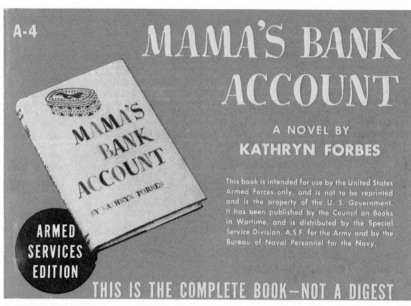

One of the first Armed Services Editions (September, 1943), designed by Sol Immerman

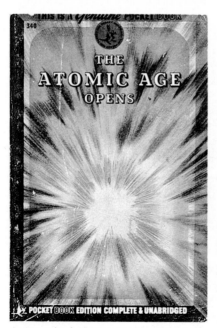

An instant book (August, 1945)

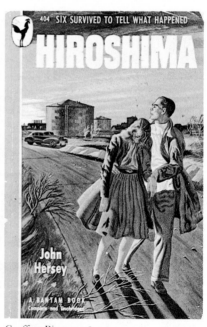

Geoffrey Biggs, 1948

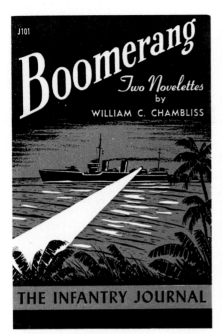

An Infantry Journal Book, 1945... ...and the 1948 dustjacket

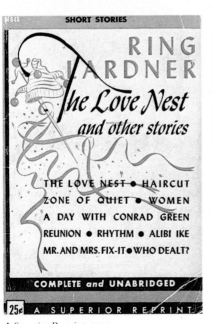

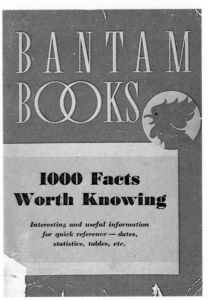

A Superior Reprint, 1945

A rarity: a Bantam (L.A.) Book from 1940

"*She tried to use her nails on me,*" the murderer explained.

This was the simple explanation. "I didn't mean to," the killer added. "I didn't mean to," but—the woman now lay dead, huddled in a crouch before the fireplace. She wore a plain black nylon nightgown, paneled with black lace, and on her feet were *a pair of scarlet satin slippers.*

Suzy tried to run. She bit, kicked, scratched, until the murderer, groping with one free hand, found a roll of rope.

"You're not going any place," the killer said.

THE SCARLET SLIPPERS
by JAMES M. FOX

3 WOMEN

can make a mess out of a man's life—

THE RIGHT ONE —*Michele,* the dark-eyed French beauty who looked like she had just stepped out of a European movie.

THE WRONG ONE—*Wilma,* the redheaded temptress who came along at the wrong time with the right invitation.

THE DEAD ONE —*Francine,* whose lifeless body was found in a rowboat in the middle of the bay.

Ed Lacy's latest suspense novel is a hard-hitting story of fast-living men and women caught in a web of passion and violence, with a stunning surprise ending.

Printed in the U.S.A.

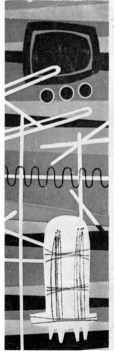

"enormously entertaining... first-rate...

So says the *San Francisco Chronicle,* joining critics all over the nation in their lavish praise for this uproarious, outrageous novel of the "big" men of Madison Ave.— the wheels within wheels in their networks, and the messes within messes in their private lives....

LION
LIBRARY
EDITIONS

19 GREAT STORY TELLERS SPIN THEIR PLOTS
masters such as Maugham, Steinbeck, Dinesen, Lord Dunsany and more than a dozen others explore in these stories the shadow world of man's mind—a terrifying though fascinating limbo which only the brave dare enter—

19 TALES OF TERROR
a brilliant and provocative collection of stories about men and women enmeshed in strange circumstances—unique, unusual stories that will shock, startle and amaze . . .

The Bestsellers come from Bantam Books
LOOK FOR THE BANTAM ROOSTER   YOUR ASSURANCE OF QUALITY!

Back covers for Dell (Walter Brooks), Avon (Roy Lagrone), Lion Books (designer not known) and Bantam (Leonard Leone)

MENTOR BOOKS
New American Library, Inc., New York

A continuation (beginning in March, 1948) of the Pelican Books (see separate listing). The first titles were called Pelican Mentors, but after number M30 (August, 1948) only the word Mentor was used. The Mentors were almost exclusively works of nonfiction, subdivided into the categories *Classics and the Arts, Anthropology and Psychology, Economics, Philosophy and Education* and *Religion*.

M26. *American Essays* –
　edited by Charles B. Shaw
M27. *Biography of the Earth* – George Gamow
M28. *Science and the Modern World* –
　Alfred North Whitehead
M29. *The Autobiography of an Ex-Colored Man* – James Weldon Johnson
M30. *America in Perspective* –
　Henry Steele Commager

Six volumes of a series entitled The Mentor Philosophers were published in 1955 and 1956; *New World Writing*, a magazine in paperback form, has appeared since 1952.

Robert Jonas provided covers for many Mentors until about 1955.

MIDWOOD BOOKS
Midwood (Tower) Publications, New York

A series of books aimed specifically at men, which began in 1957 and was advertised as: "The best in Dynamic, Virile Fiction—MID-WOOD BOOKS that are Fastpaced, Bold, Lusty and packed with Excitement!" Only four titles are known, the first two of which were unnumbered.

(1) *There Oughta Be a Law!* –
　Al Fagaly and Harry Shorten
(2) *I Take What I Want* – Hal Ellson
3. *Call Me Mistress* – Tomlin Rede
4. *There Oughta Be a Law!* –
　Al Fagaly and Harry Shorten

MONARCH BOOKS
Monarch Books, Inc., Derby (Connecticut)

A series of often erotic paperbacks which appeared between 1958 and 1965. There were two separate numbering systems, one beginning with number 101 and one with K50.

101. *Dark Hunger* – Don James
102. *Winter Range* – Alan LeMay
103. *Love Me Now* – Fan Nichols
104. *Rawhider from Texas* – Dean Owen
105. *Shadow of the Mafia* – Louis Malley

NOVEL LIBRARY
Diversey Publishing Corporation, New York

Soft-core porno novels, published beginning in 1948 by this subsidiary of Avon Books. A to-tal of 46 titles were issued.

1. *Three Gorgeous Hussies* – Jack Woodford
2. *Ecstasy Girl* – Jack Woodford
3. *Free Lovers* – Jack Woodford
4. *Passionate Princess* – Jack Woodford
5. *Wanton Venus* – Maurice Leblanc

OVERSEAS EDITIONS
Overseas Editions, Inc., New York

Published under the auspices of the Council on Books in Wartime between 1943 and 1947, this series was produced exclusively for distribution abroad; the simple white covers carried a Statue of Liberty colophon and the text: "This edition of an American book is made available in various countries only until normal free publishing, interrupted by Axis aggression, can be reestablished."

Like the Armed Services Editions (see separate listing), the Overseas Editions were numbered using a combination of letters and numbers. They measured 12 cm wide by 16.3 cm tall (roughly $4\frac{3}{4}'' \times 6\frac{1}{2}''$), a somewhat broader format than standard paperbacks. The texts were printed in English or French. It is possible that Overseas Editions in languages other than English and French may have appeared, but this has not been confirmed.

PELICAN BOOKS
Penguin Books, Inc., New York

A nonfiction series published by Penguin Books (see separate listing). The first titles were released in January, 1946; in February, 1948, the series title was changed to Pelican Mentor and, in August, 1948, to Mentor Books (see separate listing).

P1. *Public Opinion* – Walter Lippmann
P2. *Patterns of Culture* – Ruth Benedict
P3. *You and Music* – Christian Darnton
P4. *The Birth and Death of the Sun* –
　George Gamow
P5. *An Enemy of the People: Antisemitism* –
　James Parkes

All covers were designed by Robert Jonas; the Pelican colophon was created by Elaine de Kooning, wife of Jonas' friend Willem de Kooning.

PENGUIN BOOKS
Penguin Books, Inc., New York

In July, 1939, the British paperback firm Penguin Books opened a branch office in New York, under the management of American Ian Ballantine. Ballantine's job was to import British Penguins (especially the Penguin Specials, which dealt with war-related subjects) from England by ship, and to distribute them in America.

When America entered the war, in December of 1941, it became impossible to continue importing books from overseas. At the same time, the u.s. demand for books (especially war-related books) increased significantly. In order to guarantee the continued availability of paper, Ballantine closed a production deal with *The Infantry Journal*; then, in March of 1942, he began to publish Penguins himself, rather than merely importing them.

These earliest American titles carried the double imprint Infantry Journal - Penguin Books (they were also known as Fighting Forces - Penguin Specials); they appeared until 1944, and were numbered s75, s81, s82 and s201-s240.

s75. *New Ways of War* – Tom Wintringham
s81. *Russia* – Bernard Pares
s82. *Aircraft Recognition* –
   R. A. Saville-Sneath
s201. *What's That Plane?* – Walter A. Pitkin
s202. *New Soldier's Handbook*

The Penguin Books series, which was not restricted to wartime subjects, also first appeared in March, 1942. The books were slightly less tall than the British Penguins.

60. *The Dark Invader* –
   Captain Von Rintelen
79. *The Rasp* – Philip MacDonald
239. *Stealthy Terror* – John Ferguson
276. *The Case of the Late Pig* –
   Margery Allingham
339. *High Rising* – Angela Thirkell

(See *The First Hundred* for the first 100 titles.)

In January of 1946, at Robert Jonas' recommendation, the format of the books was changed: both newly-released titles and new printings of earlier volumes were now printed in a slightly taller size.

Numbers 503, 538, 545, 575, 586 and 618 were subsequently reissued with dustjackets.

From March through July, 1948, the books were labeled as being Penguin Signets. Beginning in August of that year, they were simply called Signet Books (see separate listing).

Robert Jonas dominated cover design at Penguin from his arrival in 1945 until the change-over to Signet. Others who delivered covers during this period were Edgard Cirlin, Arthur J. Hawkins, Jr., H.L. Hoffman, Lester Kohs, David Triggs, Michael Loew, George Salter and Arthur Getz.

A single Penguin Guide was released in July, 1947; two years later, in July of 1949, a single Mentor Guide was released as well.

G1. *The Penguin Guide to California* –
   Carl Maas
G2. *How to Know and Enjoy New York* –
   Carl Maas

PENNANT BOOKS
Bantam Books, Inc., New York

A paperback series established by Bantam in 1953. A total of 78 titles were released, numbered P1-P47 and P49-P79. The line was discontinued in July, 1955.

P1. *Navajo Canyon* – Thomas W. Blackburn
P2. *The Last of the Plainsmen* – Zane Grey
P3. *Epitaph for a Spy* – Eric Ambler
P4. *Stamped for Murder* – Ben Benson
P5. *In Those Days* – Harvey Fergusson

PERMA BOOKS
Permabooks, Inc., New York

Originally a series of hardcovered books published in a paperback format. The early titles, released beginning in 1948, were primarily "how-to" books and were edited by George DeKay.

1. *Best-Loved Poems* – edited by MacKenzie
2. *How to Write Letters for All Occasions* –
   Alexander L. Sheff and Edna Ingalls
3. *Best Quotations for All Occasions*
4. *Common Errors in English* –
   Alexander W. Witherspoon, Ph.D.
5. *The Standard Bartender's Guide* – Duffy

In 1950, Permabooks began publishing paperbacks priced at 35 cents instead of hardcovers and added other types of books to its list; the format used remained the same, however, and the numbering continued uninterrupted. The hardcovers were numbered 1-92, 94-97 and 99-101; number 93 was not used and number 98 was a paperback, as were all volumes beginning with number 102.

Chuck Gabriel was the series' art director. Covers were illustrated by, among others, Cardiff, Rafael Palacios and, especially, George T. Erickson, who worked exclusively for Permabooks for two years.

In 1952 two new lines were introduced: Perma Star and Perma Special. The Stars retailed for 25 cents, while the Specials were quality books and cost 50 cents.

The publisher was bought out by Pocket Books in 1954. As of 1955 a smaller format (identical to the standard Pocket Books format) was again used, and a new numbering system (M1000, M1600, M2001, M3002-M5014 and M7500) was introduced. Sol Immerman became art director, and Pocket Books cover artists (including Stan Borack, Tom Dunn, Robert Maguire, James Meese and Bill Rose) began drawing for Perma as well. Spines were colored silver in 1957, gold in 1958 and brown in 1961.

PHANTOM MYSTERIES
(Publisher unknown)

A single title appeared in 1942.

1. *Rocket to the Morgue* – H.H. Holmes

Not to be confused with Phantom Books, a digest series published by the Hanro Corporation in the early '50s.

POCKET BOOKS
Pocket Books, Inc., New York

Pocket Books were the first American paperbacks to be distributed on a large scale. The firm was founded in 1939 by Robert F. DeGraff, M. Lincoln Schuster, Leon Shimkin and Richard L. Simon, after the marketing of 2,000 copies of a test edition of Pearl S. Buck's *The Good Earth* in the autumn of 1938. The first 10 titles, released in 1939, were printed in editions of 10,000 copies each (except for number 6, Dorothy Parker's *Enough Rope*, of which only 7,600 copies were printed).

1. *Lost Horizon* – James Hilton
2. *Wake Up and Live!* – Dorothea Brande
3. *Five Great Tragedies* – William Shakespeare
4. *Topper* – Thorne Smith
5. *The Murder of Roger Ackroyd* –
   Agatha Christie

(See *The First Hundred* for numbers 1-100.)

Number 259, Ellery Queen's *Halfway House* (1944), was published in an oblong format and set in two columns, just like the Armed Services Editions; this experiment was not repeated. Numbers 268, 307, 321 and 324 were published with dustjackets.

Production supervisor James Jacobson originally functioned as art director and hired artists to produce cover illustrations. When Jacobson was called up for military service, his position was taken over by Ed Rofheart, who gave cover assignments to design-oriented artists like E. McKnight Kauffer, Leo Manso, Jeanyee Wong and George Salter.

Sol Immerman, who had been doing cover work for Pocket Books on a freelance basis, was appointed full-time art director in 1947; he remained in that position until 1975, the year the firm was bought by Gulf & Western. Over the years, Immerman worked with the following artists: H.L. Hoffman, Leo Manso, Stanley Meltzoff, Harry Barton, Roswell Keller, Paul Kresse, Frank McCarthy, Casey Jones, Carl Bobertz, George Erickson, Harry Bennett, Tom Dunn, John Groth, Victor Kalin, James Meese, Gerald McConnell, Don Neiser, Barye Phillips, Verne Tossey, Lou Marchetti, Paul Bacon, Charles Binger, Richard Powers, Sam Savitt, Robert Schulz, Charles Skaggs, Stanley Zuckerberg, Bob Abbett and Robert McGinnis.

Pocket Books (G.B.) Limited was established in London in August, 1949; the first titles were released the following spring.

B1. *Ming Yellow* – John P. Marquand
B2. *Pro* – Bruce Hamilton
B3. *The Lost Weekend* – Charles Jackson
B4. *Mink Coat* – Kathleen Norris
B5. *The Anatomy of Murder* –
   Dorothy L. Sayers and others

The British Pocket Books resembled their American cousins in format and graphic approach, but their cover illustrations, being of British origin, were of a lower quality. The series was abandoned in 1953.

By 1951, the price of 25 cents per volume could no longer be maintained for all Pocket Books; as a forum for higher-priced books, the Cardinal Editions (see separate listing) entered publication in that year, priced at 35 cents; in 1952, the 50- or 75-cent Cardinal Giants were added. The difference between the Cardinals and the standard Pocket Books was indicated by a colored band along the spine: Pocket Books had a silver band, while the more expensive Cardinals had gold bands.

In January, 1951, Pocket Books' series for young readers, which had appeared under the imprint Comet Books since 1948 (see separate listing), was renamed Pocket Books, Jr.

J-35. *Ski Patrol* – Montgomery Atwater
J-36. *Long Lash* – Bertrand Shurtleff
J-37. *The Adventures of Tom Sawyer* –
   Mark Twain
J-38. *Baldy of Nome* – Esther Birdsall Darling
J-39. *Sponger's Jinx* – Bert Sackett

After 43 titles (numbered J-35 through J-77), the Junior line was discontinued as a result of disappointing sales.

The first titles of the Pocket Books Art Series appeared in 1953.

A1. *Degas* – Daniel Catton Rich
A2. *El Greco* – John Matthews
A3. *Toulouse-Lautrec* – Samuel Hunter
A4. *Cézanne* – Theodore Rousseau, Jr.
A5. *Dufy* – Alfred Werner

And in May, 1954, the Pocket Library series was introduced. These books, which cost 35 or 50 cents, bore unvarnished offset-printed covers and were advertised as being "books of classic literary stature."

PL-1. *Man and the State: The Political Philosophers* – Robert N. Linscott
PL-2. *Man and Man: The Social Philosophers* – Robert N. Linscott
PL-3. *Man and the Universe: The Philosophers of Science* – Robert N. Linscott
PL-4. *Man and Spirit: The Speculative Philosophers* – Robert N. Linscott
PL-5. *The Imitation of Christ* –
   Thomas à Kempis

PONY BOOKS

Stamford House, Stamford (Connecticut)

In this series, 22 titles are known to have been released between December, 1945 and June, 1946. They were numbered from 45 to 66.

45. *Your Life in the Atom World* – Captain John Craige
46. *The Singing Corpse* – Bernard Dougall
47. *The Orange Divan* – Valentine Williams
48. *The Narrow Cell* – Dale Clark
49. *The Corpse with the Redheaded Friend* – R.A.J. Walling

POPULAR LIBRARY

Popular Library, Inc., New York

Founded by Ned L. Pines, of Pines Publications, in 1942. The editor was Charles N. Heckelman, and the first titles appeared in February, 1943. The first three volumes were unnumbered.

(1) *Saint Overboard* – Leslie Charteris
(2) *Danger in the Dark* – Mignon G. Eberhart
(3) *Crime of Violence* – Rufus King
4. *Murder in the Madhouse* – Jonathan Latimer
5. *Miss Pinkerton* – Mary Roberts Rinehart
(See *The First Hundred* for numbers 1-100.)

The first 76 titles were reprints of successful mysteries and thrillers. Afterwards, Westerns, adventure stories and other novels were also published.

The first 125 books were designed by Sol Immerman's studio, with H.L. Hoffman doing most of the work: with five exceptions, Hoffman was responsible for the first 86 releases. An illustrator named Fiedler also produced Popular Library covers during this period. The typeface used on the covers of numbers 30-100 was Lydian; Sol Immerman handled the typography.

Ed Rofheart was named art director in January, 1952. He modernized the Popular Library "look" and gave cover assignments to Rafael DeSoto, A. Leslie Ross, Bob Fink, Paul Kresse, George Meyers, Norman Saunders, George Erickson, Lou Marchetti and Harry Schaare. In 1956, Rofheart designed a new colophon for Popular Library covers, a pine tree, which symbolized (obviously) Pines Publications.

The Popular Giant series, costing 35 cents, began in 1952 with number G100. A total of 104 Popular Library Eagle Books, numbered EB1 through EB104, appeared between November, 1953 and February, 1958.

POST YARNS

The Saturday Evening Post, Philadelphia

A series of paperbacks, published in 1944 and 1945, which reprinted short stories from *The Saturday Evening Post*. The cover illustrations also originated in the magazine.

PREMIER BOOKS

see *Fawcett Premier Books*

PYRAMID BOOKS

Almat Publishing Corporation, New York

The name "Almat" comes from the first names of the corporation's founders, Alfred R. Plaine and Matthew Huttner. Their paperback series began with number 11 (and skipped over number 13) in the autumn of 1949.

11. *Passionate Virgin* – Perry Lindsay
12. *Reckless Passion* – Gordon Sample
14. *Blonde Mistress* – Hall Bennett
15. *Palm Beach Apartment* – Gail Jordan
16. *Set-up for Murder* – Peter Cheyney

The Pyramid Royals, numbered PR10-PR26, first appeared in March, 1956.

QUICK READER BOOKS

Royce Publications, Chicago

Published in 1944 and 1945. All books were 128 pages long, bound with staples (like the Dell 10-cents Books) and illustrated. The first volume was numbered 101.

101. *Stories of Guy de Maupassant*
102. *The Killers* – Stewart Edward White
103. *Nana* – Emile Zola
104. *The Chillers* – Dorothy L. Sayers and others
105. *You'll Laugh Your Head Off*

Royce Publications also published the Trophy Books (see separate listing).

READERS CHOICE LIBRARY

St. John Publishing Company, New York

A series of popular novels, probably totaling 22 titles. Some volumes used the digest format; the first five paperbacks were:

3. *Gina* – George Albert Glay
7. *Shoe the Wild Mare* – Gene Fowler
8. *Green Light for Death* – Frank Kane
11. *Stranger than Fruit* – Vera Saspary
12. *Nightmare* – William Irish

The following numbers are known to have been used: 2-5, 7, 8, 11-20, 24, 25, 33 and 37-39.

RED ARROW BOOKS

Columbia Art Works, Inc., Milwaukee

This series included 12 titles, all published late in 1939. Numbers 1-5 had red covers and were mysteries, numbers 6-10 had green covers and were travel and adventure stories, and numbers

11 and 12 had blue covers and were straight novels.

1. *Thirteen at Dinner* – Agatha Christie
2. *Murder-on-Hudson* – Jennifer Jones
3. *Murders in Praed Street* – John Rhode
4. *Death in the Library* – Philip Ketchum
5. *Death Wears a White Gardenia* – Zelda Popkin

RED CIRCLE BOOKS
Lion Books, Inc., New York

A series of novels published in 1949. They were numbered 1-7, 12 and 13; numbers 8-11 carried the imprint Lion Books, and it was under that name that the series was continued (see separate listing).

1. *Sex Life and You* – Maxine Sawyer
2. *Passionate Fool* – John Moroso
3. *Leg Artist* – Gene Harvey
4. *Blonde Menace* – Don Martin
5. *Body or Soul* – Royal Peters

RED SEAL BOOKS
Modern Age Books, Inc., New York

Paperbacks published around 1937, at the same time as the Blue Seal and Gold Seal Books (see separate listings). Typography was by Robert Josephy.

1. *Travels in the Congo* – André Gide
2. *Twelve Against the Gods* – William Bolitho
3. *Suspicious Characters* – Dorothy L. Sayers
4. *The Leavenworth Case* – Anna Katherine Green
5. *They Shall Inherit the Earth* – Morley Callaghan

In 1938, the three Modern Age series were combined under the imprint Seal Books (see separate listing).

RED SEAL (GOLD MEDAL) BOOKS
Fawcett Publications, Inc., New York

Founded in 1952, discontinued in 1953; 23 titles were issued, beginning with number 7. Retail price was 35 cents.

7. *The Sky Tramps* – Dennison O'Hara
8. *Each Life to Live* – Richard Gehman
9. *This Woman* – Albert Idell
10. *Naked in the Streets* – Ryerson Johnson
11. *Out of the Sea* – Don Smith

Covers were illustrated by Barye Phillips, Carl Bobertz and others.

SEAL BOOKS
Modern Age Books, Inc., New York

Fiction, nonfiction and children's books; reprints and originals. Beginning in 1938, the Seal Books were a combined continuation of the Blue Seal, Gold Seal and Red Seal Books (see separate listings), which Modern Age had estab-lished the previous year. As he had done for the three earlier series, Robert Josephy handled the typography. The books were unnumbered.

(1) *The Wall of Men* – William Rollins, Jr.
(2) *The Story of Sweepstakes, Lotteries and Contests* – Eric Bender

SIGNET BOOKS
New American Library, Inc., New York

A continuation of the Penguin Books (see separate listing). The first Signets appeared in August, 1948; they were priced at 25 cents. Signet Giants (35 cents) and Signet Double Volumes (50 cents) were introduced in 1950, and Signet Triple Volumes (75 cents) were added in 1953.

Between March and July of 1948, the transition period between Penguin and Signet, a few titles were released under the imprint Penguin Signet Books. The first true Signet Book was numbered 660; later reprintings of earlier Penguins took on the Signet imprint but retained their original (lower) numbers.

660. *100 American Poems* – edited by Selden Rodman
661. *Tragic Ground* – Erskine Caldwell
662. *Invitation to the Waltz* – Rosamond Lehman
663. *As Good as Dead* – Thomas B. Dewey
664. *Portrait of the Artist as a Young Man* – James Joyce

(See *The First Hundred* for the first 100 titles.) John Legakes was named art director at NAL in 1949. He made designs for all covers and did the lettering and, occasionally, the layout himself. It was under his direction that the characteristically dark and brooding Signet covers came into being; these covers were James Avati's trademark, but they were also produced by Stanley Meltzoff, Alan Harmon, Cardiff, Stanley Zuckerberg and Barye Phillips. Covers were also provided by Mike Hooks, Carl Bobertz, George Erickson, Lou Kimmel, Harry Schaare, Victor Kalin, Robert Maguire, James Meese, Clark Hulings, Bob Abbett and James Bama. Illustrations were always either square or rectangular; until 1956, they were bordered at top and bottom by colored bands.

The Signet Key Books, which first appeared in 1954, cost either 25, 35 or 50 cents; they were numbered from K300 through KD373, except for number 366, which was not used. The Signet Classics were introduced in August, 1959, and numbering began with CD1.

SUPERIOR REPRINTS
Superior Publishing, Inc.; The Military Service Publishing Company, Harrisburg (Pennsylvania)

This series, produced in cooperation with Penguin Books (see separate listing), consisted of 21 paperbacks published between November, 1944 and September, 1945; they were numbered from M637 through M657.

M637. *White Magic* – Faith Baldwin
M638. *Ol' Man Adam an' His Chillun* – Roark Bradford
M639. *Unexpected Night* – Elizabeth Daly
M640. *An April Afternoon* – Philip Wylie
M641. *Family Affair* – Ione Sandberg Shriber

Covers were illustrated by Robert Jonas and others.

Numbers M642, M646, M649, M650, M654-M656 and M659 were dustjacketed and rereleased as Bantam Books in 1948.

TRAVELLERS POCKET LIBRARY BEST SELLERS
Ward-Hill Books, Inc., New York
Two titles were published, in 1949.
100. *Passion is a Gentle Whip* – Milton H. Gropper
109. *Venus in Furs* – Leopold Sacher-Masoch

TROPHY BOOKS
Royce Publications, Chicago
Only two titles are known, both issued in 1946.
401. *Smile Brother Smile* – an anthology
402. *The Pilditch Puzzle* – W. B. M. Ferguson
Royce Publications also published the Quick Reader Books (see separate listing).

ZENITH BOOKS
Zenith Books, Inc., New York
Approximately 50 paperback titles appeared in this series, which began publication in July of 1958.
ZB-1. *The Sisters* – Charles Jackson
ZB-2. *All Over Town* – George Milburn
ZB-3. *Johnny Purple* – John Wyllie
ZB-4. *Die Screaming* – Jo Pagano
ZB-5. *The Best Cartoons from "Argosy"*

The First Hundred

When they are known, the names of cover illustrators of first printings are given in parentheses after the names of authors.

Pocket Books 1-100: 1939-1941

1939

1. Lost Horizon – James Hilton (I.N. Steinberg)
2. Wake Up and Live! – Dorothea Brande (I.N. Steinberg)
3. Five Great Tragedies – William Shakespeare (I.N. Steinberg)
4. Topper – Thorne Smith (Frank J. Lieberman)
5. The Murder of Roger Ackroyd – Agatha Christie (I.N. Steinberg)
6. Enough Rope – Dorothy Parker (Frank J. Lieberman)
7. Wuthering Heights – Emily Brontë (I.N. Steinberg)
8. The Way of All Flesh – Samuel Butler (I.N. Steinberg)
9. The Bridge of San Luis Rey – Thornton Wilder (Frank J. Lieberman)
10. Bambi – Felix Salten (Frank J. Lieberman)
11. The Good Earth – Pearl S. Buck
12. Great Short Stories – Guy de Maupassant
13. Show Boat – Edna Ferber
14. A Tale of Two Cities – Charles Dickens
15. The Story of Mankind – Hendrik Willem Van Loon
16. Green Mansions – W.H. Hudson
17. The Chinese Orange Mystery – Ellery Queen
18. Pinocchio – Carlo Collodi
19. Abraham Lincoln – Lord Charnwood (I.N. Steinberg)
20. The Return of the Native – Thomas Hardy
21. Murder Must Advertise – Dorothy L. Sayers
22. The Swiss Family Robinson – Johann Wyss
23. The Autobiography of Benjamin Franklin (I.N. Steinberg)
24. The Corpse with the Floating Foot – R.A.J. Walling
25. Treasure Island – Robert Louis Stevenson
26. Elizabeth Essex – Lytton Strachey
27. Appointment in Samarra – John O'Hara
28. Jeeves – P.G. Wodehouse (I.N. Steinberg)
29. A Christmas Carol – Charles Dickens
30. The Little French Girl – Anne D. Sedgwick (Eve Rockwell)
31. The Hunchback of Notre Dame, Vol. 1 – Victor Hugo (I.N. Steinberg)
32. The Hunchback of Notre Dame, Vol. 2 – Victor Hugo (I.N. Steinberg)
33. The Watchman's Clock – Leslie Ford
34. Gulliver's Travels – Jonathan Swift

1940

35. Beau Geste – Percival C. Wren (Eve Rockwell)
36. The Three Musketeers, Vol. 1 – Alexandre Dumas (I.N. Steinberg)
37. The Three Musketeers, Vol. 2 – Alexandre Dumas (I.N. Steinberg)
38. The Mystery of the Blue Train – Agatha Christie
39. Great Tales and Poems – Edgar Allan Poe
40. The Man Nobody Knows – Bruce Barton
41. The Constant Nymph – Margaret Kennedy (Eve Rockwell)
42. Autobiography of Benvenuto Cellini
43. The Lodger – Marie Belloc Lowndes
44. Mother – Kathleen Norris (I.N. Steinberg)
45. The Light That Failed – Rudyard Kipling
46. The Bowstring Murders – Carter Dickson
47. Bring 'Em Back Alive – Edward Anthony & Frank Buck (Allen Pope)
48. Scarlet Sister Mary – Julia Peterkin (Eve Rockwell)
49. Dr. Ehrlich's Magic Bullet – Paul de Kruif
50. The House Without a Key – Earl Derr Biggers
51. Thunder on the Left – Christopher Morley
52. The House of Seven Gables – Nathaniel Hawthorne (Eve Rockwell)
53. The Best of Damon Runyon (Allen Pope)
54. The Great Prince Shan – E. Phillips Oppenheim
55. Our Town – Thornton Wilder
56. The Green Bay Tree – Louis Bromfield (D.E.)

57. After Such Pleasures – Dorothy Parker
58. Tom Brown's School Days – Thomas Hughes
(Van Doren)
59. Think Fast, Mr. Moto – John P. Marquand
(Allen Pope)
60. The Scandal of Father Brown – G.K. Chesterton
61. Bob, Son of Battle – Alfred Ollivant
62. The Pocket Book of Verse – M.E. Speare (ed.)
63. Pride and Prejudice – Jane Austen
64. While the Patient Slept – Mignon G. Eberhart
65. The Four Million – O. Henry (Allen Pope)
66. National Velvet – Enid Bagnold
67. Heidi – Johanna Spyrl
68. How to Win Friends and Influence People –
Dale Carnegie
69. The Thirty-nine Steps – John Buchan
70. The Mystery of the Dead Police –
Philip MacDonald
71. The French Powder Mystery – Ellery Queen
72. Anne of Windy Poplars – L.M. Montgomery
73. The Case of the Velvet Claws –
Erle Stanley Gardner (Frye)
74. The Unpleasantness at the Bellona Club –
Dorothy L. Sayers
75. Little Men – Louisa May Alcott
76. Sunset Gun – Dorothy Parker
77. The Roman Hat Mystery – Ellery Queen
(Allen Pope)
78. Oh, You Tex! – William MacLeod Raine
79. Murder in the Calais Coach – Agatha Christie
80. Up from Slavery – Booker T. Washington
81. The Red House Mystery – A.A. Milne
(Allen Pope)
82. Captain Blood – Rafael Sabatini
83. A Puzzle for Fools – Patrick Quentin
84. The Riddle of the Sands – Erskine Caldwell
85. Clouds of Witness – Dorothy L. Sayers
86. The Red Widow Murders – Carter Dickson
87. Mister Glencannon – Guy Kilpatrick
(I.N. Steinberg)

1941
88. The A.B.C. Murders – Agatha Christie
89. And Now Good-Bye – James Hilton
90. The Case of the Sulky Girl –
Erle Stanley Gardner (Pierre Martinot)
91. The Pocket Book of Short Stories –
M.E. Speare (ed.) (Miriam Woods)
92. The Pocket Bible
93. Goodbye, Mister Chips! – James Hilton
94. Greenmantle – John Buchan
95. The Sherlock Holmes Pocket Book –
Arthur Conan Doyle
96. Believe It or Not! – Robert L. Ripley
97. The Werewolf of Paris – Guy Endore
98. The Circular Staircase – Mary Roberts Rinehart
99. The Adventures of Ellery Queen – Ellery Queen
100. The General Died at Dawn – Charles G. Booth

Avon Books (1)-100: 1941-1946

1941
(1) Elmer Gantry – Sinclair Lewis
(2) The Rubáiyát of Omar Khayyám –
Edward Fitzgerald
(3) The Big Four – Agatha Christie
(4) Ill Wind – James Hilton (Pol)
(5) Dr. Priestly Investigates – John Rhode
(6) The Haunted Hotel and 25 Other Ghost Stories –
Wilkie Collins
(7) The Plague Court Murders – John Dickson Carr
(8) The Corpse in the Green Pajamas –
R.A.J. Walling
(9) Willful and Premeditated – Freeman Wills Crofts
(10) Dr. Thorndyke's Discovery – R. Austin Freeman
(11) Count Bruga – Ben Hecht
(12) Mosquitos – William Faulkner

1942
(13) Mystery at Spanish Hacienda – Jackson Gregory
(14) Call Her Savage – Tiffany Thayer
(15) The Avon Book of Modern Short Stories
(16) Murder at Midnight – R.A.J. Walling
(17) The Agony Column – Earl Derr Biggers
(18) The Man Who Murdered Himself –
Geoffrey Homes
(19) 48 Saroyan Stories – William Saroyan
(20) The League of Frightened Men – Rex Stout
(21) The Avon Book of Detective and Crime Stories –
John Rhode (ed.)
(22) The Redheaded Woman – Katharine Brush

1943
(23) Suspicious Characters – Dorothy L. Sayers
(24) Ashenden, or The British Agent –
W. Somerset Maugham
(25) Trumpet in the Dust – Gene Fowler
(26) Seven Footprints to Satan – A.A. Merritt
(27) The Avon Book of Puzzles
(28) Tonight at 8:30 – Noel Coward
(29) The Sabotage Murder Mystery –
Margery Allingham
(30) Gorgeous Ghoul Murder Case –
Dwight V. Babcock
(31) Doctor's Son – John O'Hara
(32) Stage Door Canteen – Delmer Daves
(33) The Corpse in the Waxworks –
John Dickson Carr
(34) The Saint Goes On – Leslie Charteris
(35) Poison for One – John Rhode
(36) (does not exist)
(37) Coffin for One – Francis Beeding
(38) The Big Sleep – Raymond Chandler
(39) Rage in Heaven – James Hilton
(40) In the Teeth of the Evidence – Dorothy L. Sayers

1944
41. The Narrow Corner – W. Somerset Maugham
42. The Passionate Year – James Hilton
43. Burn Witch Burn – A.A. Merritt
44. The Saint in New York – Leslie Charteris
45. Germany: Past, Present and Future –
Lord Vansittart
46. Death on the Nile – Agatha Christie
47. Shoe the Wild Mare – Gene Fowler
48. The Road to Victory – Francis J. Spellman
49. The London Spy Murders – Peter Cheyney

50. Cakes and Ale – W. Somerset Maugham
51. Nobody's in Town – Edna Ferber
52. The Man Who Had Everything – Louis Bromfield
53. The Mystery of the Red Triangle – W. C. Tuttle
54. See What I Mean? – Lewis Browne
55. Presenting Lily Mars – Booth Tarkington
56. Theatre – W. Somerset Maugham
57. The Hills Beyond – Thomas Wolfe
58. Winged Victory – Moss Hart

1945
59. Heaven's My Destination – Thornton Wilder
60. Double Indemnity – James M. Cain
61. Murder in Three Acts – Agatha Christie
62. Over My Dead Body – Rex Stout
63. Five Murderers – Raymond Chandler
64. Back Stage – Vicki Baum
65. Now I'll Tell One – Harry Hershfield
66. Little Caesar – W. R. Burnett
67. Action This Day – Francis J. Spellman
68. A Homicide for Hannah – Dwight V. Babcock
69. The Stray Lamb – Thorne Smith
70. Poirot Loses a Client – Agatha Christie
71. The Saint Intervenes – Leslie Charteris
72. The Avon Story-Teller
73. A Goodly Heritage – Mary Ellen Chase (L. A. Corrado)
74. The Ghost Patrol and Other Stories – Sinclair Lewis
75. The Mysterious Affair at Styles – Agatha Christie
76. Atomic Energy in the Coming Era – David Dietz (Lester Kohs)
77. The Long Valley – John Steinbeck

1946
78. To Step Aside – Noel Coward
79. Catherine Herself – James Hilton
80. You Can't Keep the Change – Peter Cheyney
81. Bad Girl – Vina Delmar
82. The Red Box – Rex Stout
83. Sight Unseen and the Confession – Mary Roberts
84. Mistress Wilding – Rafael Sabatini (L. Werter)
85. The Regatta Mystery – Agatha Christie (L. A. Corrado)
86. Avon Mystery Story-Teller
87. The Private Affairs of Bel Ami – Guy de Maupassant
88. Five Sinister Characters – Raymond Chandler
89. Death in the Air – Agatha Christie
90. Avon Ghost Reader – Herbert Williams (ed.)
91. The French Key Mystery – Frank Gruber
92. Loose Ladies – Vina Delmar
93. The Dark Street Murders – Peter Cheyney
94. Butterfield 8 – John O'Hara
95. Black Orchids – Rex Stout
96. Black Angel – Cornell Woolrich
97. Wedding Ring – Beth Brown
98. The Virgin and the Gypsy – D. H. Lawrence
99. The Embezzler – James M. Cain
100. The Secret Adversary – Agatha Christie

Penguin Books 60-595: 1942-1946

1942
60. The Dark Invader – Captain Von Rintelen
79. The Rasp – Philip MacDonald
239. Stealthy Terror – John Ferguson
276. The Case of the Late Pig – Margery Allingham
339. High Rising – Angela Thirkell
501. Murder by an Aristocrat – Mignon G. Eberhart
502. Pygmalion – Bernard Shaw
503. Death of a Ghost – Margery Allingham
504. All Concerned Notified – Helen Reilly
505. The Mother – Pearl S. Buck
506. Two Survived – Guy P. Jones
507. The Physiology of Sex – Kenneth Walker
508. Walden – Henry David Thoreau
509. The Pastures of Heaven – John Steinbeck
510. Trent's Own Case – H. Warner Allen & E. C. Bentley
511. Cause for Alarm – Eric Ambler
512. Miss Annie Spragg – Louis Bromfield
513. The Catalyst Club – George Dyer
514. Tombstone – Walter Noble Burns

1943
515. The Confidential Agent – Graham Greene
516. Genghis Khan – Harold Lamb
517. Philosopher's Holiday – Irwin Edman (Busoni)
518. The Middle Temple Murder – J. S. Fletcher
519. A Blunt Instrument – Georgette Heyer
520. The Saga of Billy the Kid – Walter Noble Burns
521. The Ox-Bow Incident – Walter Van Tilburg Clark
522. Sabotage – Cleve F. Adams
523. Leaves of Grass – Walt Whitman (Busoni)
524. Pencil Points to Murder – W. A. Barber & R. F. Schabelitz
525. The Penguin Book of Sonnets – Carl Withers (ed.)
526. My Own Murderer – Richard Hull
527. The Telephone Booth Indian – A. J. Liebling (Dave Huffine)
528. The Blind Barber – John Dickson Carr

1944
529. Kitty Foyle – Christopher Morley
530. The Ministry of Fear – Graham Greene
531. Drawn Conclusion – W. A. Barber & R. F. Schabelitz
532. Hag's Nook – John Dickson Carr
533. The Purple Sickle Murders – Freeman Wills Crofts
534. Black Plumes – Margery Allingham
535. The Old Dark Horse – J. B. Priestly
536. In Hazard – Richard Hughes
537. Out of This World – Julius Fast
538. The Laughing Fox – Frank Gruber
539. Laughing Boy – Oliver LaFarge (H. L. Hoffman)
540. My Name is Aram – William Saroyan (after Don Freeman)
541. Mr. Pinkerton Grows a Beard – David Frome
542. Murder Enters the Picture – W. A. Barber & R. F. Schabelitz (R. F. Schabelitz)
543. Shell of Death – Nicholas Blake (Busoni)
544. The Ten Holy Horrors – Francis Beeding
545. The Talking Clock – Frank Gruber
546. O'Halloran's Luck and Other Stories – Stephen Vincent Benét

547. Death of My Aunt – C.H.B. Kitchin
548. Black-Out in Gretley – J.B. Priestly
549. Murders in Volume 2 – Elizabeth Daly
550. To Walk the Night – William Sloane
551. Mr. Littlejohn – Martin Flavin
552. Murder in Trinidad – John W. Vandercook

1945
553. Nine Times Nine – H.H. Holmes
554. Tales of Piracy, Crime and Ghosts
555. Dr. Toby Finds Murder – Sturges Mason Schley
556. The Mycenaid – C. Everett Cooper
557. McSorley's Wonderful Saloon – Joseph Mitchell
558. Porgy – DuBose Heyward
559. Death of a Saboteur – Hulbert Footner
560. Murder in Fiji – John W. Vandercook
    (Robert Jonas)
561. Young Man with a Horn – Dorothy Baker
    (Robert Jonas)
562. Simon Lash, Private Detective – Frank Gruber
    (David Triggs)
563. Appointment in Samarra – John O'Hara
    (Robert Jonas)
564. Maigret Travels South – Georges Simenon
565. Step in the Dark – Ethel Lina White (Lester Kohs)
566. Say Yes to Murder – W.T. Bollard (Lester Kohs)
567. Trouble in July – Erskine Caldwell (Robert Jonas)
568. Night Flight – Antoine de Saint-Exupéry
    (Edgard Cirlin)
569. Conceived in Liberty – Howard Fast
    (Robert Jonas)
570. And Berry Came Too – Dornford Yates
    (Robert Jonas)
571. Death Down East – Eleanor Blake (Robert Jonas)

1946
572. The Good Soldier Schweik – Jaroslav Hašek
573. The Turning Wheels – Stuart Cloete
    (Robert Jonas)
574. A Passage to India – E.M. Forster (George Salter)
575. The Cask – Freeman Wills Crofts (H.L. Hoffman)
576. The Lovely Lady – D.H. Lawrence
    (George Salter)
577. Manhattan Transfer – John Dos Passos
    (Robert Jonas)
578. Bread and Wine – Ignazio Silone (George Salter)
579. The Patience of Maigret – Georges Simenon
580. Pal Joey – John O'Hara (Robert Jonas)
581. God's Little Acre – Erskine Caldwell
    (Robert Jonas)
582. Thunder on the Left – Christopher Morley
    (Robert Jonas)
583. Vein of Iron – Ellen Glasgow (Robert Jonas)
584. Dead Reckoning – Francis Bonnamy
    (Arthur J. Hawkins)
585. Winesburg, Ohio – Sherwood Anderson
    (Lester Beall Studio)
586. The Rasp – Philip MacDonald (Robert Jonas)
587. Martin Eden – Jack London (Robert Jonas)
588. The Unvanquished – Howard Fast (Robert Jonas)
589. Back Street – Fannie Hurst (Robert Jonas)
590. Orlando – Virgina Woolf (George Salter)
591. Mildred Pierce – James M. Cain (Robert Jonas)
592. Malice in Wonderland – Nicholas Blake
    (Arthur J. Hawkins)
593. Handbook of Politics – Lowell Mellett
    (Robert Jonas)

594. Heavenly Discourse – Charles Erskine Scott Wood
    (Robert Jonas)
595. Cabbages and Kings – O. Henry (Michael Loew)

Popular Library (1)-100: 1943-1946

1943
(1) Saint Overboard – Leslie Charteris
    (H.L. Hoffman)
(2) Danger in the Dark – Mignon G. Eberhart
    (H.L. Hoffman)
(3) Crime of Violence – Rufus King
4. Murder in the Madhouse – Jonathan Latimer
    (H.L. Hoffman)
5. Miss Pinkerton – Mary Roberts Rinehart
    (H.L. Hoffman)
6. Three Bright Pebbles – Leslie Ford
    (H.L. Hoffman)
7. Death Demands an Audience – Helen Reilly
    (H.L. Hoffman)
8. Death for Dear Clara – Q. Patrick (H.L. Hoffman)
9. The Eel Pie Murders – David Frome
10. To Wake the Dead – John Dickson Carr
    (H.L. Hoffman)
11. The Stoneware Monkey – R. Austin Freeman
    (H.L. Hoffman)
12. Death Sits on the Board – John Rhode
    (H.L. Hoffman)
13. Valcour Meets Murder – Rufus King
    (H.L. Hoffman)
14. The Criminal C.O.D. – Phoebe Atwood Taylor
    (H.L. Hoffman)
15. The Third Eye – Ethel Lina White (H.L. Hoffman)
16. The Dead Don't Care – Jonathan Latimer
    (H.L. Hoffman)
17. The House on the Roof – Mignon G. Eberhart
    (H.L. Hoffman)
18. Tragedy in the Hollow – Freeman Wills Crofts
    (H.L. Hoffman)
19. The Crooked Hinge – John Dickson Carr
    (H.L. Hoffman)
20. Murder in Shinbone Alley – Helen Reilly
    (H.L. Hoffman)

1944
21. The After House – Mary Roberts Rinehart
    (H.L. Hoffman)
22. Murder Masks Miami – Rufus King
    (H.L. Hoffman)
23. S.S. Murder – Q. Patrick (H.L. Hoffman)
24. Reno Rendezvous – Leslie Ford (H.L. Hoffman)
25. Out of Order – Phoebe Atwood Taylor
    (H.L. Hoffman)
26. Mr. Pinkerton Has the Clue – David Frome
    (H.L. Hoffman)
27. From This Dark Stairway – Mignon G. Eberhart
    (H.L. Hoffman)
28. The Burning Court – John Dickson Carr
    (H.L. Hoffman)
29. Weekend with Death – Patricia Wentworth
    (H.L. Hoffman)
30. There's Trouble Brewing – Nicholas Blake
    (H.L. Hoffman)
31. Murder by the Clock – Rufus King
32. The Wheel Spins – Ethel Lina White
    (H.L. Hoffman)

33. McKee of Centre Street – Helen Reilly
(H.L. Hoffman)
34. Mr. Pinkerton at the Old Angel – David Frome
(H.L. Hoffman)
35. The Mystery of Hunting's End –
Mignon G. Eberhart (H.L. Hoffman)
36. Death and the Maiden – Q. Patrick
(H.L. Hoffman)
37. Mother Finds a Body – Gypsy Rose Lee
(H.L. Hoffman)
38. The Dark Ships – Hulbert Footmer (H.L. Hoffman)
39. In the Balance – Patricia Wentworth
(H.L. Hoffman)
40. The Stars Spell Death – Jonathan Stagge
(H.L. Hoffman)
41. The Smiler with the Knife – Nicholas Blake
(H.L. Hoffman)
42. Murdered: One by One – Francis Beeding
(H.L. Hoffman)

1945
43. The Fatal Kiss – Rufus King (H.L. Hoffman)
44. The Brass Chills – Hugh Pentecost
(H.L. Hoffman)
45. The Wrong Murder – Craig Rice (H.L. Hoffman)
46. Sound of Revelry – Octavus Roy Cohen
(H.L. Hoffman)
47. Return to the Scene – Q. Patrick
48. Mr. Smith's Hat – Helen Reilly (H.L. Hoffman)
49. Tiger Milk – David Garth (H.L. Hoffman)
50. Green Shiver – Clyde B. Clason (H.L. Hoffman)
51. The Whispering Cup – Mabel Seeley
(H.L. Hoffman)
52. Murder by Prescription – Jonathan Stagge
(H.L. Hoffman)
53. Cancelled in Red – Hugh Pentecost
(H.L. Hoffman)
54. Her Heart in Her Throat – Ethel Lina White
(H.L. Hoffman)
55. Murder in the Willett Family – Rufus King
(H.L. Hoffman)
56. Dead for a Ducat – Helen Reilly (H.L. Hoffman)
57. The Twelve Disguises – Francis Beeding
(H.L. Hoffman)
58. The Turquoise Shop – Frances Crane
(H.L. Hoffman)
59. The Case of the Solid Key – Anthony Boucher
60. The Corpse in the Snowman – Nicholas Blake
(H.L. Hoffman)
61. The Mad Hatter Mystery – John Dickson Carr
(H.L. Hoffman)
62. The Yellow Taxi – Jonathan Stagge (H.G.)
63. Sing a Song of Homicide – James R. Laugham
(H.L. Hoffman)
64. They Can 't Hang Me – James Ronald (H.G.)
65. The Woman in the Picture – John August
(H.L. Hoffman)
66. The Blind Side – Patricia Wenteworth
(H.L. Hoffman)
67. Murder on the Yacht – Rufus King
(H.L. Hoffman)
68. The Cat Screams – Todd Downing
(H.L. Hoffman)

1946
69. The Listening House – Mabel Seeley
(H.L. Hoffman)

70. Mr. Polton Explains – R. Austin Freeman
(H.L. Hoffman)
71. Hell Let Loose – Francis Beeding (H.G.)
72. Who Killed Aunt Maggie? – Medora Field (H.G.)
73. Hasty Wedding – Mignon G. Eberhart
(H.L. Hoffman)
74. Murder in Season – Octavus Roy Cohen
(H.L. Hoffman)
75. She Faded into Thin Air – Ethel Lina White
(H.L. Hoffman)
76. Fog – Valentine Williams & Dorothy Rice Sims
(H.L. Hoffman)
77. Buckaroo – Eugene Cunningham (H.L. Hoffman)
78. Timbal Gulch Trail – Max Brand (H.L. Hoffman)
79. Rolling Stone – Patricia Wentworth
(H.L. Hoffman)
80. The Golden Box – Frances Crane (H.L. Hoffman)
81. Three Thirds of a Ghost – Timothy Fuller
(H.L. Hoffman)
82. The 24th Horse – Hugh Pentecost (H.L. Hoffman)
83. The Black-Headed Pins –
Constance & Gwenyth Little (H.L. Hoffman)
84. Challenge for Three – David Garth
(H.L. Hoffman)
85. Trouble Shooter – Ernest Haycox (H.L. Hoffman)
86. Bucky Follows a Cold Trail –
William MacLeod Raine (H.L. Hoffman)
87. Fatal Descent – John Rhode & Carter Dickson
(Fiedler)
88. Romance in the First Degree –
Octavus Roy Cohen
89. The Right Murder – Craig Rice
90. The Scarlet Circle – Jonathan Stagge
91. The Sea-Hawk – Rafael Sabatini
92. All Over but the Shooting – Richard Powell
(Fiedler)
93. The Blue Lacquer Box – George F. Worts
94. The Mortal Storm – Phyllis Bottome
95. The Red Law – Jackson Gregory
96. Singing River – W.C. Tuttle
97. A Variety of Weapons – Rufus King (Fiedler)
98. Dividend on Death – Brett Halliday
99. Dead of the Night – John Rhode
100. The African Poison Murders – Elspeth Huxley

Dell Books 1-100: 1943-1946

1943
1. Death in the Library – Philip Ketchum
(William Strohmer)
2. Dead or Alive – Patricia Wentworth
(William Strohmer)
3. Murder-on-Hudson – Jennifer Jones
(George Frederiksen)
4. The American Gun Mystery – Ellery Queen
(Gerald Gregg)
5. Four Frightened Women – George Harmon Coxe
(Gerald Gregg)
6. Ill Met by Moonlight – Leslie Ford
(Gerald Gregg)
7. See You at the Morgue – Lawrence G. Blochman
(Gerald Gregg)
8. The Tuesday Club Murders – Agatha Christie
(George Frederiksen)

9. Double for Death – Rex Stout
(George Frederiksen)
10. The Lone Wolf – Louis Joseph Vance
(Gerald Gregg)
11. Hearses Don't Hurry – Stephen Ransome
(Gerald Gregg)
12. Wife vs. Secretary/Friday to Monday –
Faith Baldwin (William Strohmer)
13. Death Wears a White Gardenia – Zelda Popkin
(Gerald Gregg)
14. The Doctor Died at Dusk – Geoffrey Homes
(William Strohmer)
15. The Golden Swan Murders –
Dorothy Cameron Disney (Gerald Gregg)·
16. The Unicorn Murders – Carter Dickson
(Gerald Gregg)
17. The Dead Can Tell – Helen Reilly (Gerald Gregg)
18. The Puzzle of the Silver Persian – Stuart Palmer
(Gerald Gregg)
19. Death over Sunday – James Francis Bonnell
(Gerald Gregg)
20. Tambay Gold – Samuel Hopkins Adams
(Gerald Gregg)
21. I Was a Nazi Flyer – Gottfried Leske
(Gerald Gregg)
22. Homicide Holiday – Rufus King (Gerald Gregg)
23. The Private Practive of Michael Shayne –
Brett Halliday (William Strohmer)
24. The Phantom of the Opera – Gaston Leroux
(Gerald Gregg)
25. Speak No Evil – Mignon G. Eberhart
(Gerald Gregg)
26. The Raft – Robert Trumbull (Gerald Gregg)
27. The Camera Clue – George Harmon Coxe
(Gerald Gregg)
28. The Mountain Cat Murders – Rex Stout
(Gerald Gregg)
29. Curtains for the Copper – Thomas Polsky
(Gerald Gregg)
30. Memo to a Firing Squad –
Frederick Hazlitt Brennan (Gerald Gregg)
31. The Fallen Sparrow – Dorothy B. Hughes
(George Frederiksen)
32. This Time for Keeps – John MacCormac
(Gerald Gregg)

1944
33. Dance of Death – Helen McCloy (Gerald Gregg)
34. Crime Hound – Mary Semple Scott
(Gerald Gregg)
35. The Cat Saw Murder – D. B. Olsen
(Gerald Gregg)
36. The Hammersmith Murders – David Frome
(Gerald Gregg)
37. Queen of the Flat-tops – Stanley Johnston
(George Frederiksen)
38. Liberty Laughs – Frances Cavanah & Ruth Weir
(Gerald Gregg)
39. Murder Challenges Valcour – Rufus King
(Gerald Gregg)
40. The Case of Jennie Brice –
Mary Roberts Rinehart (Gerald Gregg)
41. The Man Who Didn't Exist – Geoffrey Homes
(George Frederiksen)
42. Murder at Scandal House – Peter Hunt
(Gerald Gregg)
43. Midnight Sailing – Lawrence G. Blochman
(Gerald Gregg)

44. Reply Paid – H. F. Heard (Gerald Gregg)
45. Too Many Cooks – Rex Stout (Gerald Gregg)
46. The Boomerang Clue – Agatha Christie
(Gerald Gregg)
47. Keeper of the Keys – Earl Derr Biggers
(Gerald Gregg)
48. The Cross-Eyed Bear Murders –
Dorothy B. Hughes (Gerald Gregg)
49. The Feathered Serpent – Edgar Wallace
(Gerald Gregg)
50. The Iron Spiders – Baynard Kendrick
(Gerald Gregg)
51. While the Wind Howled – Audrey Gaines
(George Frederiksen)
52. The Body That Wasn't Uncle –
George Worthing Yates (Gerald Gregg)
53. Blood Money – Dashiell Hammett
(Gerald Gregg)
54. Harvard Has a Homicide – Timothy Fuller
(Gerald Gregg)
55. The D.A.'s Daughter – Herman Petersen
(George Frederiksen)
56. The Frightened Stiff – Kelley Roos (Gerald Gregg)
57. Murder at the White Cat –
Mary Roberts Rinehart (Gerald Gregg)
58. Murder for the Asking – George Harmon Coxe
(Gerald Gregg)
59. Turn on the Heat – A. A. Fair (Gerald Gregg)
60. Thirteen at Dinner – Agatha Christie
(Gerald Gregg)
61. The Clue of the Judas Tree – Leslie Ford
(Gerald Gregg)
62. The Strawstack Murders –
Dorothy Cameron Disney (Gerald Gregg)
63. Mourned on Sunday – Helen Reilly
(Gerald Gregg)
64. Blood on the Black Market – Brett Halliday
(Ben Hallam)
65. Scotland Yard Department of
Queer Complaints – Carter Dickson
(Gerald Gregg)
66. A Talent for Murder – Anna Mary Wells
(Gerald Gregg)
67. Hidden Ways – Frederic F. Van de Water
(Gerald Gregg)
68. Juliet Dies Twice – Lange Lewis (Gerald Gregg)

1945
69. Death from a Top Hat – Clayton Rawson
(Gerald Gregg)
70. The Red Bull – Rex Stout (Gerald Gregg)
71. Murder in the Mist – Zelda Popkin
(Gerald Gregg)
72. The Man in the Moonlight – Helen McCloy
(Gerald Gregg)
73. Week-end Marriage – Faith Baldwin
(Gerald Gregg)
74. The Murder That Had Everything –
Hulbert Footner (Gerald Gregg)
75. The Affair of the Scarlet Crab – Clifford Knight
(Gerald Gregg)
76. Death in the Back Seat –
Dorothy Cameron Disney (Ben Hallam)
77. G.I. Jokes – Lou Nielsen (Gerald Gregg)
78. Murder Wears a Mummer's Mask –
Brett Halliday (Gerald Gregg)
79. The Hornet's Nest – Bruno Fischer
(Gerald Gregg)

80. Prescription for Murder – Hannah Lees
(Gerald Gregg)
81. The Glass Triangle – George Harmon Coxe
(Gerald Gregg)
82. Curtains for the Editor – Thomas Polsky
(Gerald Gregg)
83. With This Ring – Mignon G. Eberhart
(Gerald Gregg)
84. Gold Comes in Bricks – A. A. Fair (Gerald Gregg)
85. The Savage Gentleman – Philip Wylie
(Gerald Gregg)
86. The Man Who Murdered Goliath –
Geoffrey Homes (Gerald Gregg)
87. Painted for the Kill – Lucy Cores (Gerald Gregg)
88. The Creeps – Anthony Abbot
(George Frederiksen)
89. Dell Book of Jokes –
Frances Cavanah & Ruth Weir (Gerald Gregg)
90. A Man Called Spade – Dashiell Hammett
(Gerald Gregg)
91. The Case of the Constant Suicides –
John Dickson Carr (George Frederiksen)
92. Suspense Stories – Alfred Hitchcock (ed.)
(David Konuro)
93. Beyond the Dark – Kieran Abbey
(George Frederiksen)
94. No Crime for a Lady – Zelda Popkin
(Gerald Gregg)
95. The Last Express – Baynard Kendrick
(Gerald Gregg)
96. Skeleton Key – Lenore Glen Offord
(Gerald Gregg)

1946
97. Trail Boss of Indian Beef – Harold Channing Wire
(Gerald Gregg)
99. Now, Voyager – Olive Higgins Prouty
(Gerald Gregg)
100. The So Blue Marble – Dorothy B. Hughes
(Gerald Gregg)

Bantam Books 1-100: 1945-1947

1945
1. Life on the Mississippi – Mark Twain
(H. L. Hoffman)
2. The Gift Horse – Frank Gruber
3. "Nevada" – Zane Grey (David Triggs)
4. Evidence of Things Seen – Elizabeth Daly
5. Scaramouche – Rafael Sabatini (Edgard Cirlin)
6. A Murder by Marriage – Robert George Dean
(Cal Diehl)
7. The Grapes of Wrath – John Steinbeck
8. The Great Gatsby – F. Scott Fitzgerald
(Edgard Cirlin)
9. Rogue Male – Geoffrey Household (Edgard Cirlir
10. South Moon Under – Marjorie Kinnan Rawlings
(Rafael Palacios)
11. Mr. and Mrs. Cugat – Isabel Scott Rorick
(Floyd A. Hardy)
12. Then There Were Three – Geoffrey Homes
(Clement)
13. The Last Time I Saw Paris – Elliot Paul
(after Maurice Utrillo)
14. Wind, Sand and Stars – Antoine de Saint-Exupéry
(Cal Diehl)

15. Meet Me in St. Louis – Sally Benson
(Edgard Cirlin)
16. The Town Cried Murder – Leslie Ford
(Robert Jonas)
17. Seventeen – Booth Tarkington (H. L. Hoffman)
18. What Makes Sammy Run? – Budd Schulberg
19. One More Spring – Robert Nathan
20. Oil for the Lamps of China –
Alice Tisdale Hobart (Rafael Palacios)

1946
21. Men, Women and Dogs – James Thurber
(after James Thurber)
24. Valiant is the Word for Carrie – Barry Benefield
25. Bugles in the Afternoon – Ernest Haycox
26. Net of Cobwebs – Elisabeth Sanxay Holding
27. Only Yesterday – Frederick Lewis Allen
(after Duffy)
28. Night in Bombay – Louis Bromfield
(Rafael Palacios)
29. Was It Murder? – James Hilton
30. Citizen Tom Paine – Howard Fast
(Charles Andres)
31. The Three Hostages – John Buchan (Bill English)
32. The Great Mouthpiece – Gene Fowler
33. The Prsioner of Zenda – Anthony Hope
(Edgard Cirlin)
34. First Come, First Kill – Francis Allan (Arnold)
35. My Dear Bella – Arthur Kober
(Thomas Ruzicka and Syd Hoff)
36. Trail Boss – Peter Dawson
37. Drawn and Quartered – Charles Addams
(Charles Addams)
38. Anything for a Quiet Life – A. A. Avery
(Bill English)
39. Long, Long Ago – Alexander Woolcott
(W. Cotton)
40. The Captain from Connecticut – C. S. Forester
(Cal Diehl)
41. David Harum – Edward Noyes Westcott
(Edgard Cirlin)
42. Road to Folly – Leslie Ford
43. The Lives of a Bengal Lancer – F. Yeats-Brown
(Cal Diehl)
44. The Cold Journey – Grace Zaring Stone
(Charles Andres)
45. A Bell for Adano – John Hersey (Cal Diehl)
46. Escape the Night – Mignon G. Eberhart
47. Home Ranch – Will James (Will James)
48. The Laughter of My Father – Carlos Bulosan
(Alexander)
49. The Amethyst Spectacles – Frances Crane
50. The Buffalo Box – Frank Gruber
51. Death in the Blackout – Anthony Gilbert
52. No Hands on the Clock – Geoffrey Homes
53. Nothing Can Rescue Me – Elizabeth Daly
54. The Love Letters – Chris Massie
55. Tutt and Mr. Tutt – Arthur Train
56. The Tonto Kid – Henry Herbert Knibbs
(Charles Andres)
57. Anything for a Laugh – Bennett Cerf
(O'Connor Barrett)
58. "Captains Courageous" – Rudyard Kipling
(Cal Diehl)
59. Wild Animals I Have Known –
Ernest Thompson Seton (Willig)
60. The Kennel Murder Case – S. S. Van Dine
61. The Bantam Concise Dictionary

62. Dead Center – Mary Collins
63. Green Mansions – W.H. Hudson
64. Harriet – Elizabeth Jenkins
65. South Wind – Norman Douglas
    (I.N. Steinberg)
66. She Loves Me Not – Edward Hope (Alexander)
67. The Bruiser – Jim Tully (Charles Andres)
68. Guns from Powder Valley – Peter Field
69. The Grandmothers – Glenway Wescott
    (Cal Diehl)
70. Lay That Pistol Down – Richard Powell
71. Mountain Meadow – John Buchan
72. No Bones About It – Ruth Sawtell Wallis
    (H.L. Hoffman)
73. The Last of the Plainsmen – Zane Grey
74. Halo in Blood – John Evans

1947

75. Cannery Row – John Steinbeck (Lester Kohs)
76. Drink to Yesterday – Manning Coles
77. Pistol Passport – Eugene Cunningham
78. Deadly Nightshade – Elizabeth Daly
79. A Tree Grows in Brooklyn – Betty Smith
80. False to Any Man – Leslie Ford (Lester Kohs)
81. Puzzles, Quizzes and Games –
    Edith Young & Phyllis Fraser
82. Ride the Man Down – Luke Short
83. Up Front – Bill Mauldin (Bill Mauldin)
84. The World, The Flesh, and Father Smith –
    Bruce Marshall (Lester Kohs)
85. Death at the Door – Anthony Gilbert
    (Lester Kohs)
86. Border Roundup – Allan R. Bosworth
    (Charles Andres)
87. Apartment in Athens – Glenway Westcott
    (Lester Kohs)
88. Trigger Kid – Bennett Foster
89. Finders Keepers – Geoffrey Homes
90. The Uninvited – Dorothy Macardle
91. The 17th Letter – Dorothy Cameron Disney
92. My Life and Hard Times – James Thurber
    (after James Thurber)
93. Dagger of the Mind – Kenneth Fearing
    (Paul Galdone)
94. The Crimson Horseshoe – Peter Dawson
95. Assignment Without Glory – Marcos Spinelli
96. The Scarab Murder Case – S.S. Van Dine
97. Swamp Water – Vereen Bell (Paul Galdone)
98. Cry Wolf – Marjorie Carleton (Paul Galdone)
99. Comanche Chaser – Dane Coolidge
    (Charles Andres)
100. The Cautious Amorist – Norman Lindsay
    (Van Kaufman)

Signet Books 660-759: 1948-1949

1948

660. 100 American Poems – Selden Rodman (ed.)
    (Robert Jonas)
661. Tragic Ground – Erskine Caldwell (Robert Jonas)
662. Invitation to the Waltz – Rosamond Lehman
663. As Good as Dead – Thomas B. Dewey
    (Robert Jonas)
664. Portrait of the Artist as a Young Man –
    James Joyce (Robert Jonas)
665. Strange Fruit – Lillian Smith (Robert Jonas)
666. The Valley of Hunted Men – Paul Evan Lehman
667. The Pinkerton Case Book – Alan Hynd
    (Robert Jonas)
668. The Dim View – Basil Heatter (T.V.)
669. The Caballero – Johnston McCulley
670. They Shoot Horses, Don't They? –
    Horace McCoy (T.V.)
671. Darkness at Noon – Arthur Koestler
    (Robert Jonas)
672. Cattle Kingdom – Alan LeMay
673. Sons of the Saddle – William MacLeod Raine
674. Mine Own Executioner – Nigel Balchin
    (Robert Jonas)
675. About the Kinsey Report –
    Donald P. Geddes & Enid Curie (ed.)
    (Robert Jonas)
676. Ariane – Claude Anet (T.V.)
677. Guilty Bystander – Wade Miller (Robert Jonas)
678. The Signet Crossword Puzzle Book –
    Albert M. Moorehead (Robert Jonas)
679. Laramie Rides Alone – Will Ermine (Rob-Jon)
680. Past All Dishonor – James M. Cain (T.V.)
681. Contract Bridge for Everyone – Ely Culbertson
    (Robert Jonas)
682. Blood of the West – Paul Evan Lehman
    (Robert Jonas)
683. The Lost Weekend – Charles Jackson (T.V.)
684. Slay the Murderer – Hugh Holman
    (Robert Jonas)
685. Lobo Law – Will Ermine (Robert Jonas)
686. A House in the Uplands – Erskine Caldwell
    (Robert Jonas)
687. Shore Leave – Frederic Wakeman (T.V.)
688. High Pockets – Herbert Shapiro
689. The Silver Tombstone – Frank Gruber
    (Robert Jonas)
690. No Pockets in a Shroud – Horace McCoy (T.V.)
691. All the Girls We Loved – Prudencio de Pereda
692. The Old Man – William Faulkner (Robert Jonas)
693. I Love You, I Love You, I Love You –
    Ludwig Bemelmans
694. Lawless Range – Charles N. Heckelman
695. Fatal Step – Wade Miller
696. The Snake Pit – Mary Jane Ward
697. Look Homeward, Angel – Thomas Wolfe
698. Black Sombrero – William Colt MacDonald
699. I, the Jury – Mickey Spillane (Lou Kimmel)

1949

700. Other Voices, Other Rooms – Truman Capote
    (Robert Jonas)
701. Finnley Wren – Philip Wylie
702. The Vehement Flame – Ludwig Lewisohn
703. Find My Killer – Manly Wade Wellman
704. Gold of Smoky Mesa – Johnston McCulley
705. A Woman in the House – Erskine Caldwell

706. Last of the Conquerors – William Gardner Smith (James Avati)
707. The Honest Dealer – Frank Gruber (Robert Jonas)
708. The Texan – Herbert Shapiro
709. Deadlier than the Male – James E. Gunn
710. The Street – Ann Petry (Robert Jonas)
711. Love in Dishevelment – David Greenhood
712. The Fighting Tenderfoot – William MacLeod Raine
713. Murder as a Fine Art – Francis Bonnamy (James Avati)
714. The Gilded Hearse – Charles O. Gorham (James Avati)
715. The Fall of Valor – Charles Jackson
716. We Were Strangers – Robert Sylvester (James Avati)
717. A Son of Arizona – Charles Alden Seltzer
718. Another Man's Poison – Hugh Holman
719. Baseball for Everyone – Joe DiMaggio
720. The Butterfly – James M. Cain
721. Night of Flame – Warren Desmond
722. Uneasy Street – Wade Miller (James Avati)
723. The Crimson Quirt – William Colt MacDonald
724. The Golden Sleep – Vivian Connell (James Avati)
725. At Heaven's Gate – Robert Penn Warren
726. The Whispering Master – Frank Gruber (Robert Jonas)
727. Trigger Justice – Leslie Ernenwein
728. Lona Hanson – Thomas Savage
729. Stranger in Town – Howard Hunt
730. The Body in the Bed – Bill S. Ballinger
731. Montana Man – Paul Evan Lehman
732. The Sure Hand of God – Erskine Caldwell (James Avati)
733. Crime and Punishment – Fyodor Dostoyevski
734. Meet the Girls! – James T. Farrell (James Avati)

735. Everybody Slept Here – Elliot Arnold (James Avati)
736. Draw the Curtain Close – Thomas B. Dewey
737. Brave in the Saddle – Will Ermine
738. Nightmare Alley – William Lindsay Gresham (James Avati)
739. Beyond the Forest – Stuart Engstrand (James Avati)
740. Whistling Lead – Eugene Cunningham
741. Life in a Putty Knife Factory – H. Allen Smith
742. Kill or Cure – William Francis
743. Intruder in the Dust – William Faulkner (James Avati)
744. The Christian Demand for Social Justice – Bishop Scarlett (Robert Jonas)
745. The Ox-Bow Incident – Walter Van Tilburg Clark
746. Human Destiny – Pierre Lecomte du Noüy (Robert Jonas)
747. Walden – Henry David Thoreau
748. Mistress Glory – Susan Morley (James Avati)
749. Forever Wilt Thou Love – Ludwig Lewisohn (James Avati)
750. Devil in the Flesh – Raymond Radiguet (James Avati)
751. Love Without Fear – Eustace Chesser, M.D. (Robert Jonas)
752. The Future Mr. Dolan – Charles Gorham (James Avati)
753. The Gamecock Murders – Frank Gruber
754. Kiss Tomorrow Goodbye – Horace McCoy (James Avati)
755. An American Tragedy – Theodore Dreiser (James Avati)
756. If He Hollers Let Him Go – Chester Himes
757. Brother of the Cheyennes – Max Brand
758. Clattering Hoofs – William MacLeod Raine
759. Everybody Does It/The Embezzler – James M. Cain (Bill Gregg)

From Amati to Zuckerberg

CHARLES ANDRES

Rudolph Belarski

EARLE BERGEY · Carl Bobertz · Cardiff

Cirlin · CLEMENT · Darcy · CAL DIEHL · Dunham

Bill English · Fickson · Fiedler · frye · HG · Getz

Glygan · BILL GILLIES

GRESSLEY · hawkins · hoffman · M. Hooks · Hulings

jonas · casey jones · Victor Kalin · van Kidder

Kinmel · Kohs · Kossin · LÁSZLÓ · Loew

MANSO · Marchetti · John Alan Maxwell

MORGAN · McConnell · palacios

PAUL · Bruyé · powers · ESE · A. Leslie Ross · Salter

Saunders · Schaare · Shoyer · R. SKEMP

Stahl · TRIGGS · T. V. Woods · Zuckerberg

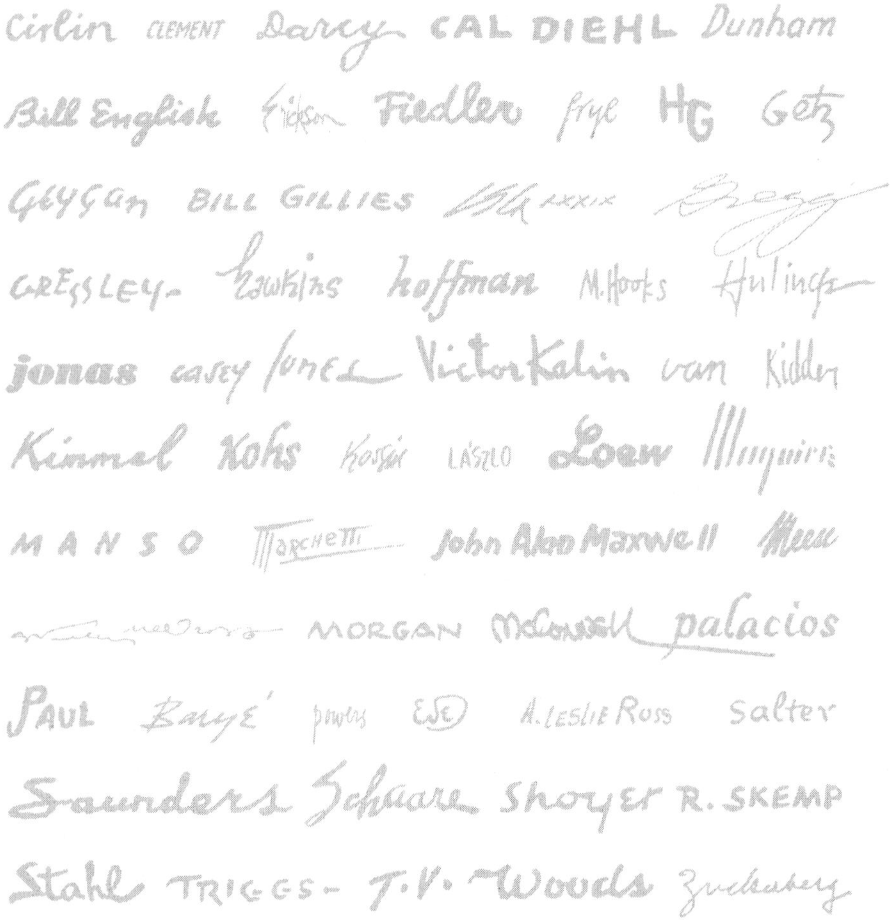

Who's Who in Cover Art

Robert K. ABBETT

Born January 5, 1926 in Hammond, Indiana; studied at Purdue and the University of Missouri and later took night classes at the Academy of Fine Art in Chicago.

Abbett began his career as a writer. He later worked as an illustrator at the Alexander Chaite Studios in New York, where he made magazine illustrations for *True*, *Argosy*, *Redbook*, *This Week*, *Reader's Digest* and *Zane Grey's Western Magazine*.

He began producing paperback covers in the late '50s. His first assignments were for Fawcett and he also drew approximately 100 covers for Bantam, 50 each for Ballantine, Pocket Books, Cardinal Editions and Dell, and about 20 for Signet.

Abbett worked in acrylics, tempera and, occasionally, in oils.

He is now a "fine" artist.

ALEXANDER

Produced humorous covers for Bantam (such as Bantam 66, *She Loves Me Not*) during Gobin Stair's tenure as art director. He also drew endpapers for Bantams 42, 48, 52, 66, 81 and 89.

Charles J. ANDRES

Born September 6, 1913 in Hastings-on-Hudson, New York; was a student under George Bridgman, Charles S. Chapman and Thomas Fogarty at the Phoenix Institute of Art, privately with Frank Reilly, between 1935 and 1938 at the Art Students League of New York and between 1936 and 1940 under Harvey Dunn at the Grand Central School of Art (also in New York).

CHARLES ANDRES

Late in 1945, Andres received his first paperback assignment from Gobin Stair and produced a cover painting for Bantam 30, *Citizen Tom Paine* (see page 174 for a color reproduction). In 1946 and 1947, he produced eight more Bantam covers; the last was for *Hot Leather*, which was published in 1948. His cover painting for Eagle Book E3, *Duchess Hotspur*, was never used. In addition to his paperback work, Andres also illustrated dustjackets for hardcover editions of Zane Grey's novels.

He worked in oils and acrylics.

In 1981, three of Andres' original paintings were displayed in the exhibit "Paperbacks, U.S.A." in The Hague, Holland.

David ATTIE

Born November 30, 1920 in Brooklyn, New York; studied at the Kansas City Art Institute and at the Cooper Union for Advancement of Science and Art in New York.

Attie produced only a small number of paperback covers: four for Bantam in 1947 and 1948 (including Bantams 120, *Secret Beyond the Door*, and 450, *Moonlit Voyage*) and a few more for Dell (1950) and Berkley (1950-1954).

In 1958, Attie did two photographic covers for Dell; he currently works as a photographer.

James AVATI

Avati's colleagues consider him the master of paperback cover art. His finest period was from 1949 to 1955, when he produced a wealth of brooding, emotionally-charged paintings for Signet Books.

Born in December, 1912 in Bloomfield, New Jersey; he studied architecture and archaeology at Princeton University.

Living in New York in the '30s, Avati supported

himself by working at various jobs and was nick-named "Brother Brush;" he ultimately built up a reputation as a designer of display windows for Fifth Avenue department stores. After his marriage to Jane Hamill and the birth of their first child, Avati was called up for military service during World War II. He spent 3½ years in the Army, serving as a radio operator in Belgium, Holland and elsewhere in Europe; in Biarritz, he gave art lessons for several months.

When he returned to America, Avati settled in Red Bank, New Jersey and decided to go to work as a commercial artist. He did illustrations for magazines such as *McCall's*, *Collier's* and *Ladies' Home Journal*, but soon found such assignments clichéd and took a job as a carpenter instead.

In 1948, agent Seymour Thompson put Avati in touch with Kurt Enoch at the New American Library; the result was Avati's first paperback cover: Signet 706, *Last of the Conquerors* (see page 80). Enoch and art director John Legakes were so impressed with Avati's style that they assigned him to produce dozens of additional Signet covers (see pages 79 and 80), including new covers for new printings of books whose original covers had been illustrated by Robert Jonas (see example on page 175). In 1949 and 1950, he also made several covers for art director Don Gelb at Bantam Books (such as Bantam 766, *Jassy*, in 1950).

An Avati "school" of paperback art quickly sprang into being. Illustrators including George Erickson, Mike Hooks, Cardiff, Stanley Meltzoff, Tom Dunn and Rudy Nappi all began to work in the dark Avati style. The flood of imitators finally became so heavy that Avati himself wound up developing a new and different approach to cover painting.

At one point, Kurt Enoch offered him the position of art director at Signet, but Avati felt that would entail too much work and he turned Enoch down. He did, however, serve for a while as consulting art director.

Many of the images on Avati's covers came from the films he remembered seeing as a boy. He suggests today that this may be one reason why his work was so popular among members of his own generation, who shared his experience of those films.

Looking back on this Signet period, his "Golden Age," Avati tends to underestimate his own talent: he claims that his success was, rather, due to a lucky combination of naïveté, despair and ambition. He dreamt of becoming a fine artist, but felt that his technique was inadequate. Like many others, his intention was to use paperback work as a sort of art school.

Avati: cover for Signet 1260, *The Farm* (1955)

He painted from photographs which he took himself, originally hiring models from the Silver Studios in New York and later taking pictures of ordinary people, nonprofessionals. He even used himself as a model on occasion.

His paintings were done in oil on prepared hardboard. Finished works were generally sized about 90 cm × 120 cm (35″ × 47″), with the head of the main figure roughly 6 cm (2½″) in diameter.

A new world of stylistic possibilities opened up for Avati when, in 1962, he again did a cover for Bantam Books. Leonard Leone was art director at Bantam by that time, and he encouraged Avati to stop doing fully-detailed paintings and to concentrate only on essentials. A man and a woman, a chair, the corner of a bed: those were the important elements, and the rest of the cover could remain white or could be used for lettering.

Reproduction and printing techniques were more advanced at Bantam, and this too was an attraction; after more than a dozen years at Signet, Avati now began working regularly for Bantam. He continued working for Leone through the '60s, and was also able to provide covers for art

Avati: 1952, 1956, 1957

director Barbara Bertoli at Avon Books.

Today, his cover paintings are done primarily for Dell and Avon.

His favorite covers are those he did for *The Farm* (Signet D1260), *An American Tragedy* (Signet 755) and *The Woman of Rome* (Signet S844). He calls his current work "phony." "I've got the skill down pat, now," he says, "and I can use it like a juggler. But it's not a part of me anymore; I don't have any emotional investment in it."

Leonard Leone says that if a second flood should come and he should get to play a modern Noah and preserve one example of everything of importance from destruction, he would pick James Avati, who he calls "an artist's artist," to represent cover art. About Avati's technique he says: "He knows you can make a picture extremely realistic if you paint it five feet tall—then, when you reduce it, everything becomes much sharper. He always brought in these enormous paintings. He also knows that when you look at someone, you always focus on one particular part of them, usually their eyes. That means that the eyes or the head have to be drawn very sharply. That's where the suggestion of clarity is, the rest of the figure doesn't need to be clear at all."

But Avati himself says he has never thought about things like that. To him, the atmosphere and the relationship between the people in the image have always been the most important considerations.

In the early '50s, Avati divorced Jane Hamill and remarried. He now lives separated from his second wife, Linda. Leigh, the woman he calls "my greatest love," died in 1978 aged 24.

In 1981, four of Avati's original paintings and 70 of his paperback covers were displayed in the exhibition "Paperbacks, U.S.A." in The Hague, Holland.

Cover artist Stanley Meltzoff sums up James Avati in this way: "Avati stands alone, not only as the great pioneer, but also as the best of us all, right up to today. He is the only one who counts—everyone else just passed through."

Paul BACON

Graphic designer. Produced many covers for Pocket Books and Cardinal Editions beginning in 1956.

James E. BAMA

Born April 28, 1926 in New York; studied for four years under Frank Reilly at the High School of Music and Art and Design and for three years at the Art Students League, both in New York.

He did his first book cover (Avon 267, *A Bullet for Billy the Kid*) in 1950, shortly after finishing school, and also did magazine illustrations for *The Saturday Evening Post*, *Argosy* and *Reader's Digest*. Between 1955 and 1971 he produced at least 450 covers for Bantam Books. He also painted several more covers for Avon, about 50 for Signet and 4 for Berkley.

In the '60s, he provided 62 enthusiastically-received covers for Bantam's Doc Savage series.

His paperback work was done exclusively in oils.

Since 1971, Bama has been a fine artist. He specializes in scenes of the American West, many of which have been reproduced in a volume titled *The Western Art of James Bama*. According to Leonard Leone, his art director at Bantam, Bama is "the most realistic painter in the world today. If there hadn't already been an Andrew Wyeth, *he* might have been Andrew Wyeth."

Frederick E. BANBERY

Illustrator, originally from England. He did covers for Pocket Books between 1948 and 1958; an example is Pocket Books 903, *Miracle on 34th Street*, released in September, 1952.

He worked mainly in watercolors.

Bacon: 1955, 1956

Bernard BARTON

Born in New York City; his childhood ambition was to replace Babe Ruth in the Yankee outfield. He made sidewalk drawings for 25 cents apiece, later advancing to commercial art and then to drawing posters for the Army Signal Corps during his hitch in the service. Afterwards, his work appeared in magazines and in advertising illustrations.

He made about five cover drawings for Bantam in 1948 and 1949, including Bantam 314, *The Yellow Room*; he did covers for Avon and Popular Library between 1949 and 1952 and for Ace between 1953 and 1958.

His work is signed "Barton."

Harry BARTON

Painted several covers for Pocket Books and Dell around 1950.

BARYE

see *Barye PHILLIPS*

Warren BAUMGARTER

Painted several covers for Pocket Books in 1950 and 1951.

Beall: 1948, 1951

C.C. BEALL

Produced covers for Bantam Books, Pocket Books and Cardinal Editions between 1948 and 1951.

Sheilah BECKETT

Made 10 covers for Dell between 1952 and 1955.

Belarski: 1949, 1952

Rudolph BELARSKI

Born March 27, 1900. At 12 years of age, Rudy Belarski was working in a Dupont, Pennsylvania coal-processing plant as a slate picker. A picture he drew on a white-washed wall near the mine entrance was seen by one of his bosses, who liked it so much that he gave young Rudy the job of painting safety posters for the company. With no time available for a formal education, Belarski taught himself from books on art, history, literature and philosophy; later, aged 21, he went to New York and was able to put himself though the Pratt Institute in Brooklyn by working as a waiter, sign painter, portraitist and private art teacher. While at Pratt, he won a number of prizes for poster and commercial art and figure drawing.

Three years after graduation, he was invited back to Pratt to teach commercial art. Meanwhile, he was doing a great deal of illustration work as a freelancer.

His first cover illustrations were done in the '30s, for pulp magazines such as *Western Round-Up*, *Terence X. O'Leary's War Birds*, *Wings*, *The Phantom Detective*, *RAF Aces*, *Thrilling Detective*, *Popular Detective*, *Mystery Book*, *Detective Novel* and *Black Book Detective*, many of which were published by Ned Pine's Pines Publications.

Ned Pines founded a paperback firm, Popular Library, in 1942, but it was not until 1948 that Belarski produced his first paperback cover, for Popular Library 154 *(The Case of the Crumpled Knave)*. Subsequently, several of his pulp covers were recycled as paperback covers, appearing on, for example, Popular Library 188 *(The Yellow Overcoat)*, 227 *(The Illustrious Corpse*; see page 171), 293 *(The Hangman's Whip)*, 302 *(The Old Battle Ax*; see page 170) and 382 *(Dark Threat)*. In all, some 50 Belarski paintings appeared on Popular Library covers by 1952, and Belarski's style strongly influenced the look of the entire line, as well as the work of Rafael DeSoto, George Rozen and other cover artists.

After 1952, Belarski began doing covers for several digests, including *Future Science Fiction* and *Venus Books*. He also drew the cover for Pocket Books 900, *Scirocco*.

In 1957, he joined the staff of the Famous Artists School in Westport, Connecticut.

tic; after painting he often used a razor blade to create special effects.

One of his original Gothic paintings was displayed in the 1981 exhibition "Paperbacks, U.S.A." in The Hague, Holland.

Bergey: 1950, 1952

Earle K. BERGEY

Began his career in the 1940s, producing cover illustrations for pulp magazines, especially for science-fiction and fantasy pulps: *Thrilling Wonder Stories, Startling Stories, Captain Future, Space Science Fiction*, even *Popular Love*. He specialized in women waering futuristic iron-clad bras and little else.

Like Rudolph Belarski, Bergey moved from the pulps to Popular Library. Between 1948 and 1952 he did a total of 16 covers for that firm, including the famous "nipple cover," number 147 *(The Private Life of Helen of Troy)* and numbers 221 *(Gentlemen Prefer Blondes)* and 273 *(The Big Eye)*. After leaving Popular Library, he painted a few covers for Pocket Books, such as number 886, *The Case of the Fan-Dancer's Horse* (1952).

Geoffrey BIGGS

Illustrated several covers for Bantam Books between 1947 and 1949; his best-known, in 1948, was for Bantam 404, *Hiroshima* (see page 178).

Charles BINGER

Born in England, Binger produced many covers for Bantam Books in 1953 and 1954. From 1955 through 1960 he did cover work for Avon, Ballantine, Cardinal Editions, Perma Books and Pocket Books.

Herman E. BISCHOFF

Did a few covers for Bantam Books in 1949 and 1950, such as number 320, *As Long As I Live* (1949).

Bennett: 1950, 1952

Harry BENNETT

Born in the Roaring '20s in Lewisboro, New York; studied in Chicago at the American Institute of Art and the American Academy of Art.

Starting around 1950, Bennett produced some 650 paperback covers for Fawcett, plus 475 for Pocket Books, 250 for Berkley, 65 for Dell and five each for Ace and Ballantine. In 1952, he drew the cover for Ballantine 1, *Executive Suite*.

Another first claimed by Bennett is that his 1960 cover for Mary Stewart's *Thunder on the Right* was the first Gothic cover, but Lou Marchetti makes the identical claim for his own 1960 cover for *Thunder Heights* and, in fact, valid Gothic covers had appeared at least nine years earlier anyway.

Bennett's Gothic covers are realistic; his fantasy covers, on the other hand, are impressionis-

Bob BLANCHARD
Art director for Ballantine Books during the years 1953-1962; he illustrated 16 Ballantine covers himself in that period, beginning with number 284K, *After the Rain*.

Wayne BLICKENSTAFF
After Sol Immerman gave him his first paperback assignment for Pocket Books, he produced covers for that firm and for Pyramid during the '50s.

Bobertz: 1955, 1951

Carl BOBERTZ
Made about 20 covers for Dell and, in 1952, also drew for Pocket Books and Signet.

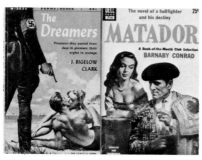

Borack: 1953

Stanley BORACK
Studied at the Art Students League of New York under Frank Reilly.

In 1952 and 1953 he worked for *Zane Grey's Western Magazine*; from 1953 through 1955 he painted about 50 paperback covers for Dell; between 1952 and 1957 he also provided covers for Pocket Books, Perma Books and the Lion Library.

Walter BROOKS
Born June 25, 1921 in Glasgow, Scotland; studied with George Salter at the Cooper Union for Advancement of Science and Art and took further courses at the New School for Social Research and the Art Students League of New York.

Brooks was art director of the Dell Books Division of Western Printing from 1952 to 1961; during this period he not only designed Dell paperbacks but executed some 100 covers himself. His first experience as a cover artist came much earlier, though, when he drew about six covers for Avon Books in 1941. After leaving Dell he produced more covers for Avon (1963-1965), and for Pocket Books (1962-1968) and Penguin Books (1968-1976) as well.

His work, which could vary from realistic (such as *History of Mexico and Peru* for Pocket Books) to stylized (such as Dell D118, *Really the Blues*), was done with acrylics and, often, woodcuts.

In addition to book covers, Brooks has also designed advertisements, film posters, magazines and postage stamps.

Al BRULÉ
Illustrated covers for Bantam Books (1948-1950) and Dell (1950-1957).

BUSONI
Cover artist for Penguin Books in 1942 and 1943.

CARDIFF
An illustrator who painted Avati-like covers for Signet and Perma Books between 1952 and 1955.

Frank CAZORELLI
Did covers for Signet and Dell in 1953 and 1954.

Ernest CHIRIAKA
Born in 1920; studied at the Art Students League and the Grand Central School of Art, both in New York.

He began his career as an illustrator for magazines like *The Saturday Evening Post*, *Esquire* and *Cosmopolitan*. Later, he moved to the West Coast and painted portraits of movie stars. In the early '50s, he provided paperback covers for Pocket Books and Cardinal Editions.

He currently lives in New York and specializes in paintings of Western scenes.

Cirlin: 1945, 1946

Cirlin

Edgard CIRLIN

Born January 16, 1913 in Montreal, Canada; Cirlin's family moved to Detroit when he was young, and he attended Cass Technical High School there. After graduation, he studied at a Detroit art school for a year, on a scholarship. Following a period of travel back and forth between Detroit and Florida, he took night classes under George Salter at the Cooper Union for Advancement of Science and Art, and graduated around 1942.

Cirlin began his career in commercial art as a freelance sign painter, working both at his Greenwich Village house and in a studio in East 35th Street which he shared with Lester Kohs. In 1945 and 1946, his circle of friends included Salter, Kohs, Riki Levinson, Philip Grushkin, Rafael Palacios, George Hornby and Gobin Stair. Stair was art director at Bantam Books at this time, and some of the others worked on cover illustrations for Bantam and Penguin Books. Cirlin's first paperback assignment was to do a cover for Bantam 5, *Scaramouche*. Although he had the ability to draw quite well, he was then using a rather clumsy drawing style which he had picked up from George Salter.

According to designer and publisher George Hornby: "He was the best calligrapher in America, but you never knew if he would deliver on time. I often had to go around there at six in the morning, practically with a pistol pointed at his head, to get him to finish things for me."

Rafael Palacios remembers: "One time Cirlin had to do a cover for a Simon & Schuster book called *Caesar and Christ*. He lettered the title beautifully, in lovely big Roman capitals, in three lines over the entire cover: *Caesar - and - Christ*. Then he had to sign it, and he put his name very small in the middle of the cover, so it read: *Caesar - Cirlin - and - Christ*! And then there's the story about why he never had to go into the Army during the war: when he was called up and they asked him what he did for a living, he said he made jackets; they thought he meant *work* jackets and, since the manufacture of work clothing was considered essential, they didn't induct him!"

Cirlin taught at Cooper Union until about 1950. In 1953 he moved out to the Los Angeles area; he was the art director for UCLA for a time, did graphic work for motorcycle and aviation magazines, designed a series of albums for the Audio Books Company and worked on "Designer and the Printing Press," a series outlining the history of typography.

He died in 1973.

CLEMENT

Produced covers for Bantam Books in 1945 and 1946.

L. A. CORRADO

Produced covers for Avon Books in 1945 and 1946.

Mel CRAIR

Studied under Frank Reilly at the Art Students League of New York, and was "discovered" there by art director Sol Immerman. Between 1954 and 1963 he drew approximately 30 paperback covers for Pocket Books, Berkley Books and Ballantine Books.

Bernard D'ANDREA

Originally a magazine illustrator, especially for *The Saturday Evening Post*. He did covers for Ace, Avon, Ballantine, Bantam, Fawcett and Pocket Books between 1948 and 1950.

DARCY

Probably a pseudonym. He (or she) produced covers for Avon, Dell, Perma Books and Pocket Books during the late '50s.

Gilbert DARLING

Born in New Zealand; studied at the California School of Fine Arts. He became a magazine illustrator and, as of 1948, also did work for the paperbacks. His first cover assignment for Bantam was number 301, *Headlined for Murder*. In 1951 he painted a single cover for Dell, for the mystery *What a Body!* (Dell 483; see page xi).

Rafael M. DESOTO

Born February 18, 1904 in Puerto Rico; studied at the Art Students League of New York.

He began doing paperback covers in 1953; his first was for Popular Library 543, *The Flesh and the Spirit*, and one of his favorites was for Popular Library 663, *Fast and Loose* (1955). He also drew covers for Ace, Dell, Lion, Pocket Books and Signet.

DeSoto worked in tempera, acrylics and oils.

He stopped doing paperback work in 1960. He now lives and paints in East Patchogue, New York.

Diehl: 1946

Cal G. DIEHL

Born in Philadelphia; studied there at the Pennsylvania Museum School of Industrial Art and the Spring Garden Institute School of Technology.

He received his first cover assignment, for Bantam 6 *(A Murder by Marriage)*, at the recommendation of his friend Charles Andres, then did further covers for Bantam while Gobin Stair was art director. For some of these covers, he did the lettering himself (see example on page 174).

He worked in tempera and watercolors.

After about 1950, Diehl stopped doing cover illustrations. He became a graphic designer and art director for several firms, and today he is a fine artist.

Bob DOARES

Magazine illustrator who made many paperback covers for Bantam Books between 1948 and 1950. Perhaps as a result of his three years in New Mexico and Arizona, Doares specialized in covers for Westerns such as *Trail South from Powder Valley* (Bantam 201), *The Tenderfoot* (202) and *Sugarfoot* (203). He also did covers for mysteries.

Stevan DOHANOS

Born May 18, 1907 in Lorain, Ohio; studied at the Cleveland School of Art.

Noted illustrator for *The Saturday Evening Post*, who provided covers for Bantam Books' two *Post* anthologies (Bantam 116 in 1947 and Bantam 555 in 1948).

Dohanos is now closely connected with the Famous Artists School in Westport, Connecticut.

Tom DUNN

Born February 10, 1922 near Gravesend Bay, New York and moved with his family at the age of 5 to Belford, a nearby coast town where he still lives today; studied at Villanova University from 1939 until America entered World War II, when he joined the Marines. On Iwo Jima, a general saw some of Dunn's sketches and assigned him to record his impressions of combat in a series of drawings. In 1948, he completed his formal education at Pratt Institute in Brooklyn.

He began his career doing advertising and television work in New York. Between 1951 and 1957 he provided cover paintings for Signet Books, then Pocket Books (where he was the firm's first full-time cover artist, filling the position which James Avati held at the New American Library and receiving a salary commensurate with the importance of his role), then Perma

Dunn: 1951, 1956

Books and then, finally, Cardinal Editions; along the way, he also did four cover designs for Dell.

In addition to his paperback work, Dunn has also painted many seascapes.

Bill EDWARDS
Drew covers for Bantam and other publishers, beginning in 1956. His cover for *The Wayward Bus* in the early '60s introduced a period in which much white was used on paperback covers.

Edmund A. EMSHWILLER
Ed Emsh, or Emshler, as he often calls himself, is a noted illustrator for science-fiction digests. Since his first cover in 1950, for *Galaxy*, he has worked for *Planet Stories, Space Stories, Startling Stories* and others.

Around 1955 he also did some science-fiction illustrations for Gold Medal, Ballantine and several other paperback firms.

Bill ENGLISH
Member of the Book Jacket Designers Guild. He worked primarily for hardcover publishers, but also designed some of the early Bantam covers.

Erickson: 1955, 1952

George T. ERICKSON
Born January 27, 1924 in Bridgeport, Connecticut; studied for seven years at the Whitney School of Art in New Haven, Connecticut and for two years at the Pennsylvania Academy of Fine Arts.

His first paperback cover was for Avon 412, *Waiting for Willy*; he produced some 30 covers for Avon in 1950 and 1951. Because he felt that

Avon's fee of $150 per cover was insufficient, Erickson went to work for Signet Books, where he received $400 per cover; he did about 35 covers for Signet between 1951 and 1954 and simultaneously worked for Pocket Books (about 12 covers in 1951 and 1952), Bantam Books (in 1952), Perma Books (about 50 covers between 1952 and 1954), Popular Library (about 8 covers in 1955), Lion, Fawcett and Dell.

His personal favorites are *Spider in the Cup, The Tattooed Heart* and *The Money Song* (all for Signet), and *Old Hell, Boy Gang, Celluloid Jungle* and *Down and Out in Paris and London* (all for Perma Books).

Jaro FABRY
Cartoonist, known for his 1947 covers for Pocket Books by Thorne Smith.

Jack FARAGASSO
Born January 23, 1929 in Brooklyn, New York; studied under Frank Reilly from 1949 through 1953 at the Art Students League of New York.

Faragasso illustrated his first paperback cover in 1952; since then he has worked for Pocket Books, Popular Library, Midwood, Berkley and Signet.

He painted in oils, tempera and watercolors, and has also produced photographic covers. He is the author of *The Student Guide to Painting in Oils*, published in 1979.

FIEDLER
Did covers for Popular Library in 1946 and 1947, using a style similar to that of H.L. Hoffman and Gerald Gregg.

Robert FINK
Drew covers for Bantam Books around 1950 and for Popular Library around 1952. His father was Denham Fink, an illustrator who was productive in the '20s and '30s.

John J. FLOHERTY, Jr.
Born in 1907 in New York City; studied at Columbia University, the Art Students League of New York and the Grand Central School of Art.

In 1942, Floherty illustrated publicity material for the Coast Guard; he later worked as a magazine artist, and began doing covers for Gold Medal Books in 1953.

Griffith FOXLEY
Art director for the magazine *Sports*; one cover produced for that magazine was also used as a paperback cover by Bantam. Between 1949 and 1954, Foxley made about 40 covers for Dell.

Gilbert FULLINGTON

Did covers for Bantam mysteries between 1948 and 1950; his first was for Bantam 304, *The Problem of the Wire Cage*.

Paul GALDONE

Drew several covers and endpapers for Bantam Books in 1947 and for Pocket Books in 1949.

William GEORGE

Produced illustrations for *Zane Grey's Western Magazine* in 1952 and 38 paperback covers for Dell between 1953 and 1957; also did several covers for Pocket Books.

Getz: 1947

Arthur GETZ

Born May 17, 1913 in Passaic, New Jersey; studied at the Pratt Institute in Brooklyn until 1934.

In 1935, Getz established his own studio in New York City. He produced more than 200 cover drawings for *The New Yorker* and, in 1946 and 1947, three paperback covers for Pen-

guin: numbers 606 *(A Rope of Sand)*, 633 *(Great Son)* and 635 *(Blood on Lake Louisa)*. The paperback assignments came his way through his friend, Robert Jonas.

Getz is also known as a muralist, painter and art teacher.

George GEYGAN

Did covers for Dell, Bantam and Ballantine between 1953 and 1955.

F. Kenwood GILES

Made 12 covers for Dell between 1948 and 1950; the first was for Dell 255, *Enchanted Oasis*.

Denver L. GILLEN

Born in 1914 in Vancouver, Canada; studied under Frederick Horsman Varley in Vancouver.

Worked in the Hudson Bay Company's art department, then became a freelance magazine illustrator, drew cartoons for *Esquire* in the '30s and '40s and produced covers for the *Reader's Digest*.

In 1948 and 1949, Gillen did dramatic/realistic and humorous paperback covers for Bantam Books; his first was for Bantam 550, *Out of My Trunk* (see page 172). He also made six covers for Dell: the first was for Dell 635, *To Wake the Dead*, and a later one (for Dell 819, *The Amazing Adventures of Father Brown*) was reprinted many times.

Bill GILLIES

Drew several mystery and Western covers for Pocket Books in 1945 and 1946.

Glanzman: 1949, 1947

Louis S. GLANZMAN

Born February 8, 1922 in Baltimore; no formal art education.

Glanzman painted about 150 covers for the major publishers between 1948 and the 1960s, when he became involved with other types of projects. He still does occasional covers for Bantam Books, and has worked with Bantam's Leonard Leone since Leone was art director for *Argosy* magazine.

Ed GRANT

Originally from Chicago.

Produced several covers for Bantam in 1948; his first was for nr. 302, *The Fabulous Clipjoint*.

Simon GRECO
Produced several covers for Pocket Books in 1950, and later for Mentor Books.

Gregg: 1946, 1949

Gerald GREGG
Born January 25, 1907 in Lamar, Colorado; Gregg attended Racine High School in Wisconsin until 1925, when he won second prize in a poster designing contest and was advised to go to art school. He graduated from the Layton School of Art in Milwaukee in 1928, but found it difficult to get work at that time. He began accepting freelance assignments, including several from the Western Printing & Lithographing Company in Racine. In 1935, when one of Western's staff artists took a temporary leave of absence, Gregg was hired as his replacement. Russell Stone, Western's art director, liked Gregg's work and offered him a regular position.

In 1943, new art director Bill Strohmer and his assistant George Frederiksen assigned Gregg to do covers for Dell paperbacks. Strohmer or Frederiksen would generally provide color sketches, which Gregg either fleshed out or adapted. He often used Western's secretaries and stenographers as models for the beautiful women on his covers. Of the 176 covers he produced for Western (see examples on pages 76 and 77), Gregg's own favorites include Dell 115, *The Broken Vase*, and Dell 239, *Candidate for Love*.

Also during his tenure at Western, Gregg drew Disney and Warner Brothers comic strips and all back covers for the Little Golden Books series.

He worked with an airbrush, and it was his extraordinary technique with that apparatus which made the Dell covers of the 1940s unique. He describes his own style as a combination of graphic design and stylized realism. In addition to his airbrush work, he also produced covers in oils and watercolors, with pen-and-ink and with photography.

Original paintings by Gregg now sell for 1,000; four of his originals were displayed in 1981 at the exhibition "Paperbacks, U.S.A." in The Hague, Holland.

Leon GREGORI
Drew two paperback covers for Bantam in 1948 and eight for Dell in the 1950s. He is a member of the Society of Illustrators and currently lives in New York.

Gressley: 1946, 1947

GRESSLEY
Made humorous covers for Pocket Books between 1946 and 1949.

George GROSS
Made covers, especially for Westerns, for Dell between 1953 and 1958; art director Walter Brooks found him "very dependable."

John GROTH
Born February 26, 1908 in Chicago; studied at the Chicago Art Institute and, in 1926-27 and 1937-38, at the Art Students League of New York. Advised by an artist to do 100 drawings a day, Groth took the suggestion literally, resulting in a phenomenal output of sketches.

He was *Esquire* magazine's first art director, and held that position from 1933 through 1936.

From 1941 through 1945 he was art director for *Parade*, and during that period he also served as an artist-correspondent for the Chicago *Sun*.

As a paperback artist, Groth worked for Seal Books and Pocket Books during the 1930s and 1940s, illustrating covers for, for example, Blue Seals 1 *(Babies Without Tails)* and 6 *(Meals on Wheels)* in 1937, and Pocket Book 489 *(I am Gazing into my 8-Ball)* in 1948. In 1956 he did pen-and-ink drawings for Bantam S1497 *(War and Peace)*, and during the '60s he produced covers for Bantam, Dell, Vintage and other publishers. He worked primarily in watercolors.

In 1967, Groth was an artist and war correspondent in Vietnam, working for the U.S. Marines Combat Art Program. Since 1978 he has regularly illustrated the covers and several of the stories for the bimonthly magazine, *Short Story International*.

Philip GRUSHKIN

Born June 1, 1921 in New York City; studied under George Salter at the Cooper Union for Advancement of Science and Art.

Cartographer, typographer, illustrator and designer, Grushkin created calligraphic paperback covers for Pocket Books and Cardinal Editions between 1948 and 1955.

He spent many years as a teacher at Cooper Union, and today owns Philip Grushkin Associates in Englewood, New Jersey.

Ben HALLAM

Made two covers for Dell: numbers 64 *(Blood on the Black Market)* in 1944 and 76 *(Death in the Back Seat)* in 1945.

Remie HAMON

Made two covers for Bantam: numbers 465 *(Bitter Forfeit)* in 1949 and 471 *(Marry for Money)* in 1950.

Alan HARMON

Made covers for Signet in 1950 and 1951. He is especially known for his cover for George Orwell's *1984* (Signet 798).

Arthur HAWKINS, Jr.

Noted designer of hardcover jackets and member of the Book Jacket Designers Guild. He also did paperback covers: for Pocket Books 266 *(Lend-Lease: Weapon for Victory)* in 1944, for Penguin 592 *(Malice in Wonderland)* in 1946 and for Penguin 626 *(The Purple Onion Mystery)* in 1947.

Hawkins: 1946

Robert HILBERT

Produced nine covers for Dell and several more for Pocket Books between 1949 and 1953.

H. Lawrence HOFFMAN

Designer and illustrator of innumerable paperback covers in a wide variety of styles.

He began his career doing drawings for the pulp magazine *Thrilling Mystery Novels*, one of Ned Pines' publications.

In the early '40s, Hoffman worked for Sol Immerman's studio at 48 West 48th Street in New York and, together with Immerman, designed the covers for the first 125 Popular Library titles. Except for numbers 9, 31, 47, 48 and 59, Hoffman executed the first 86 of these covers himself.

He made covers for Pocket Books beginning in 1942, for Penguin between 1944 and 1946, and for Bantam beginning in 1945 (see pages 74 and 75); the first Bantam release *(Life on the Mississippi)* carried a Hoffman cover. Sol Immerman became art director at Pocket Books in 1947, and the sig-

Hoffman: 1943, 1944

M. Hooks

Mitchell Hillary HOOKS

Born in 1923 in Detroit; attended Cass Technical High School.

Mike Hooks made illustrations for books and magazines and, beginning around 1950, drew paperback covers for Avon, Bantam, Cardinal Editions, Dell, Fawcett, Pocket Books, Popular Library and Signet (see page 173).

nature IM-HO on a paperback cover sometimes stands for Immerman and Hoffman.

Hoffman also designed many dustjackets for hardcover publishers Macmillan, Morrow, The World (Tower Books), Random House, Scribners, Knopf, Rinehart and Little, Brown. He did much research for historical illustrations, and was an avid collector of books, Americana, illustrations and old photographs. He lived in Seacliff, on Long Island, and died in 1976.

Robert HOLLY

Around 1942, Holly became the first employee of Sol Immerman's West 48th Street studio. As with some covers created by Immerman and H.L. Hoffman, some covers created by Immerman and Holly were signed IM-HO. Most of Holly's IM-HO covers were done in 1941 and 1942 for Pocket Books (such as Pocket Books 133, *The Black Camel*), but also in 1943 for Popular Library.

Clark HULINGS

Grew up in Spain; studied drawing under Sigismund Ivanovsky and, at the Art Students League of New York (where he was "discovered" by Sol Immerman), under Charles Bridgman and Frank Reilly; he also received a degree in physics from Haverford College.

Because of ill health, Hulings moved out West, to Santa Fe, New Mexico. In 1946 he moved again, to Louisiana, and established himself there as a portraitist. By 1951 he was working as a freelance illustrator.

He produced paperback covers for Avon, Cardinal Editions, Dell, Fawcett, Lion Books, the Lion Library, Pocket Books and Signet.

In 1957, he returned to Santa Fe. Today he is a fine artist; one of his landscapes recently sold for $179,000!

Hooks: 1957, 1958

IM-HO: 1941, 1943

IM-HO

see *Sol IMMERMAN, H. Lawrence HOFFMAN* and *Robert HOLLY*

Sol IMMERMAN

Born in New York; attended a public school in 119th Street. His original ambition was to be a dentist, but he later changed his plans and, in 1928, graduated from New York University as an art major.

Immerman often hung around his father's nightclub in Harlem, and he came to know many musicians and songwriters there. It was through these connections that he got his first job, as a designer of sheet music covers. He was extremely successful: at one point his signature could be found on some 80% of all sheet music published in New York.

He later switched from sheet music work to book cover work; his first paperback cover was for Pocket Books 123, *Dr. Jekyll and Mr. Hyde.*

He established his own design studio, located at 48 West 48th Street, in 1942; his partner was H. Lawrence Hoffman, their first employee was Robert Holly, and the signature IM-HO, which can be found on several Pocket Book and Popular Library covers, stands sometimes for Immerman and Hoffman and sometimes for Immerman and Holly. The studio produced covers for both hardcover and paperback publishers, and had some 40 firms as clients.

After several years of serving as part-time art director at Pocket Books in addition to his duties at the studio, Immerman became full-time art director for that house in 1947 and turned the studio over to Hoffman. He stayed at Pocket Books through 1975. A colleague says that, although Immerman was a good artist and calligrapher, he was often too busy to produce good work. There were times when he had to design five covers himself and supervise the design of a dozen others, all in the space of a few days. Some of his own covers were quite good; others, to be kind, were not.

In the late '70s he was employed as art director for Penguin Books. He is now a consultant, working out of his home in Yonkers, New York.

William George JACOBSON

Made covers for Dell during the years 1947-1951.

Raymond JOHNSON

Illustrated many covers for Popular Library between 1948 and 1952; in addition, he worked for Avon, Bantam and Dell.

Robert JONAS

Born in New York on August 25, 1907; attended the Fawcett Art School in Newark, New Jersey. After a period of working in factories and holding a number of other jobs, including painting nightclub scenery, he began to study at New York University, supporting himself by working in

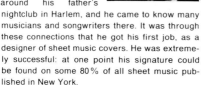

the display workshop of the A.S. Beck shoestores. It was there that he met Dutch painter Willem de Kooning. In the friendship that followed, he met and became associated with the avant-garde artists who were later to become the core of the "Abstract-Expressionist" movement.

Early in 1945, Jonas was interviewed by Kurt Enoch, vice-president of the American branch of Penguin Books, Soon after, he did his first paperback cover, for Penguin 560 *(Murder in Fiji),* which was released in July of 1945. Further 1945 covers for Penguin included numbers 563 *(Appointment in Samarra),* 567 *(Trouble in July)* and 569 *(Conceived in Liberty);* he also was assigned some covers for Superior Reprints, such as number M654 *(On Ice).*

Meanwhile, president Ian Ballantine and art director Gobin Stair left Penguin to found Bantam Books, and several Penguin illustrators went with them. Jonas also made two cover designs for Bantam, one of which was ultimately used: *The Town Cried Murder* (Bantam 16). According to Gobin Stair: "Bob Jonas was a dominant and successful cover artist. He developed an idea and projected it powerfully without getting trapped by compromise. His designs worked year after year."

Jonas: 1945, 1946

Jonas stayed with Penguin, on into the Signet years; his cover designs (sometimes incorporating photo montage) and typography determined the look of all nonfiction and most fiction titles the house released. Before Signet hired its first art director, it was Robert Jonas who effectively filled that function (his title "type director" came later, though).

In 1949, James Avati began doing paperback work; soon, Jonas was asked to begin delivering realistic covers for Westerns and other types of books. Jonas himself, feeling that this was not his métier but under the pressure of making a living, made an indifferent try with some titles and, rather than associating himself with them, adopted the nom-de-plume "Rob-Jon." Art director John Legakes recalls: "Before I arrived at Signet, he attempted illustrating some of the fiction covers realistically, which in my opinion was a disaster. I still wonder how some of those covers ever went tot print."

He continued providing covers for Mentor Books through around 1955, and also worked for Pocket Books and Perma Books during that time; in 1952 he made a single cover for Dell, for *The Mysterious Mr. Quin* (Dell 570). Of all his cover designs, his personal favorite is Penguin 596, *The Heart is a Lonely Hunter* (see page 71).

In the latter half of the 1950s, Jonas turned from paperback to hardcover work, and designed covers for Frederick Ungar, Macmillan, Random House, Dolphin, Grove Press and other publishers. He works today in design and photography.

Five of his paintings for Penguin and 60 paperbacks with his covers were displayed in the 1981 exhibition "Paperbacks, U.S.A." in The Hague, Holland.

His colleague, James Avati, has this to say about Robert Jonas: "Excellent. His covers were very simple, technically speaking, but they had an enormous psychological power."

Jones: 1948, 1951

Yankee Storekeeper, which was Bantam 456. He made further covers for Bantam (see page 172) and, later, for Pocket Books as well, but he was not particularly productive in the paperback field. "They never used me very much," he says, "because my stuff was basically on the slightly satirical, humorous side, and the truth about the matter is those books never sold well." *My Flag is Down* (Bantam 419), however, for which Jones provided the cover illustration, was a million seller.

Currently he does advertising work exclusively: drawings and storyboards for television commercials.

Victor KALIN

Born January 19, 1919 in Belleville, Kansas; graduated from the University of Kansas with a B.F.A. in 1942 and taught painting and drawing there in 1941 and 1942.

During World War II, Kalin worked as a field correspondent for *Yank* magazine in the Azores; he also made maps, did artwork for training manuals and produced three-dimensional assembly drawings. He met his wife, Catherine Bryan, on the island of Santa Maria, where she was a Red Cross worker in charge of the enlisted men's club.

His first illustrations after the war were done for magazines such as *American Weekly*, *Collier's*, *Liberty* and *Esquire*. In 1949, his work for *Esquire* caught the eye of a paperback house's art director and led to Kalin's first paperback cover assignments. He worked for Avon, Pocket Books, Signet and Dell (where he created covers for all of Mary Roberts Rinehart's books).

Casey JONES

Began his career in 1945 as an advertising artist, working for, among others, the Charles E. Cooper Studios, which he called "the most glamorous, fancy studio anywhere in the country." At Cooper, he did illustrations for magazines like *Collier's* and *Today's Woman*.

He drew his first paperback cover in 1948, for

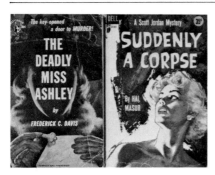

Kalin: 1951, 1956

Kauffer: *Flight*, woodcut, 1916

Discussing his early paperback illustrations, Kalin says, "They were lurid and tasteless, and I considered the whole thing something of a lark, certainly not a serious business." In spite of that attitude, however, he painted at least one cover per week and sometimes as many as three or four.

Today, in addition to creating record album covers, book illustrations, portraits, and surreal and abstract paintings, Kalin still paints an occasional paperback cover.

Owen KAMPEN
Did covers for Perma Books and Popular Library between 1952 and 1955. In 1955, his cover for *The Gathering Darkness* (Popular Library G131) was displayed at Columbia University's School of Library Service exhibition, "The Evolution of American Publishing in Paperbacks."

Jules KARL
Made seven covers for Bantam Books in 1948 and 1949, including Bantam 355, *The Man Within*.

E. McKnight KAUFFER
Born December 14, 1890 in Great Falls, Montana and grew up in Evansville, Indiana. In 1907 he moved to San Francisco and worked in Paul Elder's bookshop, where he met Joseph E. McKnight, professor of elementary education at the University of Utah. McKnight was so impressed with Kauffer's artistic talent that he offered to send him to Paris to study painting; as a gesture of gratitude, Kauffer took on his benefactor's last name as his own middle name.

So, as Edward McKnight Kauffer, he traveled

through Chicago, where he saw an exhibition of Cubist and German Expressionist paintings, and Munich, where he was impressed by the posters of Ludwig Hohlwein, to Paris. He met many contemporary artists there, but when World War I broke out he went to England, where he decided to settle.

Kauffer developed as a painter in England, and also as a designer of posters, tapestries, vignettes and illustrations for books and advertisements. He became a protégé of Frank Pick, director of the London Underground, who commissioned him to design a total of 150 London Trans-

Kauffer: 1945, 1946

port posters between 1915 and 1940. Kauffer abandoned painting in 1921 to concentrate fully on design and commercial work; over the next two decades he produced posters for a number of firms, including Great Western Railways and Shell-Mex B.P. Ltd.

In July of 1940, unable to contribute to the war effort in England, he left for the United States. He established a studio on 57th Street in New York, where he made a large number of war posters and also began designing book jackets for Modern Library, Knopf, McGraw-Hill, Random House, World, Harcourt Brace, Pantheon, Harper & Brothers, Macmillan, Henry Holt and other publishing houses.

In 1944, art director Ed Rofheart asked him to do a paperback cover for Pocket Books. The result was an illustration for number 259, *Halfway House*; some seven further Pocket Books covers followed, including a well-known one in 1945 for number 320, *The High Window*.

His last jacket designs were made in 1954, for Modern Library and Viking Press. Most of his work was done with poster paints.

Ted Kauffer's posters and illustrations have influenced many American cover artists, including Robert Jonas, Leo Manso and Walter Brooks. He was a precise man, in his work and in his appearance. Even faced with the most pressing of deadlines, he always had time for a bath and a manicure and kept his room immaculately clean.

Late in life, though, he was a heavy drinker. On October 22, 1954, he died.

Van KAUFMAN

Did seven humorous covers for Bantam between 1947 and 1949 (see page 172); in 1950 he did a single cover for Dell 393, *The Code of the Woosters*.

He currently does illustration work for advertising agencies.

Lew KELLER

Illustrated several covers for Pocket Books in 1950 and 1951, such as number 762, *Swing, Brother, Swing*.

Roswell KELLER

Made covers for Pocket Books between 1947 and 1952; his first was for number 491, *Border Kid*.

Rockwell KENT

Born June 21, 1882 in Tarrytown Hts., New York.

Wrote and illustrated numerous books. In 1929, he made covers and endpaper illustrations for Boni Paper Books and Bonibooks.

Harvey KIDDER

Drew many covers for Pocket Books between 1948 and 1951, specializing in mysteries.

Lou KIMMEL

Born in 1905 in Brooklyn, New York; studied at the Pratt Institute in Brooklyn and under Pruett Carter and George Luks.

As a freelance illustrator for *The Saturday Evening Post*, *Country Gentleman*, *Woman's Day* and other magazines, he specialized in Westerns.

Kimmel returned to school in 1950, obtaining a degree in order to be able to teach commercial art at Hunter College and the Commercial Illustrators School in New York.

During the '50s, he painted paperback covers for Avon, Gold Medal and Signet, plus a single cover for Dell D169, *Roads from the Fort* (1956). For Signet he did covers for most of Mickey Spillane's novels, such as *I, the Jury* (Signet 699).

He died in Queens, New York in 1973.

Kohs: 1947

Lester KOHS

Calligrapher, designer and illustrator, friend of Edgard Cirlin, Nettie King and Gobin Stair in the 1940s. Together with Cirlin, he had a studio in New York's East 35th Street; he taught during the day and spent his evenings working on assignments.

He made Penguin and Bantam covers for art director Gobin Stair between 1943 and 1947; the lettering was sometimes provided by Ava Morgan. In 1945, Kohs designed a single cover for Avon: number 76, *Atomic Energy in the Coming Age*.

Tony KOKINOS

Did cover illustrations for Signet around 1956.

Paul KRESSE

Born in Brooklyn, New York; studied for about five years at the Pratt Institute of Fine Arts in Brooklyn.

Made covers for Avon, Graphic Books, Pocket Books and Popular Library between 1949 and 1956, specializing in mysteries. His work was extremely realistic; he stopped doing paperback covers because he was always required to introduce "a strong element of shock, violence and sex." His personal favorite is his cover for Popular Library 470, *Headline Crimes of the Year*.

He worked in oils and watercolors.

Norbert J. LANNON

Did covers for Avon, Bantam and Popular Library between 1947 and 1949; his first Bantam cover was for number 122, *Certain French Doctor*.

Frank J. LIEBERMAN

Designer who drew the first Pocket Books kangaroo: he called her Gertrude, he says, because that was his mother-in-law's name. In 1939, he illustrated the covers for four of the first 10 Pocket Books: *Topper* (number 4), *Enough Rope* (6), *The Bridge of San Luis Rey* (9) and *Bambi* (10).

Currently, he works as a designer in Woodstock, Vermont.

Michael LOEW

Born May 8, 1907 in New York City; studied at the Art Students League of New York and the Académie Scandinavie in Paris.

At Robert Jonas' recommendation, Loew worked on cover assignments for Penguin and Signet between 1947 and 1949.

He is today a prominent painter.

Mike LUDLOW

Drew paperback covers for Pocket Books beginning in 1950, for Dell from 1952 to 1954 (plus one more in 1960), and for art director Leonard Leone at Bantam Books beginning in 1955.

Frank C. McCARTHY

Born in 1924 in New York City and grew up in Scarsdale; studied at age 14 under George Bridgman at the Art Students League of New York and later at the Pratt Institute in Brooklyn.

In 1948, McCarthy set up his own studio in New York and began painting paperback covers. He provided hundreds of covers for Pocket Books (primarily mysteries and Westerns) and Signet (war books, Westerns and science fiction), and his fame in the paperback field led to illustration assignments for magazines, advertising and the cinema. In 1969 he began painting Western

McCarthy: 1950

scenes for galleries; by 1971 he was no longer doing commercial art.

Today, McCarthy lives in Sedona, Arizona; when exhibited, his paintings "sell out in ten minutes," says Leonard Leone, art director at Bantam Books. "He earns more than any of them nowadays," Leone continues, "because he can work so fast. He's a real pro."

McCarthy paints in oils over casein underpainting over gesso preparation on masonite panels.

Gerald McCONNELL

Born May 17, 1931 in New York; studied under Frank Reilly at the Art Students League of New York.

McGinnis: 1961

Since 1954, he has done more than 1,200 paperback covers for Ace, Avon, Beacon, Dell, Fawcett, Hillman and Pyramid. His specialty is Westerns and he works in watercolors.

John R. McDERMOTT

Born in 1919 in Pueblo, Colorado; attended high school in Hollywood, California.

Worked as a cartoonist and animator for the Walt Disney Studios and Columbia Pictures until World War II, during which he was a combat artist and drew relief maps for an engineering unit in the South Pacific. This wartime experience led to his employment as an illustrator for *Blue Book* magazine.

In the early 1950s he did some paperback covers for Pocket Books, specializing in action scenes.

Robert E. McGINNIS

Born February 3, 1926 in Cincinnati; studied at Ohio State University in Columbus and the Central Academy of Commercial Art in Cincinnati, and furthered his education as an employee of the Walt Disney Studios.

Beginning in 1956, he produced more than 1,500 paperback covers for Avon, Bantam, Berkley, Dell, Fawcett, Popular Library, Signet and other houses; his first was for one of Dell's Mike Shayne novels.

Art director Walter Brooks says: "Al Allard at Fawcett and I were the first to give him assignments. He was a friendly man, pleasant to work with; later, though, when he became more popular, it was more difficult to drag work out of him. He was a master of realistic portraits of elegant

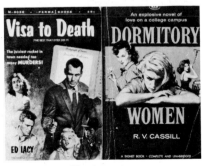

Maguire: 1956, 1959

women." (For two examples, see page 173.)

His best-known covers were done for Dell's Mike Shayne series and Signet's Carter Brown series. Around 1960 he made magazine illustrations for *The Saturday Evening Post* and *Good Housekeeping*, and more than 50 film posters (for, for example, James Bond pictures).

Robert MAGUIRE

Studied under Frank Reilly at the Art Students League of New York.

Maguire (or McGuire, which is his family name) produced covers for Pocket Books beginning in 1953, for Signet between 1954 and 1958 and Dell between 1954 and 1967, for Berkley between 1955 and 1960 and for Monarch between 1959 and 1964; he also did covers for Lion Books and Hillman Books.

Manso: dustjacket for *The Stone of Chastity*, 1945

Leo MANSO

Born April 15, 1914 in New York City; studied at the Educational Alliance in New York in 1929 and at the New School for Social Research.

He shared a studio with Pierre Martinot in West 16th Street at the end of the '30s; during the war years he was art director at The World Publishing Company, which published both Tower Books and Forum Books.

Manso also worked for Harper & Row, Simon & Schuster, E.P. Dutton, Farrar Straus, Viking,

Manso: 1943, 1957

Macmillan and other hardcover firms; through his work with Simon & Schuster he became involved with Pocket Books, for whom he produced so many covers during the years 1943-45 (see pages 167-169) that his impact on the appearance of that company's books was almost as decisive as Robert Jonas' impact at Penguin.

In the late '40s, Manso was one of the founders of the Book Jacket Designers Guild; the group was largely composed of people who had gathered around calligrapher and designer George Salter at the Cooper Union for Advancement of Science and Art. Via Salter, Manso began teaching at Cooper Union in 1947; in 1950, he started teaching at Columbia University and New York University as well.

Lou MARCHETTI

Born in Italy and moved to the United States at the age of 14; studied under Frank Reilly at the Art Students League of New York and was "discovered" there by Sol Immerman, who he refers to as "The Godfather."

Beginning in 1955, "Gino" Marchetti produced

Marchetti: 1957

paperback covers for Avon, Cardinal Editions, Dell, Lion Books, Pocket Books, Popular Library and Pyramid. At first, he was strongly influenced by James Avati; he also owes debts of thanks to James Meese and Barye Phillips (who, says Marchetti, "made a professional out of me").

As does Harry Bennett, he claims to have painted the first Gothic cover in 1960. Like Bennett, he is probably wrong: valid Gothic covers were sighted at least nine years earlier.

Phil MARINI
Drew covers for Dell between 1953 and 1955.

Pierre MARTINOT
In the late 1930s, he shared studio space with Leo Manso in West 16th Street. He became friendly with artist Isador Steinberg and Pocket Books executive Philip Van Doren Stern and was assigned to produce several Pocket Books covers, which he signed either "martinot" of "m." He also designed hardcover jackets for Simon & Schuster.

He currently lives and works in New York City.

John Alan MAXWELL
Illustrator and painter who, beginning in 1942, made covers for Avon, Dell, Pocket Books and several hardcover publishers as well.

According to George Hornby: "John Alan Maxwell consciously separated his life into two phases: during the first half of his life he earned money doing things that he didn't enjoy, and during the second half he *spent* money doing the things that he *did* enjoy. Making paperback covers was part of the first half."

Earl MAYAN
Did covers for Bantam Books in 1951, such as Bantam 911, *Vengeance Valley.*

George MAYERS
Did covers for Avon, Dell, Pocket Books and Popular Library between 1950 and 1956.

James MEESE
Beginning in 1952, made covers for Avon, Cardinal Editions, Dell, Gold Medal, Perma Books, Pocket Books and Signet.

Stanley MELTZOFF

Born March 27, 1917 in New York City; studied at the National Academy, the Art Students League of New York, the Institute of Fine Arts in New York and elsewhere. Meltzoff studied art history with the idea of becoming an art historian; he came to see, however, that he would not make a particularly *good* art historian, and decided to become an artist instead.

As a magazine illustrator, he worked for *Stars and Stripes* (1940-45), *Life, McCall's, The Saturday Evening Post, National Geographic* and *Sports Illustrated.*

Between 1947 and 1950 he drew about 10 paperback covers for Pocket Books; afterwards, he began to work for Signet (see page 78). In the early '50s he met James Avati at the offices of the New American Library, and they decided to share studio space on the top floor of a building on the corner of Main Street and Broad Street in Red Bank, New Jersey. Meltzoff's 1956 painting "Avati at easel" captures this shared environment wonderfully (see page 81); the original was displayed in 1981 at the exhibit "Paperbacks, U.S.A." in The Hague, Holland.

After 1955 Meltzoff made about 10 covers for Fawcett; after 1962 he did five more for Bantam. His personal favorites include his Signet covers for science-fiction books by Robert Heinlein and Ray Bradbury; he was one of the first illustrators to specialize in science-fiction themes.

His signature, either "S.M." or "Meltzoff," was often worked into his cover illustrations in inter-

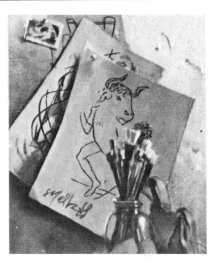

Meltzoff: detail of cover for Signet 927, *Renée* (1952)

esting and unusual ways, as graffiti on a fence or initials on a mailbox, for example. He wanted his signature to be an actual element within the scene, rather than something foreign to the scene and added onto it. Another frequently recurring image on Meltzoff covers was the artist's wife, Alice, who he often used as a model.

Today, Meltzoff paints underwater scenes of big game fish, either for private sale or as illustrations for *National Geographic.*

Robert W. MEYERS

Born in 1919 in New York City; studied under Ivan Olinsky and at the Grand Central Art School.

Did magazine illustrations for *True, Argosy, The Saturday Evening Post* and *Reader's Digest.*

Between 1948 and 1950, he created 16 paperback covers for Dell, mostly Westerns; his first was for number 217, *Gun Smoke Yarns.*

In 1955, one of his illustrations was named to a list of the year's 100 best posters. Both that year and in 1956, the Society of Illustrators in New York devoted one-man shows to his work.

In 1960, Meyers moved to a ranch near the Shoshone River in Wyoming, where he spent the rest of his life painting Western scenes.

Don MILSOP

Did covers for Avon Books around 1946.

Ava MORGAN

Studied under George Salter at the Cooper Union for Advancement of Science and Art; while study-

Meltzoff: 1950, 1951

ing, she also worked as a lettering assistant for Lester Kohs, and later became a lettering assistant for Edgard Cirlin.

During the early years of Bantam Books' existence, Morgan drew several covers and endpapers. Her main work, however, was done for hardcover publishers, who occasionally reused her illustrations on paperback editions without her knowledge or approval. Later, as art director at Macmillan, she instituted a policy that cover designs could not be reused without the permission of the artist and, when necessary, the payment of an additional fee.

Using her married name, Ava Weiss, she now works as art director for Greenwillow Books, the children's book department of William Morrow.

Rudolph NAPPI

Studied under Frank Reilly at the Art Students League of New York.

In a style suggestive of James Avati, he made covers for Avon and Signet around 1952 (see page 78). He also worked for Berkley between 1955 and 1957.

Donald NEISER

Did covers for Pocket Books and Dell during the first half of the '50s.

Jon NIELSEN

While employed at Sol Immerman's design studio in the '40s, he made several covers for Pocket Books.

Casimer NORWAISH

Known as "Cass" Norwaish, he illustrated several covers for Bantam and Pocket Books beginning in 1948; his first was Bantam 138, *Murder Cheats the Bride.*

Rafael PALACIOS

Born and raised in Puerto Rico in the 1930s.

Worked for American newspapers as an illustrator and a translator of comic strips. When he translated a novel, *Lydia Bailey*, into Spanish, he also designed a cover for its Spanish edition.

Around 1945, Palacios *palacios* shared a studio with Edgard Cirlin, Ava Morgan and Riki Levinson. Cirlin's agent, Nettie King, obtained a number of freelance assignments for him, and Gobin Stair, art director at

Palacios: calligraphy, 1981

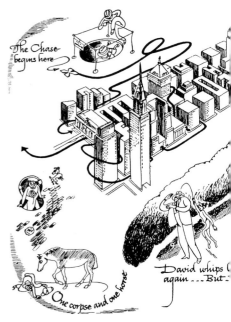

Palacios: 1945, 1952

Palacios: endpaper for Bantam 2, *The Gift Horse* (1945)

Bantam Books and friend of the group, had him do covers for Bantam; the first was for number 10, *South Moon Under*. For some Bantams, Palacios did both cover and endpapers, often putting a diagram or map on the latter (see page 66).

Later, he concentrated exclusively on cartography; his maps for Dwight Eisenhower's *Crusade in Europe* were, in 1949, his breakthrough into that field. He has also done hardcover jackets for Doubleday and other firms, using a noteworthy combination of figurative design and cartography.

Julian PAUL
Did covers for Lion Books and Pyramid between 1950 and 1954.

Peter PAUL
Did several covers for Bantam in 1949.

Ed PAULSEN
Did five covers for Bantam in 1949; the first was for number 422, *Office Nurse*.

Raymond S. PEASE
Drew for Pocket Books, Signet (1950-52), Dell (1952-53) and, in 1953, for the digest *Original Novels*.

Phillips: 1952, 1959

Barye PHILLIPS
In the early '40s, he worked for Columbia Pictures' advertising department. He was "discovered" there by Sol Immerman who, since H.L. Hoffman was not very skilled at drawing glamorous females, was looking for someone who could do "beautiful women with low necklines" for the covers of historical novels.

During World War II, Phillips worked on the production of training pamphlets and propaganda materials. He discovered at this time that he was able to turn out his best work under pressure.

He began painting paperback covers around 1943. Al Allard, art director at Fawcett, met him shortly after the end of the war and gave him many assignments for Fawcett's Gold Medal Books. He worked so quickly and was so productive that he was referred to as "The King of the Paperbacks" throughout the industry. His signature, "Baryé," can be found on releases from Avon, Bantam, Dell, Pocket Books (see page 177), Signet and several hardcover publishers, as well as on Gold Medal Books.

"Barye was ideal for this field," Al Allard remembers. "He was good. He was fast. He had imagination. He always met deadlines. He photographed his models, and then worked from the photos. Revision and composition followed later. He had the rare gift of being able to change his style." Allard found that ability a blessing; otherwise, he says, the early Gold Medal covers would have looked too much like each other and he would have been in trouble with the firm's management. (Incidentally, Phillips also worked with-

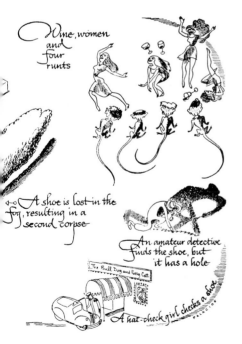

Phillips: from *Mr. Adam*, Pocket Books 2498, 1955

out models on occasion.)

Towards the end of the Korean Conflict, he took a few months away from paperback work in order to go to Southeast Asia and make sketches and paintings for the Army.

During the 1960s he served two terms as president of the Society of Illustrators in New York. With his scarf, his blazer and his checkered pants, he was himself an artistic figure. He died in 1968 or 1969.

Allen POPE

Produced many covers for Pocket Books in 1940, including numbers 47 *(Bring 'Em Back Alive)* and 53 *(The Best of Damon Runyon)*.

Powers: 1953, 1960

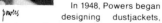

Richard G. POWERS

Born in 1921 in Chicago; studied at the Art Institute of Chicago and the University of Illinois, worked with Julian Levi at the New School for Social Research in New York and took private lessons from Jay Connaway in Maine and Vermont.

In 1948, Powers began designing dustjackets, generally in two or three colors, for the science-fiction genre which was at that time beginning to blossom; his employers included Knopf, Rinehart

and Harcourt Brace. He also did covers for the magazines *Star Science Fiction* and *Beyond Science Fiction*.

His agent soon began to get him assignments for Ballantine Books as well; his first characteristic science-fiction cover for Ballantine was for number 52, *Expedition to Earth*. Between 1953 and 1963, he produced almost 100 covers for Ballantine (see page 173); beginning in 1954, he also did 88 covers for art director Walter Brooks at Dell.

Says Brooks: "Dick Powers once did a painting which I thought was great. It was abstract. I asked him if I could hold on to it for a while. We didn't have any use for it, though, until about a year later we published the book *Asylum*. Dick's painting fit it exactly. He adapted a few small things and the cover was finished. It was totally different from the usual covers of that time." The book was released in 1954 as Dell 802.

Powers also worked for Pocket Books, Medallion, Belmont, McFadden and Gold Key Comics. He occasionally used the pseudonym "Terry Gorman" (Gorman is his middle name).

Two of his paintings were displayed in 1981 in the exhibit "Paperbacks, U.S.A." in The Hague, Holland.

Ken RILEY
Born in 1919 in Waverly, Missouri; studied at Parsons Junior College, the Kansas City Art Institute and the Art Students League of New York.

Riley enlisted in the Army in 1942 and made eyewitness sketches of the action at Tarawa. After the war, he worked as an illustrator for *The Saturday Evening Post*.

In 1949 he did some paperback covers for Bantam Books, including *The African Queen*, which was Bantam 712; he has also worked for Avon.

Today he is a fine artist.

Eve ROCKWELL
Cover artist for Pocket Books in 1939 and 1940; Pocket Books 48, *Scarlet Sister Mary*, is an example of her work.

Rofheart: 1943, 1945

Ed ROFHEART
Pocket Books' art director between 1942 and 1945; he designed several covers himself during that period.

William ROSE
Made covers for Avon, Cardinal Editions, Dell, Perma Books, Pocket Books and Pyramid between 1954 and 1958; also did magazine covers.

Ross: 1951, 1956

A. Leslie ROSS
Drew comics in the '30s and illustrated pulps in the '40s (for example, Street & Smith's *The Avenger*).

In 1948 he did several Western covers for Bantam Books, and in 1949 he began providing cover drawings for Popular Library and Signet. His cover for the November, 1944 issue of the pulp *Thrilling Western* was recycled in 1949 as the cover of Popular Library 171, *Chaffee of Roaring Horse*; this cover was displayed in 1955 at Columbia University's exhibition, "The Evolution of American Publishing in Paperbacks."

Al ROSSI
Worked for Avon and Bantam around 1955.

George ROZEN
Drew pulp covers for *The Shadow* in the 1930s and paperback covers for Popular Library in 1951 and 1952.

Hy RUBIN
Illustrator for *The Saturday Evening Post*.

Beginning in 1947, he did paperback work for Bantam; later, he also worked for Ballantine.

Tom RYAN
Born in 1922 in Springfield, Illinois; studied under Frank Reilly at the Art Students League of New York.

Around 1955 he painted three Western covers for Dell, including number 858, *Bury Me Not*.

Between 1954 and 1962 he did historical scenes of the American West for an art gallery; since 1964 he has painted Western scenes for calendars.

Bernard SAFRAN
In 1949, he made several covers for Pocket Books and one for Bantam: *One More Unfortunate*, which was number 360.

George SALTER

Born in 1897 in Bremen, West Germany and moved with his family at an early age to Berlin; studied at the Municipal School of Arts and Crafts in Charlottenburg from 1919 to 1921, and afterwards worked in stage and costume design. In 1927 he began *Salter* his career as a graphic designer, producing book jackets through 1933; from 1931 until 1934 he was the director of the commercial art division at the Graphic Arts Academy in Berlin.

He emigrated to the United States in 1934, arriving in America on a Friday. The following Monday, Simon & Schuster hired him to design jackets for five hardcover books. In all, he designed some 600 covers for Knopf, Harper & Row, Random House, Viking, Little, Brown, Fischer, Bobbs-Merrill and E.P. Dutton.

From 1938 through 1957, at Lawrence Spivak's Mercury Publications, he served as art director for such digests as *Bestseller Mysteries*, *Mercury Mysteries*, *Mercury Publications* and *Ellery Queen's Mystery Magazine*. His job was to take care of the cover illustrations and lettering, all interior typography and all logos (see page 166).

Salter also created paperback covers: three for Pocket Books (including number 300, *Franklin Delano Roosevelt*), eight for Penguin in 1945 and 1946 (including number 590, *Orlando*), 10 for Berkley in 1961 and 1962, and one for Pyramid in

1962 *(So Love Returns)*. His favorite typeface for book jackets was Caledonia.

Although his drawing style was somewhat clumsy, he had many followers, primarily because of his great skill as a calligrapher. Many of his students at Cooper Union in New York (where he taught from 1937 through 1967, using Alfred Fairbank's *A Handwriting Manual* as a textbook) went on to become book jacket designers: Edgard Cirlin, Jeanyee Wong, Miriam Woods, Philip Grushkin, Meyer Miller, Anita Karl, Riki Levinson, Rafael Boguslav, Milton Glaser and Walter Brooks.

Rafael Palacios says this about Salter: "He was a giant, he was highly respected, publishers always approached him first. He earned a lot of money, not only because he was good, but also because he could work quickly."

Salter died in New York in 1967. His last cover, completed by Philip Grushkin, was published in 1968.

Norman B. SAUNDERS

Born January 1, 1907 in Minneapolis; studied under Harvey Dunn at the Grand Central School of Art in Minneapolis.

From 1928 through 1934 he worked for Fawcett magazines such as *True Confessions*. Afterwards, he was a free- *Saunders* lance illustrator for pulps; one example, in 1938, was Street & Smith's *Pocket Detective*, which was published in paperback format. During the war, he served in the Army.

Beginning in 1948, Saunders produced covers

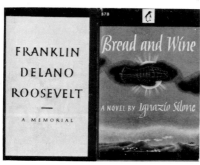

Salter: 1945, 1946

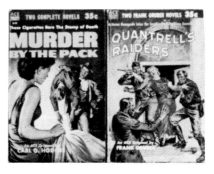

Saunders: 1953

for a number of paperback houses: Ace (for the first Ace Double Novel, *The Grinning Gismo/Too Hot for Hell*, he drew *two* front covers), Ballantine, Bantam (about 10 Westerns), Dell, Handi-Books, Lion, Popular Library and Readers Choice.

Sam SAVITT

Born in 1917 in Wilkes-Barre, Pennsylvania; studied at the Pratt Institute in Brooklyn and the Art Students League of New York.

Savitt's career in commercial art began in 1947; he illustrated book jackets, Western comics, Christmas cards and puzzles. Starting in 1950, he did paperback work as well. His first paperback cover was for Pocket Books, Jr. J-50, *Tiger Roan*; he continued working for Pocket Books through 1960. His specialty was drawings of horses.

Schaare: 1949, 1953

Harry J. SCHAARE

Born May 23, 1922 in Jamaica, New York; studied in 1940 at the New York University School of Architecture and further at the Pratt Institute of Fine Arts in Brooklyn. After a stretch as a pilot in the European theater during World War II, Schaare graduated from Pratt and established his own studio.

He illustrated stories for *The Saturday Evening Post* and, in October of 1949, drew his first paperback cover for Bantam 713, *Murder Listens In*.

Since then he has produced a total of around 450 covers for Bantam (1949-80), Avon (1955-64), Pyramid (1956-70), Popular Library (1957-80) and Dell (1958-79), plus additional covers for Ballantine, Berkley, Fawcett, Lion and Signet.

His personal favorites include Popular Library G184 *(The Last Voyage of the Lusitania)* and Bantams A1017 *(Ann Carmeny)*, A1137 *(The Lute Player)*, A1146 *(The Gallery)* and F1165 *(The Angry Strangers)*.

Alex SCHOMBURG

Known especially for his covers for comics and pulps such as *Startling Stories, Future Science Fiction, Science Fiction Plus, Thrilling Wonder Stories* and *Amazing Stories*.

In the early '50s he made three Popular Library covers, including number 236, *Pikes Peek or Bust*.

His work was sometimes signed with the pseudonym "Xela."

Robert SCHULZ

Born in 1928 in Cliffside Park, New Jersey and confined to bed for several years as a child because of illness; studied art and philosophy at Princeton University while painting pinups for the campus magazine *Princeton Tiger*. Schulz also studied under Joe Brown, Alden Wicks and Jerry Farnsworth and, from 1948 through 1952, under Frank Reilly at the Art Students League of New York, where he was "discovered" by Sol Immerman.

One of his first paperback assignments was a science-fiction cover which featured a gigantic hand. From that point on, Schulz was known to art directors as "the hand man."

Beginning in 1953, he was active as a cover artist for Ballantine, Dell, Perma Books and Pocket Books (his cover for *Ride the Dark Hills*, Pocket Books 1048, was displayed at Columbia University's School of Library Service exhibition in 1955); his specialties were World War II and action scenes and, especially, Westerns. In the '60s he illustrated covers for a series of Zane Grey novels published by Pocket Books. Living in Stockholm, New Jersey, he used his friends and neighbors as models for his paintings; his wife Evelyn did necessary research.

In the late '60s, Schulz found himself able to devote more time to fine art. In 1977 he decided to work exclusively on a series of paintings to be titled "Man's Place in Nature." He had completed three of these pictures when, three days after his fiftieth birthday, he died of a heart attack.

A memorial exhibition of his work was held at the Grand Central Art Galleries in New York in 1979.

H.W. SCOTT

Famed for his covers for pulps during the '30s, such as Street & Smith's *Wild West Weekly* and

The Avenger, and also for his covers for the Western comics published by the Western Printing & Lithographing Company. In 1951, he drew the cover for *Trumpets West!*, the first Dell 10-cents Book.

Earl SHERWAN
Born December 17, 1917 in Shorewood, Wisconsin; studied at the Layton School of Art in Milwaukee.

After delivering a test assignment of four covers, he was hired in March of 1946 by the Western Printing & Lithographing Company in Racine, publishers of Dell Books. Through the early '50s he produced dozens of Dell covers, which were lettered by his wife Marguerite. During this same period, he also illustrated covers for Western's *Zane Grey's Western Magazine*.

He worked in pastels, charcoal, watercolors and tempera.

William SHOYER
Active cover artist for Bantam between 1948 and 1950; his first illustration was for Bantam 366, *The Hound of the Baskervilles*.

In 1950 and 1951, he worked for Pocket Books.

SILTEN
Did several Pocket Books covers in 1941 and 1942, such as number 185, *The Nine Tailors*.

SILVER STUDIOS
A commercial photography studio headed by brothers Henry and Stanley Silver; they worked out of one story of a building at 131 West 51st Street in New York City.

In the early '50s, James Avati often used their pictures as models for his paperback covers. Around the same time, Sol Immerman put Silver Studios photos on a number of Pocket Books covers (see page 171).

Charles E. SKAGGS
Noted calligrapher and member of the Book Jacket Designers Guild.

Around 1950 he was occasionally brought in by Sol Immerman to do covers for Pocket Books, generally for books which had to look rather chic (for example Pocket Books 708, *The Pocket History of American Painting*).

He lives now in Leitchfield, Kentucky.

Robert Oliver SKEMP
Born August 22, 1910 in Scotsdale, Pennsylvania; studied under Thomas Hart Benton and George Bridgman at the Art Students League of New York.

Made about 22 covers for Bantam between 1949 and 1953; his first was number 477, *The Fascination*.

He currently lives in Connecticut and Arizona and works as a painter and illustrator, specializing in marine painting.

Stahl: 1949, 1950

Benjamin Albert STAHL
Born September 7, 1910 in Chicago; learned illustration in a studio in his home town.

Beginning in 1937, he worked for magazines such as *Woman's House Companion*, *Esquire*, *Cosmopolitan* and *The Saturday Evening Post*.

Made covers for Bantam starting in 1949. Reproductions of his painting for the cover of *Midnight Lace* (Bantam 753) were offered for sale to readers, priced at $2 a copy (see page 136).

Stahl was the first paperback artist to receive $1,000 for a single cover painting.

He is now fine artist, and shuttles back and forth between homes in Connecticut and Mexico.

Robert STANLEY
Cover designer for Dell Books whose paintings, both before and during Walter Brooks' tenure as art director, were a major ingredient of the Dell "look" of the 1950s.

Stanley often used himself and his wife Rhoda as models for his cover work (see page 84); his father and daughter also served as models from time to time, and Rhoda acted as his

Stanley: 1950

agent and photographer.

He produced about seven covers, mainly Westerns, for Bantam in 1949 and 1950 (his first was for number 212, *Fighting Man*), then worked for Dell between 1950 and 1959. During the years 1951-53, he produced 19 cover illustrations for *Zane Grey's Western Magazine*; he also worked for Lion and Beacon books, and probably for Signet as well.

In Westport, Connecticut, he was a member of the Westport Artists Group.

Isador N. STEINBERG

Born June 14, 1900 in Odessa, Russia; studied at the Art Students League of New York, under John Sloan and Max Weber at New York University, and at the Grande Chaumière in Paris.

Although his "first and greatest love" has always been painting, he has also done much commercial art. In 1939, his graphic work was represented in a listing of "50 Books of the Year." He was a friend of Philip Van Doren Stern at that time, and Stern commissioned him to produce covers for the first three Pocket Books releases, plus numbers 5, 7, 19, 23, 28, 31, 32, 36, 37, 68 and dozens more.

During the war, he was a consultant on book production and illustration to the Pentagon. He illustrated many manuals for the Army and Navy, and wrote, designed and executed Army courses in botany, surveying, lettering, mechanical drawing and other subjects.

After the war he created covers and endpapers for Bantam Books; *South Wind*, released in 1946 as number 65, is one example. He also worked for hardcover publishers Simon & Schuster, Harcourt Brace, Random House, Viking, Macmillan and Little, Brown.

Steinberg currently owns York Studios on East 75th Street in New York, and winters in Palm Beach, Florida.

STRICK
Worked for Avon around 1947.

Arthur SUSSMAN
Born March 30, 1927 in Brooklyn, New York; studied at Syracuse University and the Brooklyn Museum School of Art.

Made about 10 covers for Dell between 1954 and 1957; his first was for number 778, *Crows Can't Count*.

Van SWEARINGEN
Magazine illustrator who made two covers for Bantam: number 112, *Hardcase*, in 1947, and number 200, *Western Triggers*, in 1948.

William TEASON
Born March 9, 1922 in Kansas City, Missouri; studied at the Kansas City Art Institute.

Began illustrating paperback covers in 1958 and has, to date, some 200 of them to his name; his first was for Dell D249, *The Man in the Brown Suit*. He did all covers for Dell's Great Mystery Library and also worked on other projects for Dell, as well as for Avon, Fawcett and Popular Library.

His personal favorites are his covers for Agatha Christie's books.

Frank TINSLEY
Noted illustrator who, in the '30s and '40s, worked for pulp magazines such as *All Detective Magazine*, *Bill Barnes Air Adventurer* and *Sky Birds*.

He provided art director Al Allard with paperback covers for Gold Medal Books from that series' earliest days.

Verne TOSSEY

Born March 29, 1920 in Detroit; studied for four years with Frank Reilly at the Art Students League of New York.

His agent, Bob Gordon, got him an assignment to paint a cover for a Doubleday adventure story in 1949. He began doing paperback covers for Avon the same year; the following year, he

Tossey: 1953

added Dell, Lion Books, Pocket Books and Signet to his list of employers, and in 1955 he began working for Ace. Tossey also did covers for Ballantine, and this was the house he preferred to work for, since they allowed him the most freedom.

He worked in oils, poster paints and tempera.

Today he paints only for collectors.

David TRIGGS

Cover artist around 1945 for Bantam and Penguin (see page 174).

TROOP

Between 1942 and 1947, this signature (sometimes spelled Troupp or TroupB) occasionally appeared on Pocket Books; number 180, *The Peacock Feather Murders*, is one example.

T.V.: 1948

T.V.

Made many covers for Signet around 1949. The initials may stand for Tony Varady, who worked for Pocket Books in 1946.

Edward VEBELL

Born in Chicago and became a professional illustrator at age 18.

During World War II he was an artist-correspondent in Africa, Italy and France for *Stars and Stripes*. He stayed on in Paris after the war, returning to the United States in 1947 to pick up his career as an illustrator.

Between 1949 and 1952, he worked for Pocket Books.

He now lives in Westport, Connecticut.

Anna WILSON

Made a few covers for Pocket Books in 1950; number 679, *Peony*, is one example.

William WIRTZ

Did primarily mystery covers for Pocket Books between 1947 and 1949 (such as number 558, *Bury Me Deep*), and for Bantam, where his name was written as "Wirts," in 1948 and 1949 (such as number 351, *The Lying Ladies*).

Milton WOLSKY

Born January 23, 1916 in Omaha, Nebraska; studied at the University of Omaha and the Art Students League of New York.

Drew several covers for Pocket Books in 1948 (his first cover was number 201, *The Case of the Stuttering Bishop*; Wolsky himself posed for the bishop), and for Bantam in 1948 and 1949 (such as number 213, *Hell or High Water*, on which he can be seen getting hit on the jaw).

He is the author of the book *Basic Elements of Painting*.

 ### Jeanyee WONG

Studied under George Salter at the Cooper Union for Advancement of Science and Art.

Her main work was for hardcover firms; she also designed some paperback covers, though, and it often happened that a hardcover publisher would, without her approval or permission, reuse her illustrations on paperback editions. In this way, a number of her Simon & Schuster covers were recycled onto Pocket Books.

Woods: 1946

Miriam WOODS

Studied under George Salter at the Cooper Union for Advancement of Science and Art. Afterwards, she worked as Salter's assistant for several years.

Her work as a cover artist was mainly for hardcover publishers (The World, Columbia University Press, Simon & Schuster, Holt, Harper and Little, Brown), but

Woods

between 1942 and 1947 she also did paperback covers for Bantam, Penguin and Pocket Books.

She was a member of the Book Jacket Designers Guild.

Cliff YOUNG

Magazine illustrator and friend of Harvey Dunn and Dean Cornwell.

In 1948 he made three paperback covers for Bantam, including number 250, *The Stagline Feud*.

Stanley ZUCKERBERG

Born September 13, 1919 in New York City and grew up in Long Beach on Long Island; studied at the Pratt Institute in Brooklyn and the Art Students League of New York.

Zuckerberg

Began his career in 1940 as an illustrator of pulp magazines; he also drew versions of *A Tale of Two Cities* and *Robinson Crusoe* for Classics Illustrated Comics and provided illustrations for *Cosmopolitan*, *Good Housekeeping*, *Redbook*, *Blue Book*, *The Saturday Evening Post*, *Argosy* and *McCall's*.

After his first paperback cover for Bantam Books in 1949, he produced about 300 more covers for Avon, Ballantine, Bantam, Dell, Fawcett, Pocket Books, Popular Library and Signet (see page 78).

He photographed his models himself, and painted in oils.

Zuckerberg's personal favorites are the covers he created for Bantam F1643 *(Jonathan Eagle)* and Signets S1023 *(Spark of Life)*, 1042 *(The Red Carnation)*, D1107 *(Days of My Love)* and S1309 *(Whispers of Love)*.

He stopped doing paperback work in 1965; since then, he has painted beaches, boats, fishermen and seagulls for New York art galleries.

Zuckerberg: 1952, 1953

Collecting Paperbacks

T HIS BOOK will be a thorn in the side of every serious paperback collector. It will put an end to the ignorance of hundreds of book dealers who, until now, have known exactly what to do with old paperbacks: toss them in a crate, price them five for a dollar and display them *outside* the shop so they don't waste valuable shelf space. It will cause thousands of readers to think twice before shipping used books off to the Salvation Army. Because of this one volume, it will be rarer and rarer that you come across old Avons, Dells or Popular Libraries at garage sales and fleamarkets. Caveat collector! Let the collector beware!

I don't like most collectors. Old men with magnifying glasses trying to decide whether a postage stamp is worth five cents or a thousand dollars and never even noticing what the thing *looks* like; crazed intellectuals carefully preserving first editions by Oscar Wilde or Charles Dickens in glass cases, not even caring that more recent printings may be better; silly goofs who fill their abundant free time buying up American paperbacks by the yard, checking off titles against a master list of the books they haven't yet "got," proudly displaying new finds without ever bothering to read them. That's the sort of people I try to avoid at all costs.

Unfortunately, I have to admit that I seem to have become one of them myself.

It begins innocently enough. One day, in a cheerful mood, you buy five or six old paperbacks, not because you really want to read them but just because they look so nice and, somehow, irresistible.

I remember, back when I only had about 75 paperbacks, how I used to assure anyone who was interested that I only bought "pretty" ones.

At that time I hadn't yet realized the mysterious magnetic attraction which pocket books seem to exert on *other* pocket books. It took me two years to gather my first hundred paperbacks; my second hundred just seemed to show up, without much effort on my part, within a few short months. When I got up around 500 volumes I found myself buying books which, earlier, I had turned down. It was quite a phenomenon: books which had been "too ugly" for me two years ago were beginning to look quite attractive. Paperbacks must begin to look better the more of them you see.

And even if a book isn't "pretty," it can still be "interesting": the first appearance of an author in paperback, a terrible cover by a fine artist, a white spine from a period when spines were always black. When you reach this point, a threshold is crossed and there is no turning back.

You're a collector.

Paperback collectors operate in a no-man's-land between two fields which, until recently, didn't have or desire to have much to do with each other: the world of books and the world of popular culture. Like other book collectors, they are interested in certain authors and in first editions, and they care about the appearance of their books. Like collectors of comic books, film posters, bubblegum cards, fruit-crate labels, 78 RPM records or postcards, their knowledge about the subject matter of their collections is usually rather limited. It is true that some expensive art books packed with full-color photographs of old pincushions, Mickey Mouse watches, Coca Cola bottles, pulp magazines and cigarette packages have popped up from time to time over the last few years, but these publications don't, as a rule, bother to include all that much *information*.

In the mid-1960s, comic books suddenly became "in." Learned articles were written for new magazines, shops specializing in comics were opened, and the comic books themselves, sometimes already "antiques" three months after publication, disappeared behind plastic covers and were dealt in at shocking prices. The same thing happened to pulp magazines about five years later, and around 1975 it all started up again, this time with old paperbacks.

This is, as far as I know, the first book on the subject, but it will certainly be followed by many more. A dignified Dutch museum exhibited 1,500 old paperbacks for nine weeks in 1981. There are two magazines for collectors in America. Mail-order firms are asking prices for pocket books which were simply unthinkable two short years ago. Comic-book collectors, who watched their market cave in at the end of the '60s when a small group of fanatics gobbled up all the really valuable comics and locked them safely out of reach in bank vaults, have switched eagerly to paperbacks. I only hope, with this current flurry of activity, that the paperback market doesn't also collapse.

In that sense, writing about paperbacks can be something of a dilemma. You really want to tell others what's interesting about these old books, but you know that your writing may affect the market and the result may be that you damage the very field you're attracted to.

If I hesitate to write about the rarity of Pocket Books 268 (*The Maltese Falcon* with dustjacket), it's not really that I grudge any collector access to the book, but just that I'm not quite sure I can trust his motives.

Since the invention of the rotary press, no book can be unique—and certainly not an American paperback. The paperback is a living example of commercialism: it exists for no other reason than to make it easier to sell the largest possible number of items at the lowest possible price.

One of the major thrills of book collecting is the opportunity of discovering a great treasure in a humble, unexpected place. And paperback collectors rarely pay more than a dollar a book for their finds: if that changes, the whole fun of it will disappear for many. You can find American paperbacks everywhere—at fleamarkets, in secondhand bookshops, at auctions. Holland and Belgium are good countries for collectors: millions of British and, especially, American pocket books turned up in and around the port cities during and after the war, and as a result you can easily build up a very interesting collection today, with a small investment, in just a few months. It's not so easy in England or in the United States. A few ambitious Americans have already put a serious crimp in the market; Melville C. Hill, for example, who has been collecting paperbacks for almost as long as there have *been* paperbacks, spends several months every year crisscrossing the country in his van, buying up whole garagefuls, shopfuls, warehousefuls of books from people in remote villages who don't know any better. Back home in Spring Valley, California, he sorts through his purchases and keeps a stock of at least 30,000 volumes on hand for mail-order sales. His prices are high, but not unreasonable considering his overhead. Another entrepreneur, David T. Alexander from Studio City, California, is one of the founders of the American Comic Book Company, which also recognizes the value of old paperbacks. Like Melville Hill, they keep 30,000 books in stock and have been reproached for high prices; unlike Hill, they sell via a catalog.

Paperbacks can be saved for about 30 years; after that their pages begin

The collecting of paperbacks has recently become a serious matter in America. This detailed advertisement appeared in a magazine for collectors.

to turn to dust. That process can be put off by storing the books in airtight plastic bags, but it can not be overcome—and even plastic can degrade, producing gasses which are themselves damaging to pulp paper. Recently, however, bags made out of synthetics have appeared, advertised as able to keep paperbacks safe indefinitely. Collectors who find all these precautions a little exaggerated should in any case remember that warmth, moisture and light hasten the disintegration process.

There are many *ways* of collecting paperbacks. Some collectors specialize in specific authors, for example; they know that many short-story collections by Dashiell Hammett (*The Creeping Siamese, Dead Yellow Women, Hammett Homicides, A Man Called Spade*—all Dell publications) are today quite valuable, because they have never been reprinted. Raymond Chandler's short-story collections *have* been reprinted, but the original editions of *Five Murderers*, of *Five Sinister Characters* and of *Finger Man*—all from Avon Books—can be worth $50 each.

Some collectors build complete sets of all books from a particular publisher. In 1976, William H. Lyles of Greenfield, Massachusetts began collecting Dells; he now has them all, most in various editions—and he also collects Dell bookmarks, Dell bookracks and other advertising materials. Lance Casebeer of Portland, Oregon started working on a set of Popular Library releases in 1975; by 1977 he had all but 10 of them and began giving parties each time he located one of those still missing. When Casebeer finally completed the series in 1979 (his last acquisition: *Crossword Puzzles, Book Two*), a hundred collectors from all over America turned up for the festivities. His wife complains that Lance's pocket books don't leave enough room for *her* in their home, but it doesn't seem to help: Casebeer is still collecting, and at this writing he's only missing one Avon, five Gold Medals, six Dells and 11 Pocket Books.

Some collectors search for items of historical interest. *The Good Earth*, which Robert DeGraff used to test customer interest in Pocket Books, is the moest sought-after prize: the going price is $135. The first volumes released by Ace, Avon, Dell, Popular Library and Checkerbooks are worth $60 each; the first edition of the first "official" Pocket Book, *Lost Horizon*, goes for $100 (because it was only distributed in New York City). Pocket Books 2-10, also with distribution limited to the Big Apple, sell for $80 each. The first Ace Double Novel, *The Grinning Gismo/ Too Hot for Hell*, is valued at $100.

Another motif for paperback collecting is cover artists. In America, covers by Rudolph Belarski, Earle Bergey, Norm Saunders, Robert Maguire and Richard Powers are especially popular; writer David Madden of Baton Rouge, Louisiana collects Jonas, and Dutchman Ed Schilders has an impressive collection of Avati. Hoffman, Phillips, Meltzoff, Salter, Hooks, Manso and Stanley are less in demand, but that is likely to change in the near future. I suppose that I belong to this category of collectors: I love it when, in the basement of a secondhand bookstore, I can fish a 40-year-old Manso out of some neglected cardboard carton. Paperback artists are friends of mine, friends I can run into anywhere—George Salter in Zurich, Robert Jonas in Amsterdam, H.L. Hoffman in New York. Who needs any *other* friends when he can find Belarski and Palacios and Gregg in every neighborhood of every city in the world?

There are also genre collectors, who specialize in covers featuring maps, skulls, naked women, peepholes, or simply puzzle books, Westerns, detective stories, or science fiction. According to Peter Manesis' 1980 catalog *Son of Paperbacks*, the most popular theme is drugs, with whips close behind and juvenile delinquency in third place.

And there are collectors who are only interested in rare books. They will readily pay $75 for *Rocket to the Morgue*, the first—and last—Phantom Mystery; they make sure they own the dustjacketed edition of *The Maltese Falcon*, worth $60; they have a shelf full of Bantam (L.A.) Books, which today have an average market value of $50. Paul Payne, of Long Beach, California, is an authority on Bantam (L.A.)—he's only missing five of them. He says: "It used to be I had to look through five million paperbacks to find one Bantam (L.A.). Nowadays I don't see *any* of them anymore, no matter how many paperbacks I go through. Well, anyway, at least I've got most of them."

Which, when you stop and think about it, is perhaps the best state of affairs for the avid collector. After all, if you ever *do* get "all of them," then what's left to collect?

Paul F. Payne's collection of Bantam (L.A.) Books

Bibliography

The following books, magazine articles and interviews were used in the compilation of this volume. The publications marked with an asterisk may be considered required reading for the serious paperback student.

The History of the Paperback

CRIDER, Bill and LEE, Billy C. *Some Notes on Movie Editions.* In: *Paperback Quarterly*, Volume 2, Number 1 (Spring, 1979)
An inventory of paperbacks with film covers.

FLOWER, Desmond. *The Paper Back: Its Past, Present and Future.* London: Arborfield, 1959
Text of a lecture given by Flower, with an introduction by Allen Lane. Provides some information on paperbacks before, during and just after World War II.

HACKETT, Alice P. *Sixty Years of Best Sellers, 1895-1955.* New York: Bowker, 1956
A wonderful book for fans, with a treasure trove of information about hardcover books and paperbacks which have sold more than a million copies.

HILL, Melville C. *Dell Dimers.* In: *Paperback Quarterly*, Volume 2, Number 2 (Summer, 1979)
An article about the Dell 10-cents Books.

LEWIS, Freeman. *A Brief History of Pocket Books, 1939-1967.* New York: Pocket Books (undated, but published in 1967)
Written by Robert DeGraff's successor, "Doc" Lewis.

MANESIS, Peter. *The Bonibooks.* In: *Paperback Quarterly,* Volume 2, Number 4 (Winter, 1979)
An article about the Boni Paper Books and the collection of same.

MORPURGO, J. E. *Allen Lane, King Penguin. A Biography.* London: Hutchinson & Co., 1979

PAYNE, Paul. *Lost and Found: L. A. Bantam.* In: *Collecting Paperbacks?,* Volume 1, Number 3 (November, 1979)
Information about Bantam (L.A.) by a devoted collector. Illustrated with color photographs of and from Payne's collection.

★ PETERSEN, Clarence. *The Bantam Story: Thirty Years of Paperback Publishing.* New York: Bantam Books, 1975
Much useful information about the history of Bantam and other publishers. A free copy of this booklet may be obtained by writing to Bantam Books, 666 Fifth Avenue, New York, N.Y., 10019.

PRONZINI, Bill. *Popular Library.* In: *Collecting Paperbacks?,* Volume 2, Number 1 (March, 1980)
A concise history of Popular Library (1942-1980), annotated by Lance Casebeer.

★ SCHICK, Frank L. *The Paperbound Book in America.* New York: Bowker, 1958
Required reading for anyone interested in paperbacks; unfortunately, it has been out of print for years.

★ SCHMOLLER, Hans. *The Paperback Revolution.* In: *Essays in the History of Publishing in Celebration of the 250th Anniversary of the House of Longman* (Editor: Asa Briggs). London: Longman, 1974
One of the best-written concise articles on paperback history, illustrated with color and black-and-white reproductions of covers. The author was once a typographer for British Penguin.

SCHREUDERS, Piet. *George Delacorte: Iedereen Kan een Boek Uitgeven.* In: *Utopia,* Number 10 (Autumn, 1978)
An interview with the founder of Dell Books. Published in Dutch.

SMITH, Roger H. *Paperback Parnassus.* Boulder: Westview Press, 1976
Based on a series of articles from *Publishers Weekly* about the world of paperback publishing. The chapter on distribution is especially interesting.

SPENCER, Herbert. *Penguins on the March.* In: *Typographica,* New Series, Number 5 (June, 1962)
About the development of the Penguin style, from Edward Young (1935) through Germano Facetti (1962), with reproductions of various Penguin colophons.

TAUCHNITZ, Bernhard. *The Harvest. Being the Record of One Hundred Years of Publishing, 1837-1937.* Leipzig: Bernard Tauchnitz, 1937
A festive publication (in a golden cover!), celebrating the 100th anniversary of the firm, with a chapter about the copyright question, the Tauchnitz list, statistics, pictures and letters to Tauchnitz from 33 authors (including Mark

Twain, Robert Louis Stevenson, Charles Dickens, H.G. Wells, Sinclair
Lewis and W. Somerset Maugham).

TEBBEL, John. *Paperback Books: A Pocket History.* New York: Pocket Books,
1964
Written to celebrate the 25th anniversary of the founding of Pocket Books.
Other publishers are mentioned, but Pocket Books itself is the star of the
show here.

TODD, William B. *Books in Series.* In: *Collectible Books* (Editor: Jean Peters).
New York and London: Bowker, 1979
Information and a bibliography regarding, among others, the Tauchnitz
Editions.

UNGER, Gerard. *Bird Watching for Beginners.* In: *Furore*, Number 1 (January,
1976)
A history of paperbacks in general and Penguin Books in particular, with
commentary by Huib Opstal. Published in Dutch.

★ WILLIAMS, William Emrys. *The Penguin Story, 1935-1956.* Harmondsworth:
Penguin Books, 1956
A history of Penguin Books, beautifully illustrated with color and black-
and-white photos. Includes an overview of all British Penguins released
through 1956.

Paperback Covers

BERNARD, Barry. *Mass Market Murmurings; Calling on the Colophon.* In: *Collecting Paperbacks?*, Volume 1, Number 2 (May, 1979)
A breezy article about the colophons used by paperback publishers, conclud-
ing with a rebus.

BONN, Thomas L. *Soft Cover Sketches.* In: *Utopia*, Number 10 (Autumn, 1978)
This article incorporates interviews with James Avati, Norman Saunders,
Lou Marchetti and Robert Jonas. Illustrated.

★ CASEBEER, Lance. *Who Drew That Girl?* A regular column appearing in all
issues of *Collecting Paperbacks?*
This column deals with cover artists, often including checklists of their
work. To date, artists covered are: Freeman Elliott, Earle Bergey, Wallace
Wood, Robert Maguire, Rudolph Belarski, H.L. Hoffman, A. Leslie
Ross, Harold W. McCauley and Frank Frazetta.

DENHOLM, Bill. *We Can All Be Joe Friday.* In: *Collecting Paperbacks?*, Volume
1, Number 6 (January, 1980)
An article about the identification of illustrators, particularly covering the
work of Robert McGinnis.

LEWIS, John. *The Paperback Explosion and the Design of the Modern Book.* In:
The Twentieth Century Book: Its Illustration and Design. London:
Studio Vista, 1967

In this chapter of his book, Lewis gives a general overview of paperback covers, with many illustrations. There is, however, little about American paperbacks.

LYLES, William H. *Rex Stout in the Dell Mapbacks.* In: *Paperback Quarterly*, Volume 2, Number 4 (Winter, 1979)
An article concerning the relationship between the maps themselves and the contents of the books they appeared on, focusing on several mysteries by Rex Stout.

OPSTAL, Huib. *Bantam: Niet ten Onrechte Haantje de Voorste Genoemd.* In: *Utopia*, Number 10 (Autumn, 1978)
A short piece on Bantam covers, primarily those of the '60s. Richly illustrated. Published in Dutch.

PITZ, Henry. *Two Hundred Years of Illustration.* New York: Random House, 1977
This book was subsidized by the Society of Illustrators in New York, and presents a well-done picture of the development of illustration in America. Some of the artists whose work is discussed and shown have also done paperback covers.

REED, Walt. *Fifty Great American Illustrators.* New York: Crown Publishers, 1979
This picture book includes text about and illustrations by Howard Pyle, Dean Cornwell, Harvey Dunn, Norman Rockwell, N. C. Wyeth and Harold Von Schmidt, all of whom exerted important influences on paperback art.

★ REED, Walt. *The Illustrator in America, 1900-1960s.* New York: Reinhold, 1966
This book discusses how tastes in illustration have changed since 1900. Includes work by some paperback artists.

SAMUELS, Peggy and Harold. *The Illustrated Encyclopedia of Artists of the American West.* New York: Doubleday, 1976
Concise biographies of more than 1,700 painters and illustrators who have specialized in Western scenes, with samples of their work. Some of the artists covered have also worked for the paperbacks.

SCHAFFER, Mark. *A Glance at Paperback History.* In: *Paperback Quarterly*, Volume 2, Number 2 (Summer, 1979)
An interesting treatment of the stylistic characteristics of paperback covers through the years. Not, unfortunately, illustrated.

SCHAFFER, Mark. *Selling Culture with Paperback Covers.* In: *Paperback Quarterly*, Volume 2, Number 4 (Winter, 1979)
An article about the connections between popular culture in general and paperbacks covers in particular.

SCHILDERS, Ed. *De Zaak U.M.C.* In: *Furore*, Number 13 (May, 1979)
During the 1960s, the Dutch publishing house Uitgeversmaatschappij De Combinatie of Rotterdam swiped and mutilated American paperback cov-

ers, adapting them for their own use. This illustrated article, in Dutch, discusses the case.

SCHILDERS, Ed. *Literaire Lichtbeelden.* In: *Utopia*, Number 10 (Autumn, 1978)
An article about the work of James Avati, uncrowned king of the paperback artists. Published in Dutch.

SCHREUDERS, Piet. *Onnavolgbare Goocheltrucs.* In: *Vrij Nederland*, Literary Supplement (September 24, 1977)
About the major difference in quality between American and European paperback covers. Published in Dutch.

SCHREUDERS, Piet. *Oog in Oog met Ontwerper van Boekomslagen Jonas.* In: *Furore*, Number 11 (October, 1978)
Interview with Robert Jonas, illustrated with original paintings and other work. Published in Dutch.

SCHREUDERS, Piet. *Rafael D. Palacios.* In: *Furore*, Number 14 (December, 1979)
Interview with Rafael Palacios, calligrapher, cartographer and cover artist for Bantam Books around 1945. Illustrated with samples of his work. Published in Dutch.

Information about Paperbacks

HANCER, Kevin. *The Paperback Price Guide.* Cleveland: Overstreet Publications, 1980
A listing of all American paperbacks published through 1959, arranged by publisher and in numerical order. Illustrated with color and black-and-white reproductions of covers, with an obvious slant in favor of pulp-like work. The book, unfortunately, suffers from a certain amount of carelessness; for example, some nonexistent titles have been carried over from Michael Burgess' index (see below).

★ REGINALD, R. and BURGESS, M. R. *Cumulative Paperback Index, 1939-1959: A Comprehensive Bibliographic Guide to 14,000 Mass-Market Paperback Books of 33 Publishers Issued Under 69 Imprints.* Chicago: Gale, 1973
R. Reginald and M. R. Burgess are, in fact, one and the same person: Michael Burgess, to be specific, a librarian from San Bernadino, California. He has been collecting paperbacks since 1964 and now owns more than 16,000 volumes. He also writes under the names C. Everett Cooper and Lucas Webb. This book is, especially when combined with Hancer's *Price Guide*, the Bible of all paperback collectors and researchers. Books are cross-indexed by author and title. A word of warning: Burgess has purposely listed a number of incorrect and nonexistent titles (such as *The Little Green Men* and *Gentlemen Prefer Corpses*) in his index, in order to catch plagiarists.

Collecting Paperbacks

Bonn, Thomas L. *American Mass-Market Paperbacks*. In: *Collectible Books* (Editor: Jean Peters). New York and London: Bowker, 1979
A chapter on mass-market paperbacks, their history, genres and motifs, with some information on collecting. Illustrated, with a list of suggestions for further reading.

Turan, Kenneth. *Passion's Plaything: Paperback Parade*. In: *New West* (March 12, 1979)
A description of the phenomenon of paperback collecting and the high market value of certain old paperbacks.

Interviews

1. James Avati. Interviewed by Thomas L. Bonn (November 3, 1971 and May, 1978) and Ed Schilders (August, 1980) in Red Bank, New Jersey
2. Ian Ballantine. Interviewed by Piet Schreuders (January 2, 1981) in Bearsville, New York
3. Walter Brooks. Interviewed by Piet Schreuders (May 17, 1979) in New York City
4. George T. Delacorte, Jr. Interviewed by Piet Schreuders (May 23, 1978) in New York City
5. Bill Gregory. Interviewed by Piet Schreuders (May 25, 1978) in New York City
6. George Hornby. Interviewed by Piet Schreuders (May 9, 1979) in New York City
7. Sol Immerman. Interviewed by Piet Schreuders (May 26, 1978) in New York City and again (January 1, 1981) in Yonkers, New York
8. Robert Jonas. Interviewed by Thomas L. Bonn (May, 1978), Piet Schreuders (May 19 and May 23, 1978 and May 3, 1979) and Ed Schilders (August, 1980) in Brooklyn, New York
9. Casey Jones. Interviewed by Bert Haagsman (May 10, 1979) in New York City
10. Roy E. Lagrone. Interviewed by Piet Schreuders (May 26, 1978) in New York City
11. Leonard Leone. Interviewed by Thomas L. Bonn (November 9, 1971) and Piet Schreuders (May 18, 1978) in New York City
12. Leo Manso. Interviewed by Bert Haagsman (May 16, 1979) in New York City
13. Helen Meyer. Interviewed by Piet Schreuders (May 19, 1978) in New York City

14. RAFAEL PALACIOS. Interviewed by Piet Schreuders (May 2, 1979) in Union City, New Jersey
15. ED ROFHEART. Interviewed by Piet Schreuders (May 23, 1978) in New York City

Questionnaires and Correspondence

In 1979, a detailed questionnaire was sent to approximately 50 artists by Thomas L. Bonn (author of *Undercover*, to be published by Penguin Books) and myself. Much of the information in this volume has come from the responses to those questionnaires, as submitted by Bob Abbett, Bernard D'Andrea, Charles Andres, David Attie, James Bama, Harry Bennett, Walter Brooks, Cal Diehl, George Erickson, Louis Glanzman, Gerald Gregg, John Groth, Paul Kresse, Roy Lagrone, Riki Levinson, Gerald McConnell, Robert McGinnis, Sam Savitt, Harry Schaare, Earl Sherman, William Teason, Verne Tossey, Jeanyee Wong and Stanley Zuckerberg.

Additional information has since then come from my correspondence with Al Allard, Charles Andres, James Avati, Ian and Betty Ballantine, Harry Bennett, Walter Brooks, Kenneth Cirlin, Rafael DeSoto, Tom Dunn, Kurt Enoch, George Erickson, Arthur Getz, Gerald Gregg, Philip Grushkin, Clark Hulings, Sol Immerman, Robert Jonas, Nettie King, Sidney B. Kramer, Paul Kresse, John Legakes, Leonard Leone, Frank J. Lieberman, Leo Manso, Pierre Martinot, Richard Powers, Agnes Salter, Earl Sherman, Gobin Stair, Isador N. Steinberg, Verne Tossey, Philip Van Doren Stern and Ava Weiss.

Magazines

★ COLLECTING PAPERBACKS? Lance Casebeer, 934 S.E. 15th Street, Portland, Oregon, 97214, U.S.A.
    Since 1979, a continuation of Louis Black's *The Paperback Collector's Newsletter*. Appears bimonthly. Subscription rate: $12 per year.
★ PAPERBACK QUARTERLY. Billy C. Lee, 1710 Vincent Street, Brownwood, Texas, 76801, U.S.A.
    Has appeared regularly since the winter of 1978. Subscription rate: $8 per year (within the U.S.); $12 per year (elsewhere).
PENGUIN COLLECTORS' SOCIETY NEWSLETTER. Andrew Dalby, 5 Primrose Way, Linton, Cambridge 6B1 6UD, England
    Has appeared twice yearly since 1974. Subscription rates: £2 (within United Kingdom); £3 (elsewhere). Checks should be made payable to the Penguin Collectors' Society and mailed to Richard W. Smith, 30 Alexandra Grove, London N4, England by January 1 of each year.

Index

A LIST OF POCKET BOOKS
THE BEST AND THE MOST FOR THE LEAST

POCKET BOOKS *include all kinds of reading—modern best-sellers, mystery stories, anthologies, biography, history, travel, inspiration, practical books for the home library, reference books, classics, and popular fiction. This is a list of titles in print.*

1. LOST HORIZON by *James Hilton.* Thousands who saw the haunting movie will want to read the whole story of this strange 'plane journey to Shangri-La, where time stood still.

3. FIVE GREAT TRAGEDIES OF SHAKESPEARE. His most famous, oft-quoted quintet: *King Lear, Romeo and Juliet, Macbeth, Julius Caesar, Hamlet*—complete texts, with special introduction.

4. TOPPER by *Thorne Smith.* A large helping of hilarious adventure, a sophisticated riot that the movie could only hint at!

12. THE GREAT SHORT STORIES of de Maupassant. *A Piece of String, The Necklace, Ball-of-Fat,* and 33 others by this Frenchman whose genius for story-telling is unsurpassed in all literature.

17. THE CHINESE ORANGE MYSTERY by *Ellery Queen.* Your favorite sleuth staring into the dead face of a nameless nobody —and everything on the dead man had been turned backward!

18. PINOCCHIO by *Collodi.* The amazing, joyous, and sorrowful adventures of a wooden puppet. A favorite of all ages in all lands.

20. THE RETURN OF THE NATIVE by *Thomas Hardy.* An overpowering love story in the mood of *Wuthering Heights.*

"I want to tell you how much my buddies and I have appreciated your books. We have just returned from two-months maneuvers in North Carolina, where everything we own we carried on our backs. Consequently, reading matter was something of a problem, except for the fact that POCKET BOOKS *were easily carried in hip pockets. One of us would buy four or five on a trip in town. Then each one would be carried by different fellows. Sort of a walking library, as it were."*
PRIVATE K. . . . T. T. . . . ., Camp Edwards, Mass.

AVON BOOKS

MANY MORE IN PREPARATION

ON SALE AT YOUR NEWSDEALER OR DIRECT FROM AVON BOOK
SALES CORP., 119 W. 57TH ST., NEW YORK 19, N. Y. ENCLOSE 25c
PER TITLE PLUS 5c EACH FOR WRAPPING AND FORWARDING.

Outstanding DELL BOOKS
in MYSTERY, DETECTIVE, ROMANCE, WESTERN and ADVENTURE
Look for These Marks on Dell Books

For any title unobtainable locally, send 25c to Dell Publishing Co., Inc., 261 Madison Ave., New York 16, N. Y., and a copy will be sent postpaid (in United States only). Order by title and number.

25 cents a copy—plus 5 cents per book for handling and mailing.

99. THE BEST FROM TRUE.
The editors of the nation's leading man's magazine selected these fact stories as the best of the year.

100. WHAT TODAY'S WOMAN SHOULD KNOW ABOUT MARRIAGE AND SEX.
This is "must" reading for any young lady who feels that she does not know all the answers to life's riddles.

101. WE ARE THE PUBLIC ENEMIES. Alan Hynd.
The peer of crime reporters writes the stories of the gangsters, from Dillinger to Ma Barker.

102. MAN STORY.
Paul Gallico, Philip Wylie, Daniel Mannix and others have written their finest true-fact stories for this book.

103. THE PERSIAN CAT. John Flagg.
Mystery! Women! Murder! The French girl loved for the sake of love, the rich blonde because she was lonely. A Yankee gets in the middle.

104. I'LL FIND YOU. Richard Himmel.
The private eye didn't believe the sad blonde when she said: "Every man I've ever touched died." He should have.

105. NUDE IN MINK. Sax Rohmer.
A mystery braided with foreign intrigue, written by the best-known author in the field.

106. STRETCH DAWSON. W. R. Burnett.
A hell-fire Western by the author of Little Caesar.

107. FLYING SAUCERS. Donald Keyhoe.
The facts—not fiction—about the celestial mystery of the century.

108. DEVIL MAY CARE. Wade Miller.
Biggo wanted the dough, the girl, and a chance to escape the assassin.

109. AWAKENING OF JENNY. Lillian Colter.
A search for passion that might be any woman's secret.

110. MILLION DOLLAR MURDER. Edward Ronns.
Sam was in love with his brother's wife. For this someone had to die.

GOLD MEDAL BOOKS
Fawcett Place,   Greenwich, Conn.

A new P A P E R B O O K is published and mailed to subscribers on the 25th of each month. The first book in the series was published in September 1929. In May, T H E B R I D G E O F S A N L U I S R E Y by Thornton Wilder was set up and printed as an example of the format.

DATE	TITLE	AUTHOR
FOR FORMAT	*The Bridge of San Luis Rey*	Thornton Wilder
SEPT 25	*The Golden Wind*	Takashi Ohta and Margaret Sperry
OCT 25	*Frederick the Great*	Margaret Goldsmith
NOV 25	*Dewer Rides*	L. A. G. Strong
DEC 26	*Prosperity: Fact or Myth*	Stuart Chase
JAN 25	*Commando*	Deneys Reitz
FEB 25	*My Reminiscences as a Cowboy*	Frank Harris
MAR 25	*The Master of the Day of Judgment*	Leo Perutz
APR 25	*Prize Poems, 1913·1929*	An Anthology
MAY 25	*The Return of the Hero*	Darrell Figgis
JUN 25	*By the Waters of Manhattan*	Charles Reznikoff
JUL 25	*All in the Racket*	William E. Weeks
AUG 25	*Margaret Fuller*	Margaret Bell
SEPT 25	*Wandering Women*	John Cournos

Cover design for this book by John Barbour.

N O T I C E O F C H A N G E O F A D D R E S S *should include the old address as well as the new, and be printed plainly to obviate error. We must have notice at least six weeks before it can be effected.*

Subscription prices for P A P E R B O O K S : *one year, for Continental United States of America $5.00; elsewhere $6.00* S I N G L E C O P I E S , *50 cents each mailed postpaid to any address.*

Charles Boni P A P E R B O O K S *New York Number 80 Fifth Avenue*

WHY YOU MUST SAVE ALL KINDS OF PAPER

Each month, 35,000,000 V-boxes go overseas to the armed forces. It requires 81 tons of supplies a month to send a soldier overseas, and these supplies are all made wrapped or tagged with paper.

> Your wastebasket scraps can help supply the needed wrapping and packaging materials—*if you make sure they are collected.*

> Your corrugated cartons and cardboard boxes can go into blood plasma containers — *if you make sure they're collected.*

Blood plasma is needed for treating the thousands of wounded and sick left in the wake of war. Every precious bottle of plasma is wrapped in corrugated paper and boxed in heavy brown paperboard.

Civilian use of paper and paperboard products has been seriously curtailed to meet all military demands for these products. Before normal civilian needs can be met again thousands of tons of waste paper will be needed by the mills.

> Your old magazines and books can help meet present vital needs—*if you make sure they're collected.*

> Your old newspapers can help return the nation to peacetime pursuits—*if you make sure they're collected.*

Industry's conversion to peacetime production and the demobilization of the armed forces will require vast supplies of paper.

EVERY SCRAP OF EVERY KIND OF WASTE PAPER IS NEEDED TODAY
U.S. VICTORY WASTE PAPER CAMPAIGN

SAVE A BUNDLE A WEEK

SAVE SOME BOYS LIFE

258

POPULAR BART HOUSE BOOKS

1. The Hand in the Cobbler's Safe *by Seth Bailey*

The cobbler finds a human hand in his safe—a girl's—and only he knows the combination! Shall he tell the police—and be accused of murder? One of eight gripping detective stories in this **volume.**

2. The Delinquent Ghost *by Eric Hatch*

A man strolling across the hot desert in evening clothes, and not a house within miles! Mansley stops his car—"Are you real?" he asks. The man laughs . . . A novel you'll never forget by the author of MY MAN GODFREY.

3. The Spy Trap *by William Gilman*

A dramatic behind-the-scenes story of espionage in the present war—tense, gripping. Read how our FBI smashes through the vicious network of international intrigue.

4. Weird Shadow Over Innsmouth *H. P. Lovecraft*

Innsmouth is a village of nameless horror. Streets deserted, its people slowly decaying. No one knows why—and strangers are warned to stay out of Innsmouth. Supernatural, eerie, fantastic.

5. Smith Hears Death Walking *Wyatt Blassingame*

Death stalks this great detective, formerly a blind man, whose ears are trained to hear footsteps even in the grass—to whom the darkness of night offers uncanny advantage. Thrilling case-book of a master sleuth.

6. Rebirth *by Thomas Calvert McClary*

Suddenly at ten o'clock one morning everyone in the world forgot everything he ever knew! Civilization was gone—the world in chaos. But—man still had his intelligence. He could learn—start all over again. An amazing story.

7. The Shivering Bough *by Noel Burke*

A huge barn burns in the dead of a winter's night. Shadowy figures steal away in the darkness. Nearby, two dead feet dangle from a shivering bough. Murder on the loose!

POPULAR
LIBRARY

DELL
BOOK
697

BB

A DELL BOOK
DELL
A DELL BOOK

A GRAPHIC MYSTERY

AN
AVON
BOOK

BART

An Original

25¢
DELL
BOOK
607

A BANTAM BOOK

pb

POPULAR
LIBRARY
"Mysteries of Proven Merit"

A
AVON
25¢
874

35¢

AVON

PYRAMID BOOKS
PB

POCKET-SIZE BOOKS
AVON
442

AN AVON BOOK

LION
LIBRARY
35¢

SIGNET
25¢
BOOKS

NAL
MENTOR
BOOKS

ACE
DOUBLE NOVEL
BOOKS

JL
JACKET LIBRARY

PERMA
BOOKS
BOOKS·TO·KEEP